Men and Sharks

HANS HASS

With 56 Photographs

JARROLDS
Publishers (London) Ltd.
FOUNDED IN 1770

Jarrolds Publishers (London) Limited
London   Melbourne   Sydney   Auckland
Bombay   Cape Town   New York   Toronto

Original edition published in 1949 by
Orell Fulssli, Zurich, under the title of Menschen und Haie.
Men and Sharks—
First Published in Great Britain November 1954
Reprinted December 1954
Reprinted January 1955

Printed in Great Britain by
WILLIAM BRENDON AND SON LTD
THE MAYFLOWER PRESS
(late of Plymouth)
WATFORD

LIST OF ILLUSTRATIONS

1

THERE were not many signs of the war in Vienna as yet. We strolled the Kaerntnerstrasse, met old friends, went to cafés, or drove out to drink new wine; the war had not yet really brought many changes. People groused about this and that but this, too, was perfectly normal, because there is always grousing in Vienna; it was the proper and expected thing to do. Novelties were the food-ration cards and the air-raid cellars, but otherwise life muddled along in the accustomed way. The same girls, the same gossip, the same for ever torn-up streets, and in the middle St. Stephen's steeple with its view of Kahlenberg and Schoenbrunn. There were still not many uniforms to be seen. We registered in proper form, and all three of us were deferred for the present to pursue our university courses. I put myself down for Zoology.

But, pleasant and familiar though life at home was, Vienna was not the right spot for my future plans. I had gone through the same thing twice before, and this third time was just the same. Whereas the reporters in New York and Tokyo had welcomed us upon our very arrival, and all the larger papers had printed stories about our expedition, nobody here gave us a second thought. People in Vienna take an interest in cultural affairs and in everything that goes on within their own four walls; as for what the cannibals or the coral fish or sunspots do, only a very small group cares at all.

"You don't say! The West Indies? Hunting sharks? Really, under water?" people said. "Now that must have been very interesting." But nobody seemed to be interested.

To induce this second thought, then, I went to Berlin, where I settled in a small pension in the Kaiserstrasse. By then there were air-raid warnings almost every night, and as the pension was under the roof, on the fifth floor, the guests unanimously went down to the cellar the moment the sirens started. This taught me about the German sense of order. As the attacks were still comparatively light—fleabites compared to what came later—I stayed in bed and went through the same performance night after night. The night-clad congregation, well-meaning, amiable, annoyed, and finally very much annoyed, strove to bring me to my senses. In Vienna, they would have said by the second evening, "Oh, all right, if he won't, let a bomb get him!"

But times change, and we change with them. Not three weeks had passed when I was going down with the others. Because the sense of order had infected me? Not at all. Because I had contrived to sell our entire collection of pictures to the *Berliner Illustrierte*. Because the then largest paper in the German language planned to publish our experiences in five instalments, and even give us a cover picture. Because nothing would have induced me not to be there when these reports hit the show windows of Vienna.

2

I HAD not been telling the managing editor of the *Berliner Illustrierte* about our experiences for five minutes when he interrupted and reached for the telephone.

"You've got to come right over," I heard him say. "I've got a fish here—That's right, a fish you've got to meet— What? You've just got back? You've got to wash?—All right, then, this afternoon. I'll bring him home with me, and you can come to tea. That's a date, now."

Thus I was served up, along with some good sandwiches, as 'the fish' to a well-known lady aviator.

"You ought to lecture," the lady said to me after I had

told her a little of my story. "You can make a lot of money that way, and you'll be able to put it to use in your next expedition. I know the manager for you—Mrs. Schneider-Lindemann, the famous Mother Explorer of Dahlem."

And she, too, went to the telephone and made an appointment for me the next day.

The Mother Explorer lived in a house in Dahlem. When I came into the garden I was first received by Kastor, a large police dog who in the course of years had sniffed at a good many globe-trotters, and always undertook the first assessment. The wagging of his tail indicated that in my case the result was favourable. He conducted me to the second floor of the house, where the Mother Explorer had her office.

Mrs. Schneider-Lindemann was enthroned behind a gigantic desk. She was rather elderly and definitely a personality. She was just on the telephone, perceptibly radiating energy. As I later had plenty of chance to learn, on this point she was a match for any man—or any youth.

"Too bad you weren't brought to my attention two years ago," were her first words. "Then you wouldn't have had to go off by guess and by God to the West Indies with no money. But it's always the same. If a man's a tenor, people fight to fill his pockets with money. If somebody risks his life for progress, nobody lends him a hand, and he even gets rooked right and left——"

She vanished for a moment to put the kettle on for tea, and meanwhile I studied the many inscribed pictures on the office walls. Everybody was gathered here: Arctic explorers, flyers, stratosphere specialists, big-game hunters, naturalists—I was particularly taken with the picture of a young man who could not have been much older than I. He had been photographed before the background of some mechanical contraption.

"How do you mean, rooked?" I asked when Mrs. Schneider came back; Berlinese was new to me.

"Why, I mean—you get cheated," she said. "When you try to sell your films or make contracts or exploit the results of your travels somehow. . . . Explorers are never good business-men, and most people take advantage of them."

Unfortunately I could not disagree with her on this score. I, too, had had my disagreeable experiences. We agreed that the Mother Explorer was to organize lecture tours for me. She would also take all business matters off my shoulders.

"You write your books, study, and lecture," she said, "and just leave everything else to me. And if you work hard, I can promise you that you'll have a ship of your own for your next expedition."

This proved to be no idle boast. Two years later, by her help, our expedition fund had grown to the point where I could buy Luckner's famous yacht, the *Sea Devil*. Unluckily we were never to sail the world in that fine vessel. As it was impossible on account of the war to get the ship from Stettin, where she lay, to the Mediterranean we had to use another ship for the expedition to Greece. And when the war reached its dramatic conclusion the yacht was removed as spoils of war, and I have never heard of her since.

"Who's that?" I asked, pointing to the picture that had taken my eye, before I said good-bye to the Mother Explorer.

"That is, or, rather, most unfortunately was, Max Vallier," she said, "one of the most gifted young men I've ever met, with the most incredible enthusiasm for his work—he was the one who developed rocket propulsion. You wouldn't believe what primitive conditions he worked under in his shed. He slaved year after year, and then, when his first rocket auto-mobile rolled along the Avus motor speedway, not he but Mr. Opel sat in it in a white leather jacket, and received the cheers of the crowd. About Vallier nobody heard a word. I can still remember how he begged to drive around the Avus just once, but they wouldn't let him. But—money, money, money! I gave him two thousand marks, all I had myself, but of course that wasn't enough. He couldn't afford even the slightest safety device, and that was what finally finished him. He was here that very morning, telling me what a terrific recoil he was getting out of his new mixture—he used to do his measuring on a set of common kitchen scales—and as he was leaving he said, 'But, you know, there's a certain amount of danger to it, too,' and that evening I was in bed, listening to the radio, and heard he had had a fatal accident. The explosion sent an iron fragment right through his heart!"

I have sometimes been reminded of Max Vallier since then. At Elephteri, when death just grazed me, and at Santorin, when my life hung on an even thinner thread, the picture of him came into my mind. As a young person one can't imagine death. And nowadays, with the war already fading into the past, as I set off to explore the newly opened world honesty forces me to admit that I've gone back to the old ways—I'm more afraid a brick might fall on my head than that something will happen to me in the sea, where there is really no lack of perils.

3

I GOT back in September; in January the lectures began. Week after week and month after month I went hither and thither, from the Rhine to East Prussia, from Hamburg to the French border, from Vienna to Stockholm. The lectures were well prepared for everywhere, and indeed usually sold out; there was much clapping, admiration, a lot of questions asked; then I would take my suitcase, board a train, and on I would go.

I came to know the public as a highly incalculable creature. At great pains I would work up a joke, laugh half the night at it myself, and then, confident of victory, I would fire it at the audience, pause briefly for effect, and—dead silence would follow. On the other hand it might happen that people would start laughing aloud at some particularly dramatic point in

my story. There was nothing for it but to adapt myself. So I
left out the prepared jokes and collected the unintended ones
as eagerly as a philatelist collects stamps; and lo, each new
day brought more success.

The introductory words were usually spoken by some leading figure of the town, the school principal, the cultural-
affairs official, or even the mayor himself. I heard some
amazing things. In Leipzig the officiating gentleman declined
to leave the platform. He had been carefully following the
stories in the *Berliner Illustrierte,* and now started telling with great
eloquence all the things that I had really been intending to tell
for myself. Perhaps not quite in such detail, but at any rate
the punch lines of the jokes. I sat there in the front row, looking at my watch and being amazed. The audience gradually
grew restless, and finally started shuffling. When the lecture
was delivered again the next day, I asked the enthusiastic
gentleman, whether in view of the length of my own dis-
quisition, he could not cut his down a little. But he interrupted
at once. Oh, he said, this time he really did know my lecture;
this time he had thought up something very special. Surely
I would let him say it? I didn't want to hurt his feelings, so
everything went exactly as it had the first day. With one difference. When the audience began shuffling again, he flung his
arms wide—rather like Lothengrin catching sight of the swan
—and cried in a loud voice: "I can only tell you, ladies and
gentlemen, it'll make cold shivers run down your spine and
come up warm in front!"

So saying, he surrendered the floor to me.

One delicate problem was the sale of pictures. This was an
idea of the astute Mother Explorer, quite on the American
pattern. Following the lectures, the finest underwater pictures
were to be sold with my autograph for the benefit of the next
expedition. At first I found this rather embarrassing, but then
I realized that the Mother Explorer was right. People were
glad to buy the pictures, the money was for a good cause, and

so there was really nothing to object to. I then found it interesting to discover how exactly the success of my lecture was
reflected in the sales of pictures. If I spoke well and established
contact with my audience, more pictures were sold; I could
soon tell beforehand. It proved to be particularly helpful if
the man who had made the introduction would return briefly
to the platform afterwards and say a few graceful words about
the pictures and the disposal of the proceeds. I formed a habit
of asking the chairmen to do me this favour, and since they
usually didn't know what to say, I would hand them a casual
little text. Once in a small town in East Prussia I unluckily
forgot this. At my last words, the cultural-affairs official
mounted the platform as requested, shook hands with me, and
said, turning to the audience, "All right, and now the lecturer
will just sell you his pictures!"

And he left me standing there.

4

ZOOLOGY, now. . . .

What do zoologists do, anyway? How do they keep busy?
What does their day's work consist of?

Why, everybody knows. Either they have a beard and go
running about the countryside with a butterfly net, which is
something one might just be able to understand; or else they
sit jammed in among bones, books, and jars of alcohol, looking absent-minded. A person can't help wondering what a
man like that gets out of life, anyway. You never see him out
taking it easy, let alone at tea or a football game; what is he
living for, after all? Of course some animals are really quite
nice—particularly dogs and cats, and maybe elephants, deer,
and birds of paradise; but as for worms, molluscs, and snakes—
ugh! To say nothing of cut-up eyes or bowels. . . . And then to
go poking around in the stuff!

If you really devote yourself to the study of zoology, sooner or later you realize that what you discover in the process is really something quite fantastic. Far more fascinating and more exciting than the wildest detective story. You see an ordinary-looking man standing at the lecture desk, telling with no great emotion what we human beings really are; how it happened that our forefathers gave up scrambling in trees with their prehensile tails; what the parts we are made of really mean; how this or that still recalls our fish forebears; how at first there was nothing but the cooling globe, and how then, out of dust, water, and sunlight, everything developed that creeps and grows and loves and twitters today. The eyes, the teeth, pain, reproduction—none of these, he says, is anything to be taken for granted. What is an instinct, a thought, a feeling? What is life, and why does it die? What is the individual, and how did it come about? What does its existence mean, and whence comes the harmony of its parts?

In Goethe's day and long afterwards there were in fact many among the zoologists who set forth with beard and butterfly net for the sole purpose of discovering and describing as many new sorts of creatures as possible. To these they would then give a Latin name, append their own, and the more such new animals a man had found, the higher his reputation among his colleagues.

Along with these men, however, there were others— including Goethe himself—who were not satisfied with that, but also compared the various animals' bodies among themselves: an insect with a butterfly, a snail with a bird, all in search of the similarities and peculiarities of their construction. Had they all a heart, a circulatory system and nerves? How were feet and muscles and noses formed here, how there? In short, how did the inner life mechanism look and function in each of the many shapes?

Improvements in the microscope made it possible to look ever deeper into the structure of living matter. In the course of the nineteenth century this brought people to three insights, which opened up such a panorama that the theory of life now became the most interesting of all branches of science.

The first insight I have already mentioned. The biologists Schwann and Schleiden were astounded to discover that all large living beings consist of similar tiny units, called cells, and that quite similar cells are to be found as independent individuals in any drop of water. We must not simply pass over this as something familiar. It is a realization more amazing than all the seven wonders of the world. Just think: we and all the higher animals are states made up of these small 'I's,' the only true ones. And more than that, it is the same with plants. All, all—bats, poplars, worms, roses, whales, and human beings —all are made up of hosts of these tiny organisms, which are indeed differently shaped, according to the formation of eyes, bark, leaves, bones, flowers, or nerves, but are completely alike in their basic construction, and in it also like those others that the astonished eye sees in a drop of water under the microscope.

A torrent of new questions and problems resulted from this discovery. At one blow the large unity that people had hitherto seen in each animal and plant now became an enormous multiplicity, a veritable ant-hill whose laws had to be deciphered. And on the other hand, again, the enormous multiplicity for which people had always taken animated nature suddenly fused in one stupendous unity; organisms, no matter how different they looked, were built of the same living bricks.

Nothing was more natural than to wonder how one of these living cellular states was formed. And in this investigation the second great miracle was revealed: that all these number-less beings out of which an animal or plant body is made are invariably descendants of just one—the germ cell.

This, too, we must not pass over as something familiar. The conclusions that result are more astonishing than love and the atomic bomb. This germ cell divides in two, then in four, then in eight, and so on, and does it with such marvellous obedience to law that the product is precisely this or that cellular commonwealth—a fish or a lime tree or a human being. Here you have germ cells under the microscope, so tiny that dozens of them would fit on the point of a pin and yet each one already contains everything that will later determine an individual, its appearance, and its behaviour. Never does a swan grow from the germ cell of a frog, never an oak from that of a violet. And so perfect is the order concealed in the germ cell that, as we see every day, even the features and characteristic traits are handed down from parents to children. If an engineer were to try to build a human body out of cells, the Empire State Building could not hold all the blueprints he would need. And nature has housed them all in a single cell! Nay, more: all the precision mechanics, doctors, and electrical engineers that our human designer would need to carry out his work are housed in that one cell. Out of itself the germ cell produces the whole tremendous principality. Nobody lends a hand. On the contrary, if the state is damaged, it restores by itself the impaired form and order of operations.

And a third tremendous problem also occupies the man who sits absently among bones, books, and jars of formaldehyde —the third of the great miracles of life, harmonizing the other two in one. Not only do all living beings consist of cells, and not only does every cell state grow from a single germ cell, but all beings and all germ cells are in turn descendants of the same primitive being who carried the first spark of life a hundred million years ago. The Creator did not, as people supposed, make animals and plants in their present shapes; they are all but branches on the same tremendous tree of life, which in the course of millions of years have spread further and further, in ever more divergent forms, round the globe.

Let us imagine that tiny body, that first primitive being. Within it everything already slumbered—the appearance of cacti, of orchids, of walruses, and purple snails; and everything to do with us human beings, our literature, our music, our

Joerg, our sharpshooter, cocks the special harpoon which does not function

Dr. Beckh, our biologist, cleans the plankton net.

Heinz, our navigator, observes the sun through a theodolite

Alfred's birthdays are dangerous affairs. His twenty-fifth ended with an air bubble in the heart; his twenty-seventh almost ended in the belly of a shark

engineering, our most delicate and ingenious instruments, everything that life has ever produced, must already have been contained somehow in that first, tiny primitive being.

It has been said that natural science leads man away from God. And indeed many a one has been so impressed by the advance of science that he felt able, with Laplace, to abandon the 'hypothesis of God'. The basic mistake here is that when something becomes explicable it by no means ceases to be divine. True, God is no longer so close to us as He once was. With each new discovery He moves a little further into the distance. As we have just seen, all of animate nature has its foundation in a speck of slime, the original cell; and yet this consists of the very same atoms as the inanimate stones and the water and the air; and all atoms in turn consist of the same tiniest elemental bits, the protons and electrons. But admit that we must thus pursue the secret of life and the mystery of creation back to the activity of these tiniest building stones of our world; even if everything, including us and our life, finds its ultimate explanation in the whirl of inconceivable elemental forces, does that make creation and life any less truly divine? On the contrary, is not the very fact that the whole cosmos is contained in every one of its own tiniest fragments—is not this the most shattering expression of what we in our dwarf human speech call 'God' or 'divine wisdom'?

The whole world suddenly seemed changed to me. Henceforth I must regard everything, no matter how familiar, with new eyes; I had to revise every attitude to these problems. For the first time I felt the icy cold of the interplanetary space in which our globe floats so utterly alone. In the boundless, shuddery nothingness, in a frozen desert without parallel, the spark of our human feeling gleams utterly forlorn. Must one not stand amazed every day that the gift of this mysterious existence was vouchsafed to us? Must one not be grateful, humbly grateful from the bottom of one's heart, for each day and each minute, no matter what it brings?

B

5

THE summer brought another chance to get to the sea. A movie company wanted to make an educational film out of our West Indian films, and since our shots included almost nothing but coral and fish, and hardly any swimming or hunting men, a few scenes of this kind were to be taken and spliced in. They asked me where this could be done, and I replied that absolutely the only possibility was Ragusa. And sure enough the movie company immediately took all necessary steps to arrange a trip for us.

Meanwhile we were doing a turn as movie actors in the Krapfenwald near Vienna. Our film was to have a plot grafted on, and so the director who was responsible for this work of art had dreamed up a story with two young Viennese girls. To them—just after getting back from our expedition, so to speak—we were to explain our outfit beside a swimming pool, put goggles and fins on them, unexpectedly push them into the water and jump after them, pursue them under water with our harpoons, and finally, reaching shore safe and sound, to sketch on one girl's back with the other's lipstick a map of Central America, after which, to the sound of Mexican music, the lipstick-painted back was to fade into the Caribbean coral reefs and the educational film proper was to begin.

It went tolerably well. The scene where Joerg sent one girl into the water with a mighty boot was highly successful. We had difficulties, however, with a scene where I was to start telling about the West Indies; it turned out that at one particular word I always twitched my left eyebrow. Since this very word was to be taken as a close-up and the director was most concerned about the artistic effect, this scene was repeated at least a dozen times. The scientifically interesting conclusion

18

was that I could say this word only if I twitched my left eyebrow. A fixation, so to speak. Either I twitched and the word
came, or I did not twitch and it didn't. Finally the director
battled his way to the conclusion that perhaps the very twitch
heightened the artistic naturalism of the performance, and so
we went on with a sigh of relief to the next scene, and soon
afterwards to a lunch break.

The trip to Dalmatia was highly dramatic. When we got
off the train at midnight in Bosnisch Brod and asked a Yugo-
slavian official about the connecting train to Ragusa he pointed
vaguely into the Stygian darkness of the railway yard. After
a brief exchange in which nobody understood a word that
anyone else said, it dawned on us that evidently a bridge had
been blown up and we would have to reach the next station on
foot. A passing German-speaking linesman confirmed this. He
said the whole line had been cut off for two weeks on account
of partisan activity, but we were in luck—next morning the
first train was going to see whether it could make Sarajevo
without getting blown up.

Shouldering bags and harpoons, we trudged through a
fairly sloppy night and across a bridge at dawn, and forced
our way into the train, which was filled to bursting with female
Bosnians. Here it turned out that it had been incautious of
us to bring along almost no provender. As we were to pick up
the film company's money in Ragusa we were provided only
with a few credit certificates, which, however, had been
declared invalid in Yugoslavia only the day before. In Vienna
nothing had been known of this or of the cutting of the line.

Promptly with the new day came a new appetite, and
this suited the tempo of the train but ill. Quaking, first timidly
inspecting each piece of track, it puffed on its way, stopping
fifteen minutes or an hour at every second station to wait for
the telephoned situation report from the 'front'. On these
occasions children invariably ran along the train with roast
chickens, chickens that appeared to be most deliciously prepared, but beyond reach by credit certificate. During the

afternoon the instinct of self-preservation drove us to lay rude hands on the (unfortunately quite unripe) plums that grew along the right of way. The consequences did nothing to make the trip more agreeable.

Gradually we drew near the critical point. Shots were audible in the distance; the crews manning the machine guns at the front and rear of the train were on the alert; the general nervousness grew ever more acute. As we were standing waiting on the platform of the last station a shot suddenly went off close beside me. With one tremendous bound I took cover in the train. Joerg and Alfred, standing a little farther away, held their sides with laughter. A barefoot Bosnian's shooting-iron had gone off; the shot had gone into the ground, missing his big toe by a hair and causing him to jump almost as far as I had.

Amid general merriment the tension relaxed, and just then the order to go on arrived. The 'front' was safely passed, and late that night we reached Sarajevo, where in our poverty we could only spend the night along with the female Bosnians in the cold train. If our hunger had already reached excessive proportions here, by the following afternoon, when we finally reached Ragusa, we felt like fakirs. A trip to the bank brought us word that no money had yet arrived. Credit certificates were no longer redeemed here, either.

We were standing downcast before the desk clerk of one of the big hotels, who had already told us everything he knew, namely that he didn't know what to tell us, and we were having considerable difficulty in tearing ourselves away, because this had been pretty well our last hope. Just then the well-nourished man's eyes looked once more pensively into the distance, and returned to us with the expression of a dawning idea. There was an American newspaper woman staying at the hotel; might I possibly. . . ?

And how I might!

I had myself announced and was soon sitting with a lady who at first was downright unfriendly, because she took me for an admirer whom she had already turned away by telephone once the day before. I soon convinced her that my intentions were entirely different, and she thereupon listened graciously to what I told her about us and our trying situation. It turned out that she was leaving that night, but had a few thousand dinars left over; she said she would be glad to do a story about us—in short, within half an hour she had our tale and we had her money.

Grossly over-estimating the buying power of the bank-note with its huge denomination, we climbed straight into a taxi and drove to a good restaurant, and then to the Lapad Pensinsula. Money? Pooh! we said to ourselves—after all, tomorrow or the day after the thousands from the movie company will be here.

And once more the sea lay before us, neat and blue, exactly as we had left it four years before. At the same spot where we had dragged our first shark ashore we went back into the water and promptly glided with luxurious fin strokes through the blue underwater landscapes, down to the rocky caves, into which we peered, swimming to all the spots we recognized from our previous stay.

"Do you suppose he's still there?" Joerg asked me as we swam out to the Graebeni Reefs.

I knew instantly who 'he' was—a grouper, a fish that had been annoying Joerg for days on end three years before. This rascal had lodged about twenty-five feet down in a hole in the rock, which, however, had so many outlets that there was no getting at him from any side. After some search we found the spot. Sure enough, the grouper was actually there. We recognized him at once by the bright stripes on his head. Just as in the old days, at the same spot and in the same attitude, he hung at the entrance to his hole. We had travelled round the world, three times the globe had circled the sun, and still he hung there, living his life, placidly fanning his fins, and retreating as of old into his hole when Joerg dived.

Joerg scrambled round the rock for a while, trying to spear him from all sides, but once more without success.

"Just you wait until we come back three years from now,"
he said when he reached the surface again, and we swam on
laughing.

Not far away, too, was the place where I had made fast
to my first bonito. I remembered how my spear had gone
through the smooth, thick body, and how the line had run
off the reel, and I had hastened ashore, while the fish, trailing
a thin thread of blood, swam on. In those days we had followed
the fish until we really bagged them in the end; meanwhile,
however, the fishy throngs of the Caribbean and the Cali-
fornia coast had spoiled us. Joerg and Alfred did dive eagerly,
but the old patience was gone. And so the result of our first
hunt was no fish.

Lying on the rocks in the sun, we argued about the new
expedition we planned. Here, with murmuring waves in the
background, we quickly reached a definite conclusion. Above
all we must seek out a region where there were sharks—that
was the one important thing. The story in the *Berliner Illustrierte*
had made friends, but it had also given rise to a lot of criticism.
More than once our pictures had been called posed shots and
our experiences with sharks an April Fool's joke. Our prime
duty was to have so many sharks swimming up and down in
front of the wiseacres' noses that they would have to own themselves beaten. First of all we must take movies, and we needed
shots where we could be seen right beside sharks, so establish-
ing that there was no disputing that sharks will actually take
flight if you swim straight at them without showing fear. The
war situation, after all, had very sharply limited the choice
of locality. We decided that the likeliest was Greece, where I
knew there were sharks, and where landscape and scenery
would be excellently suited to a movie. I would undertake the
organization of the enterprise immediately. We had not much
time, anyway, because it was evident that all students would
soon be called up.

"There are excellent grapes in Greece, too," Joerg put in.

"And very pretty girls," added Alfred, whose hair had at

last grown again after having been shaved on the way home round the world.

We began taking our movies, and I made use of the opportunity for the following experiment. I took a colour shot of a tomato as it sank slowly from the surface to thirty feet down. When we ran the film afterwards you could plainly see the tomato going through, as it were, a reverse development. It grew paler and paler, and finally, at thirty feet, was grass-green. This is the difficulty in underwater photography. Owing to the absorption of red and yellow light by the water only green and blue tones reach the film at a depth of more than thirty feet. And it does little good to use filters, because where no red or green is present even a filter cannot conjure it up. Artificial light is the only solution.

Unfortunately Joerg and I shortly afterwards got word that we were urgently needed for one day in Vienna. Of the money from the movie company there was still no sign; furthermore, partisan fighting had flared up once more and the railway was cut off again, so that suddenly overnight there was no bread in Ragusa. Joerg barely managed to steam away on the last regular train; I followed him two days later on hazardous by-paths by way of Metkovitz, leaving Alfred behind with our blessings and the unpaid hotel bill.

If I should ever become weary of life you would only need to remind me of this journey to put me in the best of humours. By comparison with those wretched days anything else must seem gloriously satisfying. I simply could not make any progress. Again and again partisans had been there just before us; again and again the line was cut and had to be repaired, which work of course went forward at Bosnian pace. In the matter of nourishment I was soon exclusively dependent on plums, alas still unripe.

Finally, when I reached Bosnisch Brod on the third day and had to wait another sixteen hours for a connexion, the night in the waiting-room so undermined my self-respect that I launched on a gallant conversation with a perfectly strange

Serbian woman simply because I had caught sight of four apricots and two tomatoes in her bag. The woman came from a frontier fortress between Serbia and Montenegro, and tried to explain to me who had been fighting against whom. So far as I could understand, there were no fewer than five groups, each of which was trying to exterminate the other four. The treatment of prisoners varied. Some merely had their eyes put out, others were hung to a tree by their own intestines, or, apparently a popular method, had their heads nailed to the front door. The Serbian woman told all this calmly, at length, and with a visible relish for detail, and when she finally reached the point of offering me one of the apricots I could only decline with thanks, my appetite having vanished despite my ravenous hunger.

I myself unfortunately had no further part in the events of the Dalmatian expedition. Owing to circumstances, I could not get away from Vienna, so only Joerg and the director went back to Ragusa. As the line was now definitely cut, they managed to cross the Karst mountains on muleback, straight through the fighting, and their courageous act had its due reward. The long-awaited money from the movie company arrived the same day they did; and when Joerg and Alfred want to annoy me they tell me how they managed to spend the whole sum within a week.

The movies were also taken.

6

I RETURNED with redoubled zeal to my lectures as the best way to bring in money for the new expedition. At the same time I placed orders for new cameras, harpoons, diving gear, and other equipment. The Zoological Institute of Berlin University was very much interested in the collecting of specimens in Greece; with this assistance I managed to overcome a good many difficulties.

I had my biggest success as a lecturer in Berlin, where I spoke to standing room only no fewer than 150 times in succession. That is to say, twice a day for more than two months, and three times on Sundays and holidays.

Now it is by no means easy to keep saying the same thing over and over again and cracking the same jokes. After my fiftieth lecture I thought I could not possibly go on.

"Surely you must understand?" I said to the Mother Explorer. "Even the projectionist knows the lecture by heart. I don't need to press the button any more—the pictures come of their own accord!"

"Why, that's fine," she said. "All the less work for you."

"But the boredom!" I cried. "You simply can't go on saying the same thing over and over again. After all, a man is not a gramophone!"

But the Mother Explorer was implacable. "One can do anything if one will," she declared. "It would be a downright sin to break off the run right now when it's just got going. Think of your ship! If you get bored, doodle or do something else, but I'm certainly not going to let you stop now."

So the lectures went on. I actually did start drawing. Even in grammar school I had had a certain talent for catching likenesses, but had never had a chance to practise afterwards. Now the chance was here. I had a reading lamp put on the platform, and while I was talking about fish and coral I would draw portraits of the people in the front row.

My thoughts, meanwhile, would travel on curious by-paths.

"And at that moment something wholly unexpected happened!" I would cry, wondering whether the brunette lady whom I was sketching was having an affair with her blond neighbour, or had only just met him at the lecture. "I had come within ten feet of the shark"—she must surely be married, and the blond man was a sort of semi-scientific admirer who sometimes took her to semi-scientific lectures; she had two children at home, her husband was in business, had a lot to do, a lot of money, and left her a good deal to herself—"and then all at once the shark made a sudden turn"—or the blond man was her brother, and here only for a week's vacation; he was a chemist in South Germany, irritable and just about to get married; he had been starting to talk about it to his sister, a fashion artist, when he lit his pipe with a newspaper and caught sight of the announcement of my lecture, and so here they were; they would have dinner afterwards at the Chinese restaurant—"and swam off again as fast as he could go!"

Gradually I noticed a regular split personality in myself. One self would tell about underwater hunting and adventures, and at the same time the other would wonder what courses I had tomorrow, and when, or why the chromosomes in the saliva glands of the Drosophila are so enormous. I reached the point where I began making notes on other subjects during my lectures. At first I had to write letter by letter, constantly switching my mind to and fro, but by the hundred and twenty-fifth lecture I could write a letter to my mother almost without pause, while at the same time my narrative went on undisturbed.

Nobody for a moment suspected any of this. Occasionally, though, there would be slips. I could tell at once from the amazed and disconcerted way that the audience pricked up their ears. I would switch quickly back and realize to my horror that, say, I had slipped unnoticed from my experience with the tuna fish into the one with the octopus. A similarity of sentence structure had caused the mistake. I had just been telling how the tuna fish had dragged me into the depths, and added immediately that he had clutched me with his slimy tentacles. Now what? Cold perspiration ran down my back.

"Well, they weren't exactly tentacles, ha, ha!" I cried. "But really, at that moment of peril I was reminded of a huge octopus, so supple, so fierce, so tempestuous was this creature —this tuna fish, dragging me behind him into the depths. . . ."

And the audience leaned back again, reassured.

7

WITH a steady growl the plane worked its way skyward.
The houses looked tiny from above. As if a sower had scattered
a few handfuls at random across the landscape.

I was feverish. The day before, I had had an injection
for typhus—a jab in the leg and a receipt for twenty-five
marks. Now I was in a plane, flying towards Athens, the first
long flight of my life. Here I sat in the belly of a fat dragonfly,
having to submit to the obvious relish with which the creature
wallowed in every air pocket.

"Well, how do you feel?" asked my neighbour, and from
his tone of voice he evidently felt splendid himself. An open
guide-book lay on his knees—the Acropolis squashed flat and
pasted on paper.

"Thanks, a little fever, that's all."

What a time lay behind me! Man is a harmless being as
long as he has no plan. The moment he has one, he turns into
a high-explosive projectile, groping with over-alert senses
through the jungle of the momentary situation. My enemy
was war. Everything revolved about guns and shooting; who
had time to worry about oceanography?

But as a matter of fact it had been the other way round.
Everything revolved about war, true enough, but for that very
reason lots of people took pleasure in the thought of a new
expedition. I had scarcely opened my mouth before help and
suggestions came from all quarters, and the building at the
Botanical Garden turned more and more into a buzzing beehive. The focal point, the queen bee, was the Mother Explorer.
She told the unskilful manufacturer what a good harpoon head
was like. She described to the tireless newspapermen just how
you behave on encountering a sting-ray. She sorted out the
letters of application, and herself answered with a categorical
no all those written in a feminine hand. And now at last things

27

were ready; I had only to find a suitable vessel and the adventure could start. An adventure that had started somehow as a tiny idea in my head, and that other ideas had attached themselves to, growing and growing and stretching—eccentric ideas that might fall upside down and be washed away by the rain, or might plant rose hedges round themselves and become the centre of new extensions.

"Ah, Athens!" sighed my companion, gazing dreamily at the tin ceiling of the dragonfly. "Ever since I was a boy it has been my dearest wish to go to Athens. I've never been keener on doing business for my firm as I am this time."

"Well, I hope your business won't end too quickly!"

"Oh, no, I don't think it'll go too fast, ha, ha!" He stretched luxuriously in his seat. "Only it's too bad we can't stop a bit in Sophia, too!"

There are some people whom destiny heeds. They have only to express a wish from the depths of the heart and it is fulfilled forthwith. Scarcely had Sophia heaved in sight when a distinct uneasiness became apparent in our pilot's compartment. Our dragonfly flagged perceptibly, and we barely reached the airport with the last feeble wingbeats. Here we were informed that there was no possibility of going on that day.

My companion beamed from ear to ear. He was particularly delighted by the fact that the air line had to pay for our involuntary stay. We collected our money and went rambling through the city. And as the motor trouble proved serious our ramble lasted three days.

Then at last we climbed again into the blue sky. With a well-rested and recuperated growl we flew over the highest mountain ranges, and suddenly a silver streak appeared in the distance, growing wider and wider, and gradually turning into a blue surface stretching towards infinity—the sea, the Gulf of Salonika, guarded by the rocky paw of Chalcidice and towering, white-haired Olympus.

Then cities, and desolate, but undoubtedly most historic,

mountains passed under us. Suddenly my neighbour cried out, pressed his nose to the glass, and sat down in my lap.

"The Acropolis! There it is—the Acropolis!" he cried, beside himself with delight.

And sure enough a grey hill with something vaguely whitish on top had come in sight.

In Athens inflation and hunger prevailed. Even when we got out of the bus that brought us into town we were surrounded by numerous children and beggars, all wanting to carry our bags for bread. All the more astonishing was the spectacle of the food shops, which were bulging with the greatest delicacies. But the prices were so high nobody could pay them.

A young Greek whom a man in Berlin had recommended to me as an interpreter for the expedition was waiting for me. He was a young, athletic man with heavily pomaded hair. We strolled together down a wide, sun-drenched street.

"It was much worse in the winter," he told me. "People starved to death on the street by the dozen. A soldier could get anything for a loaf of bread."

"And didn't anybody do anything to help?"

"Oh, yes. Swedish relief ships come."

"Well, and. . . ?"

"Well, the things just mostly don't seem to go where they ought to." He laughed. "That's a peculiarity hereabouts."

I looked down the shady narrow lanes that we passed. A regular tropical city—ragged, dirty women and men, screaming pedlars, junk shops, fruit stands, and occasionally carefully dressed gentlemen and ladies in between. Black-eyed children tumbled like jolly small animals in the gutters.

The Greek lived in a large, almost empty house, where he was waited upon by a pretty girl with black curls, who, oddly enough, slept in a sort of hen coop—in a wooden crate hanging below the ceiling of one room, accessible only by a ladder.

For supper there were Greek vegetables with canned meat, which I had contributed; then I told the Greek about our intentions, and he immediately knew all about everything. For us, he said, there was only one really good place in the Ægean where we would find clear water and fish in sufficient numbers; this was Anaphe, the southernmost of the Cyclades.

"Are there any sharks?" I asked.

"No, no. Of course there are no sharks!" the Greek hastened to assure me. "You needn't worry about that."

"Oh, well, that's a shame, now. We were particularly looking for sharks."

"Oh, I see! Well, of course on the north side of the island, where you don't usually go, you can find sharks. Fairly many, in fact."

When I had really caught fire and could see us in my mind's eye already swimming about in this fishy paradise, the Greek revealed to me that there was really a most fortunate coincidence. He himself happened to own a sailing ship at Anaphe that would be suitable for our purposes, as well as a house, which he was also willing to put at our disposal. Both ship and house, indeed, were requisitioned by the Italians at the moment but surely it would be a small matter for me to remedy this situation for our scientific purpose?

In the months that followed I met Greeks enough, but scarcely one who ever showed enthusiasm without having an ulterior motive or two. As will subsequently appear, I was often during the expedition a mere plaything of outside interests. Anyhow, I saw through this matter of Anaphe at once. I was merely expected to pull the good man's chestnuts out of the fire. Later I also found out that Anaphe is in fact a fairly dismal piece of rock, where storms were almost constantly raging at this time of year.

"Awfully kind of you," I said. "I'll give the matter my careful consideration."

The ensuing days brought little of cheer. The situation here was considerably more difficult than it had looked from a distance. The introductions I had with me made little impression. Most of the ships were requisitioned, and the authorities concerned showed little sympathy. On top of this came the inflation, with prices out of all reason, and the difficulty of getting food supplies in quantities sufficient to outfit a ship. Nor could we possibly just go cruising at large among the islands, I was assured. The Ægean was a war area, and fish were the smallest things being hunted there now.

Particularly bad was the paralyzing heat, which seemed to kill any initiative. All the more delightfully unexpected, then, my good fortune in finally hitting upon an influential man who saw what I was getting at. Through him the affair was soon put on the right track. He called my attention to the *Universitas*, the former research vessel of Vienna University, which happened to be at the Piræus and was ideal for the purpose. The mate of the ship, whom we visited at once, was very much taken with our plans, and together we managed within a few days to clear up all official difficulties. The vessel was just in the shipyard for an overhaul, having a more powerful engine installed, but in three or four weeks she would certainly be ready for sea. The *Universitas* was some seventy-eight feet long topside, and had sleeping quarters for no fewer than twenty people round a large central cargo space. Thus we could well use some of the cabins for ourselves and the rest to stow our equipment.

The question of fuel and provisions was finally solved also, and so, when I flew back to Berlin after ten days, I could be well pleased with the results of my trip.

8

JUST before my departure I had met a man at the Archæological Institute, who called my attention to the book, just out, on *Pirate Fishermen in Hellas*. It described the adventurous life of an Austrian who had lived for years among the notorious Greek dynamite fishermen.

"You may be interested to know that it is not fiction," he said to me. "This Xenophon, as he's called in the book, really exists, and I happen to know that he's in an interpreters' detachment at Berlin. Mightn't he be the right interpreter for you?"

A week later I had found the man up in Berlin, and arranged a meeting with him. I could hardly wait. In the course of the book this Xenophon had knocked his terrible adversary Psarathanas, a wicked poacher who had treated him like a slave, dead one starry night with his bare fist. So emphatically that the man's skull cracked like a "brittle wood splitting", and only "a sack of withered flesh and now nerveless bones" was left lying at his feet.

I was not disappointed. The man whose hand I soon shook looked like a knotty oak, and there was something in his eyes that pleased me from the first. Here was a whole man, I could feel. A man who loved nature and the great, wide adventure of life, and went precisely the way that pleased him. Close-cropped and gaunt as he was, he looked like a tuberculous highway robber; and at the same time he had the manners of a prime minister. His every motion was, as it were, saturated with calm assurance. Every word he uttered seemed to have some deep meaning.

As we paced along the Havel Canal by night he told me that he was painting murals in the orderly room of the inter-preters' company, and how he was going about it. Between times he was modelling for a painter. Towards evening, when he was off, he spent his time in a park under a certain weeping willow, a spot exactly suited to meditation. He declared you could live very well in Berlin on one mark a day and be happy. He felt the best form of meditation was to put each hand up the opposite sleeve.

Just as he amazed me with these and other remarks, I astounded him when I talked about sharks and our habit of swimming among the creatures. He could not repress a smile. His manner made it quite evident that I need not try such

The starfish, which crawled across the rock was, technically speaking, deformed

Although I was quite familiar with all these animals, they appeared somehow changed to me

Do we mind if the mate eats before us? No, we don't mind at all

Off we go! Xenophon knows every leaf here, every stone and every bush

fairy tales on an old fisherman like him. Nevertheless the matter seemed to interest him—particularly the chance of getting back to his beloved Greece. He told me that he was well able to lead us to all the places that might interest us. On the coast of Pelion he knew a spot where at certain times there were great octopi; seals lived in deep caves on the shore of the isle of Piperi; near Psathura there was a sunken city on the bottom of the sea. Near Steno there were as many sharks as we pleased —he could not help smiling again grimly—and furthermore there was a hole in the bottom that went two hundred feet straight down. He could also show us giant rays, whose poisoned barb alone was ten inches long, and of course turtles, tuna fish, and mackerel in unlimited quantities.

I mentioned Anaphe, but he only laughed. He would have none of the Cyclades or Crete at all. No, he said he knew every island, every rock, and we could just leave it to him. He had spent fifteen years along those shores, and only the Northern Sporades had the clear water we needed, and only there, in his second homeland, would we find what we were looking for.

I strolled home that evening profoundly satisfied. Xenophon would guide us. To giant rays, sharks, seals, and even to a sunken city. Anaphe? I had to smile when I thought about the Greek.

9

"SHARKS are always suspicious, and every shark will attack man if he is hungry, wounded, or both. . . . Of the three species of shark that most frequently attack man, the striped tiger shark, the whale shark, and the blue shark, the latter is the most dangerous. But all three species simply go after anything that comes in their way." (John D. Craig, *Danger is My Business*.)

"Though many accounts are exaggerated, numerous cases have been attested to in which human beings were attacked by sharks and succumbed to their wounds." (Brockhaus, *Lexicon*.)

"Once in the South Atlantic our boat was smashed by a sperm whale, and our crew of six was compelled to keep afloat on oars and planks for perhaps two hours, right amongst the most terrific sharks. Restless as the sea itself, rising and diving, they circled round us, but although our number included some coloured men, supposed to be a delicacy for them, we were not bothered." (Pechnel-Boesche.)

"In our eyes they are rightly considered creatures alike harmful and terrible. Along with the few Cephalopods, whose size probably gave rise to the myth of the sea monster, they are almost the only marine beasts of prey that really attack man and devour him. These robber beings have always stirred us to vengeance and rendered us their implacable foes." (Brehm, *Life of Animals*.)

"Soon his bloody maw, set with sharp triangular teeth, appeared at the rail; a yank, and the beast was on board, leaping in all directions and laying about furiously with his tail. Now was the moment for caution, lest one come too close to the mouth or the far more dangerous tail fin. The boatswain rushed up with a heavy club, the carpenter with an axe, while others tried to loop a cable round the tail, which was finally caught and drawn tight round a tackle block. Only with difficulty were the crew restrained from slashing the creature to bits and destroying it. The shark is the sworn enemy of the seaman, and never have I heard more savage curses than were bestowed upon the chained ruler of the seas. People spat at him, and at last asked for the favour of cutting off the end of the tail, from which blood poured forth in fat streams." (Chun.)

"A knife whizzed through the air, and the Kanaka had

chopped off the shark's tail. The other boys danced like children round the disabled foe, roaring unflattering names at him. At a word of command the line was slacked off, the man in the boat cut the hook out of the awful maw, and the shark had his freedom. He was free—and yet as good as dead. If his companions did not instantly devour him, he must soon have been so weakened by loss of blood that he could not survive it. I cannot, however, remember a single case where a mutilated shark was not immediately devoured by his brothers in great bites, tail first." (William E. Young, *Shark! Shark!*) (Hurst & Blackett.)

"When we speak of their insatiability, this is to be taken literally. They are actually driven by a ravenousness that can never be satisfied. All the food they devour is passed off only half-digested, and thus they are compelled to keep refilling the stomach as it constantly and swiftly empties itself— The stomach of one specimen contained half a ham, a few sheep bones, the rear quarter of a pig, a quantity of horse meat, a piece of burlap, and a paint-scraper." (Brehm, *Life of Animals*.)

"Kako Head on the south coast of the Island of Oahu is considered a particularly dangerous corner. A white man travelling among the islands was reported missing soon after we had started business in Honolulu. . . . Two days later some South Sea Islanders who lived outside the entrance to Honolulu Harbour raised a great outcry: 'Catch shark, big shark, man's foot inside!' Herb and Jack and I had been vainly searching the waters round Koko Head for hours to find the missing fisherman or his body. . . . 'Well, there you are, Bill,' Jack growled. 'There's your fisherman! And some people still claim sharks don't eat men!'— 'Maybe a mistake,' I admitted, 'but then we might find it's so—come on!' And so we went towards the group of Kanakas that stood round the dead shark. On the ground lay a shark, already partly cut open, with a human foot and shoe sticking out of the belly." (W. E. Young, *Shark! Shark!*) (Hurst & Blackett.)

"There has been a lot of nonsense written about sharks, and even now one often hears it asserted that they never attack human beings. . . . There are numerous authenticated accounts, as for instance the awful death of sixteen-year-old Adeline Lopez in the harbour of Kingston, Jamaica. Before the eyes of numerous people she was standing in the shallow water between the Myrtle Bank Hotel and the Yacht Club, holding her small nephew by the hand, when she was attacked by a shark that no one had seen. In mortal terror she cried, 'Father! Father!' He plunged into the water and brought her up. Her right leg had been completely severed from the body. I still own the bathing suit she was wearing and it shows where the shark's teeth cut through the material like a razor. There are awful stories from Panama, Costa Rica, Savannah la Mur in Jamaica, Santa Marta in Colombia, and likewise from the Australian coasts and the South Sea Islands." (F. A. Mitchell-Hedges, *Battles with Giant Fish*.)

"I was formerly very sceptical, and paid little heed to warnings, until while bathing on the coast of Tamatave I witnessed an awful scene, while a travelling companion in my immediate neighbourhood was instantly killed by a bite. I followed the unfortunate victim, a hopeful young man, to the grave, and since then have really believed in the peril." (Keller, *The Life of the Sea*.)

"The jaws, provided with dagger-like teeth, are terrible cutting instruments, whose outward-slanting position admirably suits them to hold and tear their prey with violent jerks of the head. The weakest point of a shark is his eyes, and the man who is able to punch his finger into the beast's eyes is saved. . . . Old robbers that have tasted human flesh obstinately pursue their booty." (H. Stelzner, *Diving Technique*.)

"Erik and I were standing side by side, waiting for a big wave, which promptly came in. When it swept over us Erik suddenly cried out loud, and when I looked in his direction I saw that a shark had bitten into his chest. I quickly grabbed Erik's hands and pulled him ashore. In the time while I was pulling him ashore the shark bit off half an arm and half a leg. I finally got Erik ashore, and he lived another two minutes.'' (Port Natal. From a letter of a ship's boy to the mother of the victim.)

"He was sitting on a piece of wood in the water, and we called out to him to come to dinner. He jumped into the water, and I went off; a few seconds later I heard him calling for help. I saw his head appear, and a lot of blood in the water; he was fighting off a big shark. I rushed to the shore, jumped into a boat, and pushed off, but did not reach him, and he dragged himself ashore alone. His right arm was bitten off close to the elbow. When I picked him up, a great piece of flesh fell out of his right thigh. He died when he reached the beach." (Sidney, Report of the Senckenberg Museum.)

10

JUST as the duck was being put on the table the phone rang.
"Hello?"
"This is Alfred."
"What do you mean, Alfred? Aren't you in Slovakia?"
"We were. We were supposed to be!"
Horrified, I rushed to the Vienna West Station. My mother had prepared a special festive dinner by way of farewell, and afterwards we were going to the theatre. It was our last evening; tomorrow morning I was flying to Athens. The five members of the expedition had departed by train with the boxes at crack of dawn. And now suddenly they were back again.

"Anything for a change!" was my greeting from Joerg, the first to meet me. "It's not so bad. We just need money for new tickets. Heinz and Alfred have no Slovak visa, and there was a real pig-headed frontier official who gave us the boot in spite of all our marine research. Well, it doesn't matter much, we'll take the other train by way of Hungary, and pick up our sleeping-car berths at Pecs."

Meanwhile the others had arrived. Besides Joerg and Alfred the expedition had gained three further members: Xenophon, the knotty oak; Dr. Beckh, a Munich biologist, who had come to our rescue at the last moment as a substitute for the ailing assistant from the Zoological Institute, and finally Heinz—the same Heinz we had hunted goats with in Curaçao. He had been pulled off the ship at Jamaica and interned, but had finally managed to beat his way to Bremen by way of Venezuela, and was now at the Mates' School. They were all in the best of spirits, and set off again at once.

"It's completely dried up and spoiled," said my mother when I got home.

And once more the duck came on the table.

11

IT was evening, and I was in Athens again. Having hastily taken my baggage to the hotel, I was drifting through the narrow streets, still warm from the heat of the day. A delicate aroma of blossoms hung in the air—the scent of the acacias among the ruins.

High above unlit windows, with black washing hanging between them, alone and silent stood the Acropolis. As though contemptuously it looked down upon the nocturnal city. Once men dwelt here whose clear intellects spread light through the world, but that time is past.

Snatches of music and bellowing sounded from a soldiers' tavern as I went by. A door was flung open and a woman tried to get out, but was pulled back, and the door shut again. Go where I would, the old beggar followed me like a shadow. The last time I had given him a loaf of bread, but this time I had nothing with me. In sign language I indicated that it was no use; he could stand me on my head and still not a bit of bread would fall from my pockets. But he promptly replied, also in sign language, that he only wanted to follow me, nothing more. Not for any particular reason. . . . Well, all right. The lonely street now led into the turmoil of the Corso at night, which snatched me up and pushed me along, mysteriously bubbling. Words, whispers, glances, perfume—heaven alone knew how all these people lived, what they felt, and what they were thinking about. A glorious sensation filled me—life, real life had begun again!

Through an old, smelly gateway I went into a little garden, a tavern where all kinds of jolly people were sitting. Over some low masonry in which a charcoal fire was going hung various important-looking copper kettles with different things cooking in them. For the fun of it I asked the price of such a meal from my long-eared host. As expected, it went far beyond my cash reserves. Converted into marks, say about half a month's income for a middle-grade government official. But it turned out that my money would do for a small bottle of *rezina*, a resinous wine that pleases Greek palates. And it turned out further that my faithful shadow, the beggar, was even more interested in a rezina than in a meal. Thus everything was fine. Jolly and contented, he stayed behind with the bottle. And I, jolly and contented, was swept on by the nocturnal stream.

12

NEXT morning reality began. Of course the ship was far from ready for sea; practically no progress at all had been made during my absence. The government offices I had to deal with were in large part on holiday; everywhere I found new faces, who showed small pleasure at having jurisdiction over our expedition in the prevailing heat.

"Oh, dear, it's all very, very difficult!" the mate assured me when I came on board. The new engine had arrived late, and still had to be installed. And then the compass would have to be compensated again, and the whole question of provisions, fuel, and an exit permit would have to be cleared up all over again. And there was no proper ship's boat, and, besides, the place was simply swarming with submarines; only a few days before, he said, they had sunk three ships near Cape Sounion.

"Well, they'll hardly waste their torpedoes on us," I said casually. "Besides, we have harpoons enough on board."

But the mate was not at all inclined to see a joke. Of course he was not afraid at all, but he would be awfully sorry if anything were to happen to his beautiful ship. The man struck me as considerably changed.

I went grimly to work, fighting all these new difficulties, a fight against a hydra that always grew two new heads whenever you cut off one. I was very glad indeed when my team arrived at Athens the second morning. I fetched them from the station in a truck. They were all in good humour, if rather sleepy and dirty.

"We've planned our route out in detail," Joerg told me as the boxes were being unloaded. "The main thing is that we've got to go to Giura. Did Xenophon tell you about that?"

Xenophon, standing silent beside Dr. Beckh, was wearing a flapping khaki suit I had lent him for the term of the expedition. It made him look like a fugitive from solitary confinement, though, it must be said, a very self-assured and determined one.

"Why so? What's there?" I asked.

"What's there? Ibexes are there! Just imagine—real ibexes! Besides, he says the place is simply swarming with seals."

"I didn't say that," Xenophon corrected him. "But there are grottoes on the neighbouring island of Piperi, and there are seals in those. I caught a young seal in my hands there myself on the eighteenth of July seven years ago."

"Most interesting as a matter of zoological geography," Dr. Beckh remarked.

"Oh, go on, zoological geography!" cried Joerg. "Just imagine—real ibexes! You knew I'd brought along my Mannlicher, didn't you?"

"Couldn't we rake up a couple of carbines?" Heinz asked eagerly.

"The ibexes are protected," Xenophon declared.

"Of course we need carbines," said Alfred.

"If for no other reason, on account of the sharks, in case we get any."

"Incidentally,"—Dr. Beckh turned to me again—"I managed to get hold of five glasses of glycerine gelatine in Munich——"

"And tracer ammunition!" cried Heinz. Joerg and Alfred joyfully seconded this proposal.

". . . which will allow us to preserve admirably even the most delicate organisms."

As soon as we reached the *Universitas*, which was now anchored at the outermost mole of the Piræus, a great bustle began. The cases were unloaded and unpacked, a hundred things were discussed and arranged. Everybody tried to be useful in his own way.

"I'll take the cabin beside the companionway."

"No, we've got to fasten the pump farther aft; you keep tripping over it here."

"You knew the harpoons weren't working, didn't you?"

"Just a minute, my dear Dr. Beckh; the formalin will have to go somewhere else—that's an awful stink!"

"If you don't mind, would you take charge of the film supply? All the boxes have got to be numbered."

"There must be cushions somewhere. . . ."

"And what about a snack, gentlemen?"

I gave each one a special set of duties for which he was to be responsible in the future. Joerg was to manage the medicine cabinet, the firearms, harpoons, and the outboard motor; Alfred the cameras and film; Dr. Beckh the scientific equipment; Heinz the diving gear, the pump, the oxygen flasks; Xenophon the nets, tools, and all the miscellaneous equipment we had brought.

"And what about you?" Joerg asked. "What are you going to do?"

"I'm assuming the special burden of conducting the expedition," I replied, never dreaming how bitterly true this would prove.

As soon as the worst of the disorder had been cleared away Xenophon asked for shore leave, which I gladly granted.

"Don't go into any saloons!" people shouted after him. "We don't want to have to bring you back on board in a wheelbarrow!"

Xenophon took note of this, and departed with sedate tread and a small parcel under his arm. Since we, too, were tired of unpacking I announced a free afternoon, and myself took Heinz and the movie camera to the harbour. I had made up my mind to let no film opportunities escape me on this trip. If anything, we had too much rather than too little film with us.

"If you ask me, the mate's a strange fellow," Heinz told me as we strolled along the quay. "I sounded him out a little, and it seems to me that he has an odd idea of navigation."

I could not help smiling to myself. Good old Heinz was probably trying to show off his navigational ability. Ever since I had appointed him my personal adjutant that morning there had been no restraining his zeal.

"Oh, I don't believe it's as bad as all that," I said. "Otherwise they'd hardly have entrusted the ship to him."

"Well, you'll see."

I set up the camera at a particularly crowded spot, swarming with human beings among the market stalls. But the moment I started taking pictures people stood still and stared into the lens.

"What's the picture supposed to show?" Heinz asked, eagerness shining from his eyes.

"A mass of humanity," I said. "All the confusion I can get. You know, a regular seaport scene!"

Heinz sniffed the air. "Is it worth a couple of drachmas?"

"Sure! Why?"

He disappeared into a shop, where, as I later discovered, he got change. Then he astonished me by mounting the parapet, and began shouting across the market place in a resounding tone: "Hey, multitudes! This way, this way!"

Children immediately came running from all directions, and Heinz tossed his change out amongst them. The situation was disagreeable, but at the same time very funny. In an instant a huge, fighting, yelling crowd formed, and even if these were not exactly the seaport scenes one had hoped for, I kept busy at the camera.

"Of course you could have got still better effects with bread," said Heinz as he scrambled down from the parapet.

We strolled back on board. Things had quietened down here somewhat meanwhile. Most of the baggage was now stowed away. Joerg and Alfred were sitting on the mole, kicking their heels and throwing stones into the water. The crew, Dalmatians all of them, were standing in a group by the galley, and gave us a friendly greeting as we passed. When the mate saw us coming he summoned us into the deckhouse and showed us a camera with which he wanted to take colour shots. We were to give him the film, and then he would let us have the use of the pictures. Only his name was to appear with them when they were published. Dr. Beckh was busy arranging the collecting glasses and unpacking and assembling the microscope.

"Too bad I didn't discover until the last moment that I was coming," he told me, "or I could have familiarized myself a little better with the subject." His real speciality was fresh-water fisheries. Particularly carp breeding.

And what was our odd friend Xenophon doing meanwhile? Where had he gone with his package?

He told me the secret long after.

First he ambled through the familiar lanes, trying to get matters clear in his own mind. He was not a person who took life as lightly as we did. For twenty-one years he had roamed the world on adventurous by-paths, and in this life without ties he had learned that duties are the most important things in life. But what was his duty now, when there seemed to be several? First of all there was the duty that war forced upon him; then the duty he had assumed towards us; and finally his duty to his chosen homeland, Greece, in accordance with his dedication at Skiathos, nine years before.

That day was still clear in his mind's eye. He was lounging barefoot, unshaven, and tattered along the sunny quay when he was summoned to a group of men. He had noticed the day before that the traces of dogs had been removed from the monument to Papadiamantis; this, as well as the visible respect that the locals showed to the strange men, indicated a visit from prominent personalities.

"So you're an Austrian," one of the strangers addressed him, "and have been living here as a fisherman for years, and are contented and happy?"

He had nodded. He had, in fact, been contented and happy.

"Then you're well off," the Greek continued, "and you owe your good fortune to this country. But how about duties? Don't you want to be naturalized? Raise a family! Become a citizen of our country, with rights and duties! If necessary, offer your life to this country!"

The stranger who spoke thus had been none other than the Prime Minister from Athens. And what had Xenophon replied?

"I know my duty, and shall do it towards your country, too," he had said. "And I'll do it without any solemn written promises."

Pondering, Xenophon wandered the streets, observing the misery that had come upon the country. Then his mind was made up; he set out to call on Mr. Vlastaris, the head of the Greek Alien Service, whom he had known well for a long time, told him about the expedition for which he was interpreter, and offered to work for the Greek secret service. After all, he was supposed to be guiding the expedition, and so he could easily arrange to have the ship go to any locality that interested the secret service.

"I'm ashamed to have to face you like this," he said, presenting Mr. Vlastaris with two pounds of ribbon noodles, which he had picked up on board. "But I want to do my best for Greece."

"You're an honourable man," replied Mr. Vlastaris, joyfully accepting the ribbon noodles. "If there actually should be anything we'll be glad to let you know. And do go on working for Greece!"

13

THE expedition did not begin under a lucky star. Like busy bees we buzzed off in all directions to master the many difficulties obstructing our departure, but new ones kept arising. The engine didn't work; the trial run had to be postponed; the man who was to adjust the compass fell ill; we had trouble with the port authorities; the radio equipment on board had to be replaced—and so on and so on. Furthermore, our own outfit worried us. All the new underwater cases of the cameras proved leaky and had to be soldered; the newly designed harpoon guns looked beautiful but they didn't shoot; an electrical fishing outfit that we had ordered was only half delivered; the outboard motor ran only when it chose, and it chose very seldom. In my notebook was a total of forty-two different things that still needed putting right.

Finally, after an exhausting week, everything was done. The ship was ready for sea, the equipment was all repaired and tested, and early next morning we were to start. By way of special celebration we were going to see Greta Garbo in the film of *Ninotchka* that afternoon. It was banned in Germany, but there was a print in Athens and a special showing had been arranged at our request. It was to start at two-thirty; the clock had just struck two and I hurried off to the port captain's secretary, who had asked me to take him along.

"Well, what do you say?" he called out as I entered; he looked as if he expected me to say a lot.

"Nothing, so far," I replied. "But I hear it's a good film."

"What? You're still going?"

"Still? Why?"

"Oh, then you didn't even know——?"

I assured him I knew nothing at all.

". . . that your ship is on fire?"

Less than a minute later I was in the car, speeding towards the Piræus. Although we ploughed through the teeming mass of humanity with terrifying speed it seemed the slowest drive I had ever taken. It simply wasn't possible. We couldn't have that much bad luck all at one time! As I had been out all the morning no one had been able to reach me. If only the outfit was still all right!

Finally the tyres squealed round the last corner and I could see the mess with my own eyes. The ship was wreathed in a thick cloud of smoke; beside it on the pier was a great jumble of things and people. Hose lay about but there was no more spraying going on. The ship was somewhat lower in the water; but apart from the cloud of smoke and the confusion things didn't look too bad.

Tousled and sooty, Alfred came towards me. "It's all over!" he panted. "But it was a damned near thing. Pure chance that we were still on board. Everything is saved."

"Yes, but how? How did the whole thing happen, anyway?"

Alfred shrugged. He looked like a stoker after a hard day's work.

"Nobody knows. It started in the engine room. I was sitting up above with Joerg, and we were writing a letter and getting ready to dress for the afternoon when I smelled something burning. It all went very fast after that. We rushed straight below, but by then you couldn't get into the engine room. So we hollared across to the guards and lugged the cases up one after another. Then the harbour emergency service arrived and simply poured water on the ship—a hell of a mess; the chairs are still floating below, and it'll be an awful job to get everything clean again; but, anyway, the fire is out. By the way, don't worry—I got pictures of the whole thing. There ought to be some quite nice shots."

Only now that I was closer could I see what a mess the pier was. Everything lay in jumbled heaps—mattresses, diving gear, cases, laundry, instruments, harpoons, life jackets, and other nautical odds and ends. The boxes of sensitive film lay in the bright sun. Joerg was just easing the microscope case from under an anchor.

When the mate saw me he came up and excitedly drew me to one side. "What about this?" he panted. "The fire was certainly set! I know those Greeks, those damned scoundrels! My beautiful new engine! I slaved for three months to get it. If the emergency service hadn't been so quick the whole tub would have gone to hell!"

Shortly afterwards I had a word with Xenophon. He was indignant at the mate's suspicion.

"That fellow!" he cried. "It's ludicrous—he wants to go sailing to compensate the compass!"

The mate's behaviour had more than once been peculiar; it almost did look as though he didn't like the sea. "I don't want to lose my head!" was his habitual phrase. On the other hand, he had been the one who from the first had done everything to make sure we got the vessel. I was never quite able to make up my mind about the man.

In the course of the afternoon tempers grew more and more frayed. As we had nothing but buckets and one very inferior pump it was hours before the lower compartments were free of water. The mate now declared it would all have to be painted again. This, however, we vigorously disputed. With much grunting and groaning the crew, under our supervision, scrubbed the cabins clean, while we strove to restore some semblance of order to our gear. Unfortunately there had been quite a bit of damage, after all. And some things were missing. The scene of the fire had indeed been roped off but some strange Greeks had been among the fire brigade.

During supper—which, to make matters worse, consisted of a scorched risotto—the mate delivered prolonged speeches on the filth, incompetence, treachery, thievery, and inferiority of the whole set of Greek rascals. He was obviously aiming this at Xenophon, who, however, ate his risotto as placidly as if the mate had been air. There apparently had been some scene between the two during the afternoon. As the rest of us were also tired and exasperated, the atmosphere at table was tense.

And suddenly it snapped.

The immediate cause was the mate's dog, a small white spitz that kept wagging round the table. Although it was by no means a beautiful animal the mate loved it dearly, and actually would eat off the same plate with it. When that plate was empty, the spitz had the unfortunate idea of jumping up on Xenophon's lap and sniffing at his food. Quite calmly Xenophon took a key from his pocket and hit the spitz on the nose. Not very hard but hard enough to make the dog squeal heart-rendingly and run in rapid circles round the deck.

The mate turned as white as a sheet. "What—what's the meaning of this?" he shouted, jumping up and reaching for his hip pocket, where he usually carried a revolver.

"Oh, but look here!" I interposed. "He didn't mean it that way!"

"I meant it exactly that way," replied Xenophon casually.

No one can tell me that the bottom of the sea is dull. For us collectors
it is an interesting field of work. But there are no fish at all

Joerg discovers a cave in the bottom of the sea and searches it for
perch, but reappears with an empty spear

"And I may as well tell you here and now, Mr. Mate, that I shall hit the brute on the nose with the key every time he gets too close to my food. The dog is the dirtiest of creatures, always poking his nose into all the filth he can find—no Greek would put up with a thing like that!"

White-lipped and muttering vague threats, the mate disappeared in his cabin, where we heard him consoling the spitz. We sat about for a while but, being tired, we soon crawled into our bunks. I tried not to attach more importance to the thing than it deserved. But I still could not get to sleep. If trouble was starting on board already, where would it end?

I heard from their steady breathing that the others were already asleep. I was still awake. It must be fairly late. All sorts of strange noises were coming from the foredeck. It sounded as though someone were making a speech, interrupted by jangling. Since I could not get to sleep anyway, I decided to investigate and took my mattress with me in order to sleep on deck.

From the roof of the deckhouse I looked down on a strange scene. The mate had distributed wine to the crew, was completely drunk himself, and was delivering to his men an endless speech in alternating German and Croatian phrases. The chief figures in his babbling rendition were his poor spitz and a certain Greek cockroach that was on board and that he intended to toss overboard like a rusty nail. I listened for a while, then crawled back and lay down on deck.

Things had been considerably simpler in the tent, alone with Joerg and Alfred. What could the crew be thinking? They were decent fellows, these Croatians, but such behaviour was bound to undermine any authority. And he even kept brandishing his revolver during the speech.

Gradually the noises on the foredeck grew fainter. The sailors' voices made it plain that they were tired and fed up with the affair. Suddenly I heard footsteps. The mate came staggering across the deck, looking for me. He hissed my name gently.

D

I pretended to be asleep. If only he would go back to his cabin and sleep off his drink! In this condition he might do practically anything.

Out of the corner of my eye I could see that he still had the revolver in his hand. For an endless moment he stood beside me, trying in a whisper to awaken me. He kept leaning farther and farther forward, until he finally lost his balance and fell full length across me. The smell of a whole wine cellar bathed me, and the hand with the revolver hit the planks right beside my head.

"What the hell goes on here?" Not too gently I set him on his feet again. I tried to take the revolver from him, but he clung to it obstinately. After a prolonged flood of apologies came another, which I was fortunately able to guide over the rail; he insisted on informing me what high personal regard he had for me, hic; but that Greek cockroach had got to go, hic; a very dangerous character indeed; he had an unerring eye for such things, hic; he would never sail in the same ship with the fellow. . . . He shook the revolver under my nose in emphatic negation.

Finally I succeeded in pushing him into his cabin. He fell like a sack into his bunk. I heard him lamenting over the spitz for a while, then at last there was quiet on board. I fell asleep with an uneasy feeling in my stomach.

14

THE next morning we got word that the port captain would call on us at noon. So the ship would have to be in order by that time. And by that time, also, the two fighting cocks would have to make it up. While I set the others to work on the first task, I undertook the second myself. But this was far from simple. The mate was still in very much of a fog, and kept repeating the business about the rusty nail.

"Him or me!" was his unvarying reply. Either the cockroach left the ship or he would not dream of sailing with us.

Xenophon, on the other hand, was perfectly open to reason-
able arguments but emphatically declined to beg the mate's
pardon about the spitz. Nevertheless I gradually succeeded in
effecting a rapprochement, so that by noon not only order
but peace and quiet were actually restored.

The port captain arrived in company with a second gentleman. He greeted us cordially, and the mate clicked his heels.
We led our guests to the table we had set, and since the meal
was good and the wine no less so the party soon grew lively.

First of all we were amazed by Xenophon, who suddenly
showed himself altogether amiable and amusing. He told the
port captain all sorts of things about Greece, which the latter
obviously found most interesting.

"The home of the Greek divers," he said, "is Trikkeri,
a marvellously pretty spot at the entrance to the Gulf of
Volos. The Trikkeriotes are known far and wide, and that's
where the man who found Poseidon came from."

"Oh?" said the port captain, at the same time praising our
bean salad.

"Yes," Xenophon went on, "it's quite a story how Poseidon
came to light. You must have heard about the drag fishermen,"
he said to us. "Well, those people know the bottom of the sea
in that neighbourhood in every detail. They know every
bump, every crag, and every wreck down below, all the way
down to seventy or eighty fathoms. Well, there's one spot they
called 'Chapalo', which means the Anchor; they always
hoisted their nets as they passed over it, or the nets would have
been torn to pieces. But only in one direction. If you sailed
past from the south, nothing happened. So obviously there was
something pointed on the bottom, sticking up diagonally.
People thought it must be an anchor."

Xenophon filled all the glasses, we drank one another's
health, and then he went on: "Well, one of the fishermen was
out, but he fell asleep—old Captain Dimitri, a good friend of

mine, I was out with him once in a terrible storm near Platania,
well, so he fell asleep, and his boy wasn't paying attention
either, and when he woke he found he was just sailing over the
Chapalo, and it was too late to hoist the nets——"

"But how could he tell exactly where it was, way out at
sea?" Alfred interrupted.

"He could see by the bearings of the various islands. There
are mountains and trees and capes that you have to line up—
I'm just about to tell you how careful you have to be. So there
was a sharp jerk at the rope and the man thought, 'Damn, now
Chapalo has torn my net apart!' But when he pulled it in the
net didn't look so bad and there was a broken arm in it—
the bronze arm of Poseidon, hurling thunderbolts!"

"Oh!" said the port captain, and the rest of us, too, felt
obliged to say "Oh!"

"Yes," Xenophon went on, "and the man, being no fool,
naturally said to himself, 'If the arm is there the rest must
be there, too,' and he made a deal with Ialeos, a sponge diver
of Trikkeri: half and half, fifty-fifty; and it shows how amazingly
those people can find their way about that old Dimitri, even
though it's thirty-five fathoms deep there, brought the diver
so exactly to the spot that the boy—the diver sent his boy down
first—landed right on the stomach of Poseidon as he lay in
the mud."

"Thirty-five fathoms?" I cried in surprise.

"Yes, thirty-five fathoms. And you may be interested to
know that divers here claim you can't get any deeper than you
go down on your first try. So he landed right on the stomach,
but didn't see anything because everything was covered with
mud, so he came back and said there was nothing but mud
down there.

" 'It's the right place!' old Dimitri insisted.

" 'Nothing but mud?' the diver asked his boy.

" 'Nothing but mud,' he answered, 'and one single gorgonian.' 'Aha, a gorgonian,' the diver thought to himself.
'How can a coral branch grow out of the mud?' You know,

Dr. Beckh, people thereabouts have their own science of the sea.

"So he didn't say anything but went down, and do you know where the gorgonian was growing? Right out of the navel of Poseidon, buried in the mud!"

This accomplishment really deserved a general toast.

"The end of the story is soon told. Naturally the diver didn't say a word, but hunted up an experienced middleman, and he went and sold Poseidon, as he lay there in the mud, to the Americans. Old Dimitri would have been taken over the jumps, but right from the start he didn't trust Ialeos. He kept watching him, months on end, and one day when he actually caught him near the Chapalo he told the police. They lay in wait a little way off, and just as the divers started raising the thing they rushed up with the motorboat, and not only took the boys' catch away from them but locked them all up. I was in on it; we unloaded at Oreoi—the old rascal weighed nearly five hundred pounds, and the coral branch kept waving from his navel at every step. Now he's all cleaned up and on show at the National Museum in Athens, and the Americans, who had paid half the price beforehand, were just stuck. Because of course they never got any of the advance back."

The port captain laughed, and the conversation turned to other subjects.

15

Is it true that you can swim under water for an hour in your new diving outfit?" the port captain asked me in rather an undertone. "My secretary was telling me about it."

"Yes, that's right."

"And you can move considerably easier with the fins you use?"

"Yes. You can swim almost a third faster. And the main

thing is you have your hands free, which is important in our work."

"Well, now, that's very interesting. And can you carry loads?"

"Yes, within limits we can. If you let a little more gas into the pouch you're that much more buoyant."

The port captain felt that the equipment would be very suitable for raising sunken ships, and particularly for hunting out wrecks and finding exactly where they lay.

"And I should think an outfit like that would be specially good for ships with some kind of damage at sea," he said. "Just think how fast a man could dive, even under the hull, and make repairs!" He asked me whether I could give him a practical demonstration of the outfit.

As it was very hot, and I had for some days been eagerly awaiting the first free moment for an undersea expedition, his request suited me admirably. I told him we could grant it at once along the mole.

When I went down to fetch the gear Alfred came after me.

"If you ask me," he whispered, "the man really has something quite different in mind. Remember how the Japanese took Hong Kong? They were supposed to have had swimming battalions that cleared the mine fields. And the English landed at Dieppe with fins, too——"

It was not impossible that Alfred was right.

We came back and set out on our way, which was not without its difficulties. As the mole at the Piræus is screened off from the sea by a high wall we had to scale the latter with a ladder, and since ungainly chunks of rock clutter the far side our party had to take some tremendous jumps. Furthermore, there was a pretty awful stink among the rocks. But of course this didn't matter; neither the port captain nor his companions paid any attention, and as for me, I promptly plunged below water, where the evil smell immediately ceased.

I had already tested the diving gear in the sea, during my first stay at Athens, on the occasion of a trip to the island of

Aegina. Before the capture of the place the Greeks had thrown all the powder from the coast artillery into the sea, long, grey rods that now lay in heaps on the bottom, eleven fathoms down. I dived with a rope, got down without any trouble, gathered up a big armful of these rods and set fire to them on shore, producing an intense, shooting flame.

Whereas the water at Aegina had been as clear as crystal, here along the mole I swam in thick soup, scarcely able to see ten feet in front of me. Fish whisked before me like shadows. The breathing valves at my back rattled steadily and reassuringly; I felt like an aeroplane in fog. I slid down along the rock wall. Suddenly all was clear.

The turbid water lay above me like a dark cloud bank. and I could see sixty or seventy feet ahead. The rock wall of the mole fell off a few more yards, then the bottom was flat; a broad, sandy floor, some of it covered with seaweed, and a few salpa and marbled bream swimming around. Once upon a time the whole bottom had looked like this; then the mole had been built and a new fauna had developed among the rock fragments. In one cleft I saw some bream, turning elaborately hither and thither. Not far away a sea anemone was spreading its flower-like ring of tentacles. In the deep spots among the stones I saw shellfish and crabs.

Although these creatures were familiar to me in the Mediterranean and Dalmatia, somehow this time they seemed changed. As long as you go hunting only with a spear you see living things as nothing but game. That white bulbous object stuck to the stone yonder, for instance, I would certainly not have noticed in the old days, whereas now it positively jumped out at me. It was a sea squirt, a creature more closely related to man than a bee or a cuttlefish. A tremendous basket gill, in which the tiniest sea dwellers get caught as if in a net, and two holes through which the water is drawn in and ejected: such is the inner structure of this, our potato-like relative. Before the sea squirt attaches itself permanently to a stone, however, and while it is still floating about, animal-like, as a grub in the sea, it has a tiny rudder tail, stiffened by an elastic rod. In the course of biological history this rod, the so-called chorda, developed into our backbone; it was the first sign of bone formation in the animal kingdom. Round this the ribs and extremities developed, and at the front end the head. The sea squirt has given up all this. When the grub settles down it casts off the tail along with the valuable chorda and spends the rest of its life like a plant, sitting in one spot and gulping the sea soup, always full of nourishing bits.

Or the little starfish, crawling across the rock below the sea squirt: it embodies, as it were, a blind alley where nature turned off in her upward march. For when the monocells started forming organisms with more than one cell there were only a limited number of mechanical possibilities for doing so. Nature tried out all these blue-prints, with very uneven success. Some designs proved uncommonly fruitful. For instance, the 'outside skeleton' that distinguishes the crabs, spiders, and insects; or the 'internal skeleton' that all vertebrates, ourselves included, possess. Others, again, offered but small chance for development, and among these are the spiny-skinned species: the peculiar sea urchins, starfish, and sea cucumbers. Their five-pronged symmetry and their open plumbing are of such impractical design that only a few types have succeeded in surviving and developing. From an engineering standpoint, the starfish crawling across the rock before my eyes was a failure. He had more organs of motion than any other creature round about—several dozen suction cups on each of his five arms—and yet he moved as slowly as a snail, which has but one foot.

For the first time, too, I realized that the empty water about me, far from being really empty, was full of countless living beings, only too tiny for my eye to make out. Radiolaria, Globigerina, Foraminifera, Diatoma—dusty names, but what an abundance of shapes they stood for! And all alike, great and small, plankton, fish, shellfish, bacteria, algae, corals, crabs, were only bits of different shapes in the huge mosaic of nature. Not one of them could be understood without all the rest. In the bitter struggle for existence only those features had been able to survive that were of advantage, or at least of no disadvantage, to the organism. Why is the sea bream's mouth shaped the way it is and not some other way? Why is the liver in his belly here and not there? Why can't his scales take on the coloration of the bottom the way the skin on an octopus does? There is a reason for everything, because everything has been shaped as it is by necessity; every living being must be understood in two aspects: on the one hand, as a reflection of its surroundings, to which it must adapt itself as much as possible, and on the other, as a variant of its original blueprint, which never allows more than certain limited possibilities of development.

I glided carefully across rocks, through submarine clefts and over waving forests of seaweed. When I happened to look at the pressure gauge on my belt I found to my horror that my oxygen was almost gone. Then I had been under water for three quarters of an hour. And I was supposed to have dived only for ten minutes.

Alack and alas, the port captain!

I shot hastily upwards, pierced the muddy cloud layer, and reached the upper world again. Joerg and Alfred were swimming a little way off, searching; they had already become seriously worried about me. The port captain and his companion gave me a chilly welcome. The heat and the stink of the rocks had annoyed the two gentlemen so much that we were barely able to persuade them to come aboard for a little refreshment. Then they took a very formal farewell.

They seemed to have lost all interest in the diving gear.

16

A BRIEF interpolation: Why marine research, anyway? From pure curiosity, or for some practical purpose?

Like all research, marine research serves primarily to satisfy a curiosity that parades, when scientifically pursued, under the name of thirst for knowledge. Since this thirst costs money, and the savants usually have none, and hardly any-one is ready to spend money to satisfy other people's curiosity —except perhaps in a limited way a State—pure research is usually combined with some practical aim. In the case of marine research such a purpose is obvious enough. The students investigate the occurrence of useful fish, their distribution, life, spawning places, and migrations; in short; anything that may help man to catch them in larger numbers. And in the same way they investigate all the other animal and plant products that man can eat or use somehow.

There have, however, also been times when science has succeeded in interesting the public in some question to such an extent that the necessary money came from private pockets. This was what happened, about the middle of the last century, when the existence of deep-sea creatures was discovered while taking soundings for the first transatlantic cable. Suddenly the most remarkable fish began coming to light. Fish consisting solely of a huge mouth with a tiny tail directly connected; others with spy-glasses instead of eyes attached to their heads; others, again, that glowed with successive colours like a traffic light. It was even suspected that quite terrible sea monsters might live in the lower depths, and in order to discover these private citizens contributed lavishly. When the monsters proved coy, however, this flow of cash dried up. Next it was polar explorations that attracted public interest and generosity; and then, except for Beebe's sphere and occasional sea serpents, general interest in things marine declined.

And then there is one last possibility of carrying out marine research, namely, on warships in peace time when they have nothing to do. To keep them from rusting, the governments send them cruising the seas, and sometimes scientists are taken, for instance, Chamisso aboard the *Rurik* and Darwin in the *Beagle*. Sometimes even an entire ship was provided, as for instance by England on the famous *Challenger* expedition, or by Germany with the *Meteor* and Austria with the *Navarra*.

Thus we must distinguish between scholarly and practical research. Truly intellectually motivated research is absolutely insatiable. It demands to know everything within the vast spaces of the ocean: every living creature that lives there, every organ of the creature, every function of the organ, and every effect of the function. Practical research, on the other hand, emphasizes what it must emphasize for economic purposes. Though its representatives would gladly take a much greater interest even in the useless sea urchin or the altogether unprofitable sense processes of the lower molluscs, they have to be constantly busy with oysters, herrings, and sardines. But they do this none the less gladly, and can still find time enough for the other, wholly unremunerative, things of the ocean.

17

WE had already concluded that our series of misfortunes was over at last, and the mate was dreading the moment when he would have no choice but to set sail on the perilous sea, when fate once more took a hand on his behalf. When we put out next morning we made less than a mile. Then the mate came rushing excitedly to us, announcing that our ship was sinking.

"It's doing what?" we asked with one voice.

"We've sprung a leak!" he declared. "We've got to get to a shipyard the fastest possible way!"

Hurrying to the engine room, we convinced ourselves that he was speaking the truth. The fire had done some damage near the propeller shaft, and the screw had enlarged this into a leak. Water was spurting into the hold in a good-sized stream. The mate and the engineer were struggling with wooden chocks and rags.

When I came on deck again Xenophon received me with more bad news.

"Tell the mate we've got to get back to Salamis as fast as possible," he said. "There'll be all hell to pay in not more than twenty minutes. A *meltem* is coming!"

I was getting past being surprised at anything. For some reason fate was not well disposed to us. So far as the *meltem* was concerned, I knew only that it signified a particularly treacherous wind. The opportunity to widen my information on this subject was coming all too soon.

Not more than five minutes had passed when a spectacle of nature beyond compare took place before our eyes. It was almost like a stage set as scraps of grey cloud rose with astonishing speed across the sky behind the flat mountain ridge of Salamis, towards which we were heading with all the speed we could muster. Soon the sun was darkened, and the sea took on a steel-grey tone. Luckily the shipyards were already well within sight. In broad, irregular patches the first squalls approached across the water. And exactly at the moment when we dropped our two anchors before the first yard the *meltem* broke loose, full force.

The storm almost seemed to be scooping water up with both hands, so quickly did waves of imposing height rise. Our sailors, who had been trying to row a cable ashore, were lucky to be able to haul their way back aboard by the cable. In less than a minute their boat was half full of water. We hoisted them on board like drowned rats.

"Hey, look! We're drifting off-shore!" cried Alfred.

Sure enough! The storm was so fierce that it was sweeping us away from shore despite the two anchors. In grey masses of foam it howled past us overhead. The *Universitas* pitched more and more alarmingly to and fro. Suddenly we heard cries for help from Dr. Beckh, who had rushed below decks. Here collecting glasses, harpoons, diving helmets, and so on had set off independently on their travels. I arrived just in time to save the microscope from a nasty fall. Everything was topsy-turvy.

Above, meanwhile, a downpour began that was by no means inferior to the one we had gone through in Trinidad. Here, too, the whole sky seemed to descend on us. At the same time the storm raged so fiercely that the drops swept almost horizontally across the waves.

Then its force swiftly faded away. This is a peculiarity of the *meltemia*, which occur only in summer. They reach their greatest force in the first rush, which is why they are so very dangerous. One moment the sky is blue, and twenty minutes later it is whistling fit to flatten you. But they pass off just as suddenly. This time it rained a little longer, then the clouds abruptly broke open, and twenty minutes later the weather was fine again.

As soon as the waves had quietened down a bit the ship was hoisted on a sledge and drawn ashore. According to the yard engineer, the repair would be done in two days. But we were beginning to doubt that we would ever get out among the Greek islands at all.

With shouldered harpoons we marched across the bare mountain ridge to the bay beyond, but the storm had stirred the water up pretty well and there was no sign of any sizeable fish in the underwater fogs. More success awaited Dr. Beckh, who had gone hunting with sharpened sticks for snakes. At least he brought back a walking-stick insect.

In the evening we sat on the deck of our vessel as she floated in the air. While gluing and pounding went on below us far into the night by torchlight, Xenophon told us about the battle of Salamis, whose details he was as familiar with as if he himself had been in the Persian camp.

"Xerxes was particularly careful," he told us, "because he had already lost several fleets. While the land army marched across the Hellespont—according to Aeschylus' drama this had particularly insulted the ocean—the Navy followed close along the coast, and he was so careful that in order to avoid circumnavigating Mount Athos he had a canal cut through the Isthmus. The Athenians under Themistocles had no choice but to evacuate the city. It went up in flames, and everyone fled over here, to Ambelaki"—he pointed to the bare, high ground where Dr. Beckh had found the walking-stick insect—"while the Persians took up their position over yonder beside the big rock I showed you on the way here." Despite the darkness, the silhouette of the rock was still visible on the far side of the bay. "There Xerxes sat down in his bright red cloak, and that's why to this day people call the rock the 'chair of Xerxes'. "

"Oh, so he sat on that rock?" asked Joerg, with suddenly awakening interest.

"Yes, on that rock, and watched his ships slowly coming into the bay. But the old boy had underestimated the incredible seamanship of the Athenians. Suddenly their ships shot forward, cutting off the retreat of the other side, and before the Persians knew what was happening to them their whole fleet was destroyed."

"Marvellous sailors, those Athenians," said Joerg, puffing at his pipe.

"Yes, marvellous sailors indeed," Xenophon agreed.

"And the most remarkable thing about it," Joerg went on in a silky voice, "is that the battle of Salamis, as any half-educated person knows, wasn't fought here but off the real Salamis on the east coast of Cyprus, about two hundred and fifty miles from here—Xenophon, I'm afraid you confused it with Italian salami."

After two days the ship was ready to be put back in the water. Returning once more to the familiar mole of the Piræus, we discovered that a few more difficulties had arisen calculated to delay our departure. But by now we were fed up and paid no further attention to anything. When the mate told us regretfully that the ship's papers were not in order we simply took them away from him and two hours later they were in order.

That evening we were sitting on deck again; this time Joerg, our doctor, was the centre of discussion. The question was whether health is a right of every citizen, and therefore the doctor ought to be an official in the service of the State, which would destroy all ambition; or whether, on the contrary, doctors had a right to demand a special fee for special ability.

"All right, listen here, Joerg," said Xenophon suddenly. "Tell me, should a person enjoy health?"

"Of course—why not?" replied Joerg, surprised.

"Can you know what warm is if you haven't felt cold?"

Joerg laughed aloud. "Had a couple too many?"

But Xenophon was not to be put off. "Can you know what health is without having been sick?"

"Bravo!" cried Alfred.

"Well, then," Xenophon completed his logical structure, "sickness is just as necessary as health, and in my eyes a doctor is no better than a high-class barber."

"Just you wait, my boy," said Joerg. "You may be coming to me some day for a haircut!"

18

I T is five o'clock in the morning; we had really meant to put out at four but the mate overslept. Or, rather, to be fair, the boatswain, who was supposed to wake the mate, overslept.

All the more briskly now the mate is at the wheel, giving the necessary commands. We stand about on deck, rather sleepily, in pyjamas, experiencing the great moment. This should, by rights, have been celebrated with more ceremony, but it really is awfully early. The screw is just beginning to turn, a gloriously full sound— What's that?

A heavy blow sets the ship trembling. An equally heavy blow must have shaken the mole. But luckily the ship is still whole. We have rammed the mole with considerable force, a manœuvre that cannot be described as completely successful navigation.

Now the screw is turning in the other direction and our ship willingly starts to the rear. What's that, Heinz? About to bump again? No, he's just going to turn, don't you see?

Wham! An almost more violent shock makes the ancient hull quiver. This time our stern has rammed the mole. But once again the ship is intact; a scar on the pier is the only trace of the little accident. The damage to the mole will be easily repaired, and we have made the decisive turn. The one obstacle that might still give us trouble is the lighthouse; but we pass it without further damage.

Before us lies the morning-smooth, the endless, the longed-for, adventure-bringing sea!

"A fine day!" I say to the mate.

"Well, yes," is the somewhat grumpy answer. As if to say, "Well, yes, but it isn't over yet."

"A fine ship, the *Universitas*," I go on.

But to this there is no answer.

We're moving! We're moving! At a respectable speed we cut the long swells. The Piræus moves off into the distance in a grey screen of haze. The houses along the coast grow scarcer. The shore becomes lonely and abrupt. The sun mounts, and gradually a stronger wind comes up.

Hoist sails! Already the sailors, our honest Croatians, are at the ropes. The sails go up with a rattle and a flap. Onward, onward—we, too, must think of work. Everything we see we are seeing not for ourselves alone, but equally for the cinema audience we hope will share our expedition. Forward, up and at the cameras! First, let's show what each of us does during the outward voyage.

At once we are all well in the midst of our work. First, the Croatians have to lower the sails again and hoist them once more. Then it's the mate's turn to stand impassively at the wheel. This shot in particular promises to be most impressive. Then it's Xenophon's turn; as our expert guide, he has to point off into the distance. We take Joerg, our huntsman, cocking the new harpoon gun in the shadow of his Tyrolean hat—an

About seventy-five feet down one begins to feel physically the immeasurable extent of the sea

There are over a hundred suction cups on each of the eight arms of the octopus. With these he sucks himself fast to his victims

To make sure the fish would not be frightened, I personally took
the anchor to the bottom

awful shame that the gun doesn't work. Alfred, our underwater cameraman, is working on the scenario, for which purpose he has donned diving gear. Next comes Dr. Beckh. He is shown fastening a plankton net to a pole, and then moving glass instruments from the table to a chair, and then back from the chair to the table. Excellent! Now for Heinz. What could he possibly do during the voyage? Oh, of course, he's a student mate; let him shoot the sun with the theodolite. As for myself, I stand in the middle of things, giving orders and gazing into the distance with the gravity and resolution befitting the leader of an expedition.

Have we forgotten anything? No, our audience now has an idea of what we do during the voyage. The props are cleared away, and we sit down, relieved, forward by the bowsprit. Nothing is so fine as sniffing the aromatic breeze and swinging one's legs high above the passing waves.

About noon the temple of Poseidon comes into view. Great excitement. Here is the chance to put the telephoto lens to use. But it's very difficult to get a solid stance on the trembling ship. Heinz's back serves as a spring prop, and so the shot is a success. At the same time Dr. Beckh reads aloud from Baedeker everything worth knowing about the temple. Xenophon amplifies this with remarks of his own, which Dr. Beckh immediately notes on the margin.

Cape Sounion is duly passed, and we now turn our back on the sun. At three o'clock, sailing splendidly, we reach the mine barrier. The coastguard ship in whose company we have been travelling leaves us here. At this our mate is beside himself. The moment we come within earshot he shouts across to the captain that he had supposed the coastguard ship was also going as far as Chalcis. The reply is quick in coming, and is not altogether flattering. In substance it says that apart from bedbugs in the mate's bunk there is positively no danger to be feared within the straits.

And in fact we reach Chalcis in good order that evening. The first night of the expedition is spent within the sea gate-

E

way, and next morning we start with new strength to negotiate the difficult passage. As soon as the bridge opens we start moving. Luckily this time Heinz is standing close beside the mate, so that at the crucial moment he can grab the wheel from him and turn it in the opposite direction—something monstrous from a seaman's standpoint, but even the crew agrees that we owe it only to Heinz that we have passed the pillar unharmed.

Now it is about eleven, and we are already quite a stretch into an area that Xenophon calls Lita Donisia. The difficult process of dropping anchor is safely behind us and we are now busy loading our boat with everything we may possibly need for our first thrust into the depths of the ocean.

"Have we got enough spare spearheads?" I cry.

"Yes, spare heads in the boat."

"And spare film?"

"Yes, spare film too. Should the diving helmet go along?"

"Yes, let's take it—you never know . . . no, better leave it here."

My instructions are promptly followed. Since this is, after all, our first excursion, everyone is busy and excited. It is the first time, furthermore, that we are not only to hunt but to do some serious scientific work. Two main aims of the expedition must be distinguished henceforth: our collecting and the movie-making. Every opportunity must be exploited in both directions.

Joerg is the only one who preserves his aplomb. With a philosopher's calm he tugs at the rope of the outboard motor, which seems determined to stall our departure. When at length it does noisily start we find Xenophon has been forgotten, so we have to go back. When shall we be back for dinner? Well, in an hour or two. Do we mind if the mate eats ahead of us? No, we don't mind at all.

Off we go.

Xenophon knows every leaf and every rock and every bush here. We are in highly volcanic territory. Between the little island before us and the cape there is always a strong current, now in one direction, now in the other; only twice a month do the currents offset each other. When is that? Always two days after the new moon, Xenophon declares. Dr. Beckh finds this very interesting from the planktonological standpoint. Alfred, please take a short note. No pencil? Well, Xenophon, please tell us this again on board. And in future we must always take a pencil along——

Well, there we are. It is a gentle little bay with black, rounded lava stones and dusty bushes above. To our left lies the cape, beside it the wreck of a small vessel and behind us the wake, leading in a straight line to the *Universitas*, which is flying a pennant at her mainmast in honour of our first trip.

As nobody can wait, the boat rocks menacingly. It turns out that even embarking and debarking in due expeditionary form have to be practised and organized. But that is only a matter of minutes. Then the five of us are swimming hither and thither, while Xenophon remains in the boat, watching us in astonishment. Joerg has the spear, Alfred the first camera, I the second film camera, Heinz the still camera, and Dr. Beckh the underwater net, which he still tends to handle like an oar. I have to show him how to swim with the fins, or he'll end up by drowning. All this takes time, but what you have to do you have to do.

Then I make haste to overtake the others, who are already playing about in the depths. Only now can I take a look at the ocean floor below me. It is mostly big, round, smooth stones, with green weeds and some sort of reddish objects among them. A single deep breath, and I am fifteen feet down and close up. They must be some sort of synascidia growing there, or possibly hard sponges. It is a glowing red crust covering the rock. Back to Dr. Beckh: I must show him this stuff. He comes at once, but it now turns out that Dr. Beckh can't dive fifteen feet. On the contrary. When he tries to plunge, he just surfaces all the more firmly. His legs shoot up, and he makes a hell of a racket.

"But you told me you were a good diver, didn't you?" I ask him reproachfully.

Dr. Beckh himself does not know how it can be. In the swimming pool he was always a good diver, in fact one of the best. Here it just doesn't seem to go. Probably it's the salt water that wants getting used to.

"Come on, you take the underwater camera. That'll pull you down all right."

But Dr. Beckh doesn't want to do that either.

So I dive alone and scrape the red crust off the rock. On the surface, I present it to Dr. Beckh, who, however, has a hard time making anything out through the water-tight goggles, because these are now half full of water. This is remedied, but as to what sort of red crust is involved, that remains temporarily a mystery.

"It might be a sponge," I say.

"That's right, a sponge," Dr. Beckh agrees.

"Or else it's a synascidia."

"Quite right, or it's a synascidia."

Outside, meanwhile, where the other ocean explorers are swimming about, fierce and excited howls are heard. Alfred has discovered a ray at a great depth, but Joerg cannot see it; hence the argument. Unfortunately I arrive too late on the scene, for now Alfred does not see the ray either. It is alleged to have been a tremendous great beast. Alfred hardly dares even guess, but does guess it was at least ten feet long. Joerg had swum off like a madman in the direction Alfred had pointed out, but there was no sign of the fleeing creature there either.

It is remarkable, incidentally, that when you take a close look there isn't really a single fish anywhere. But you can't call the ocean floor uninteresting; there are any amount of interesting shells and sponges and corals, an inexhaustible field for our collecting activites; but no fish whatever. Hence Joerg looks rather out of place with his lance, whereas the rest of us can at least use our cameras to photograph and take pictures of one another. But Dr. Beckh is shouting again! While Xenophon inquisitively rows after me, I hurry back. It turns out that Dr. Beckh has withdrawn to a part of the sea

where he can reach bottom; it is only three feet deep. Here
he has discovered among the rocks a strangely gelatinous
creature. This time we jointly detach it from the rock, and
Dr. Beckh then personally fetches it up in the hand net. We
exchange views again, but no doubt about it the ocean fauna
is a hard nut to crack.

Two hours are passed in hunting, filming, and exploration,
a third in persuading our outboard motor to bring us back
aboard the ship. The views about the success of the expedition
are divided. From the hunting standpoint Joerg utters a single
expressive word, which cannot, however, be put on paper;
Alfred is still excited about the giant ray, and keeps on producing new details of its appearance. The only real enthusiast
is Dr. Beckh. He has a large jar full of interesting sea creatures,
which we will now examine more closely on board, a fine
beginning for our collections.

So far as Heinz and Xenophon are concerned, they devote
themselves jointly and successively to the provender. With it
they eat oysters, which Heinz has fetched up from the bottom
at Xenophon's suggestion, and which are alleged to taste
wonderful with olive oil. Heinz further maintains he has taken
some splendid underwater pictures, and this rounds off the
day's success. Ha! We are back at the ship. Easy, Joerg, or
we'll all capsize! And now, our work done, it's dinner for us!

19

As we wanted to reach Skiathos before evening we went on
right after lunch. But we did not get far. Something was out
of order again. This time, for a change, the radio transmitter.
It had suddenly balked, and the mate declared he must report
this to Athens at once. The next place where this could be done
was Oreo. Half an hour later we were there and cast anchor
off the picturesque little town. While the mate was waiting

for his telephone call to Athens we took a walk through the surrounding vineyards. After three hours the reply finally came. The mate had great difficulty concealing his satisfaction. He had instructions from Athens that the transmitter absolutely must be repaired before going on. As this was possible only in Chalcis, the ship would have to go back there immediately.

We held an immediate and embittered expeditionary council.

"It doesn't matter a bit," declared Xenophon. "I know a beautiful, solitary spot near here, where we can put up our tents. And there are two sunken ships in the neighbourhood. We'll simply wait there until the *Universitas* comes back; that way, you can make good use of the time."

The proposal was unanimously accepted. Heinz, however, was to remain on board and take care that the mate did not stay any longer in Chalcis than was absolutely necessary. We calculated that if the ship left early next morning it could easily be back in two days. With some grumbling the crew, already growing weary, hauled in the 125 foot anchor chain again. We set off, and reached Xenophon's place at dusk. It was in fact most idyllic, a flat, wooded bay beside a cape, off which lay two small, rather abrupt little islets. The sea was now perfectly still. Great birds circled over the outer islands.

We put ashore everything we would need—tents, blankets, diving gear, guns, harpoons, cameras, provisions, and so forth —and set up a pretty camp among the trees along the beach. Everyone was in the best of moods. By the light of our little lamp Dr. Beckh and I scrutinized the creatures we had taken. Joerg and Alfred played cards. Xenophon, meanwhile, prepared a Greek supper, which we immediately consumed with relish.

As there was no fear of rain, and no mosquitoes here, we put down our rubber mattresses in the open air outside the tents. Shouts came across to us from the ship for a while. The mate was moving around with two sailors in a boat, turning a spotlight on the water, and trying to spear fish with a trident.

"Hey, look here! Here's the ray!" we heard him shout several times.

Then there was gradually quiet, and we heard only the steady rush of the sea. The starry sky arched infinitely wide and infinitely glittering above us. The smell of the dying fire mingled with the perfume of the blossoming shrubs. . . .

I fell blissfully asleep.

20

My awakening was anything but blissful. I gave a fearful cry, and danced about in a circle like one possessed. I'd never felt such a terrible pain. In addition, there was the fright, for I had been sound asleep when the scorpion bit me in the thigh.

I flung the revolting creature from me, remembering as I did so that the bite of a scorpion is supposed to be deadly. But Xenophon was immediately to hand, reassuring me. So long as you had the scorpion itself, it was all right. You had only to crush it and rub it on the wound, and the pain would subside within an hour.

Joerg gave a grisly laugh when he heard of this method of treatment, but I was ready for anything that might relieve my pain a little, and I gladly accepted Xenophon's ministrations. He gleefully trod on the scorpion, and smeared the pulp over the sting, which had swollen up a good deal even in this short time.

"Now please just don't tell me that it's really getting better!" Joerg implored. But I could not oblige him. It actually did get better, and in less than an hour all was over.

"That'll bring good luck," declared Xenophon as we ate breakfast.

It had occurred to us to take the painful awakening for our expeditionary film, if not in the original, at least convincingly acted. In the process we saw history repeat itself. To get a good background for the shots Alfred walked into the the water with the camera, and missed by a hair stepping barefoot on a *Petermaennchen*—a little spotted fish, with a poisoned dorsal finspine, whose wound produces a dreaded delirium. In the case of both scorpion and Petermaennchen this was the only specimen we caught sight of during the entire expedition.

"To be consistent," said Joerg, "we ought to take a picture of Alfred jumping while he's taking a shot of you jumping."

Dr. Beckh came with two small nets, and we surrounded the Petermaennchen from all sides and drove it ashore. The fish would always take a little jump, then dig so adroitly into the sand that only its eyes and the poisoned spine stuck out. Finally Dr. Beckh clapped the net over it and we put the creature in our aquarium.

Meanwhile, not far from the cove, two fishing boats had turned up, in one of which Xenophon thought he recognized an old fisherman friend. In this connexion he explained the peculiarities of the region to us. He said the outer of the two islands off the cape, Ari Ronisi, was named from the fact that pirates had once buried there a treasure of silver; it had actually been found thirty years before. The straits between it and the other little island were an interesting territory for us because sometimes schools of fish would pass through; besides, the two sunken ships were there. He said the fishermen were busy catching octopi, which they lured out of their holes with bait.

This was enough for us to begin with. We quickly loaded all our diving gear into the boat and put off. Dr. Beckh stayed behind. He wanted to observe and sketch the captured Petermaennchen.

As soon as we approached the straits we saw bonitos jumping up. Their plump bodies, glittering in the sun, appeared one after another on the surface. There must have been twenty of them. They were playing. Instantly Joerg and Alfred seized their harpoons and slid into the water.

"You swim over to the left," said Joerg excitedly, "and out yonder we'll try to get them between us."

"Shall I come after?" asked Xenophon.

"Don't you do anything! Just keep still!" The two were on fire with hunting fever.

We watched them swimming in great curves, but the fish always popped up exactly where the men were not. Xenophon, who obviously did not think it possible to do a fish any harm under water with a spear, watched these exertions with a suppressed smile.

I buckled on the diving gear and slid into the water myself. The sea was wonderfully clear here. I could see every detail on the bottom, thirty feet below. There was a flat, rocky ridge going under water from one islet to the other, and sinking away into the deep sea at a fairly sharp angle on the side where we were. I saw no signs of any large fish. Only directly below me a few giant pinna mussels, recognizable by the black crack in their shells, and in deep water, at the limit of my visibility, a vague jumble. . . . Well, I would soon be down there.

I slid away almost without motion. By now I was so familiar with the gear that I scarcely had to think about it. When increasing depth compressed the breathing pouch at my back, so that my specific gravity increased and I sank faster, a brief squeeze on the valve of the oxygen flask fastened to my belt was enough; instantly fresh gas would rush into the breathing pouch, my descent would be checked, and I would hang once more without weight in the water. The gear was so small that it did not hinder my motions in any way; its centre of gravity was so adjusted that I could move in any position I liked, even backwards and downwards. A glance at the pressure gauge would always show how much oxygen was left in the flask. If I had used up a certain amount, or sunk a few feet deeper, I pressed the button; that was all I had to do.

I floated down like a Christmas angel towards the undersea landscape. My breathing was calm and steady. It was always the same cycle. When I breathed out, the used air went through the right-hand breathing tube into the potassium cartridge on my back; there the resulting carbonic acid was absorbed, and the oxygen, purified, went back through the left breathing tube into my mouth. Breathing pure oxygen is by no means harmful, as people often suppose; test subjects have lived more than twenty-four hours in pure oxygen without suffering any harm. On the other hand, one gains no special strength by it, as is sometimes also supposed; the red blood corpuscles can absorb only a limited quantity of oxygen, and no more. For the diver, pure oxygen has this advantage over air, that the lungs receive no nitrogen, whose easy solubility in blood produces the dreaded caisson disease. If you breathe air you must come back to the surface only very gradually, or else the nitrogen bubbles in the blood. In severe cases this may cause death, and at all events terrible pain and sometimes paralysis. In that case the diver must be brought as quickly as possible under the same pressure as before, and then, when the bubbles in the blood have disappeared, must be returned more slowly to normal pressure. Breathing pure oxygen, I ran no such risk. I could dive and come up as fast as I liked, and another advantage of pure oxygen was that my eight-tenths litre flask, under 200 atmospheres, was enough for a full hour, whereas for the same time I would have needed about twenty times as much air, and accordingly a much bigger flask. Scientists had warned us, however, against diving below sixty feet; here, they said, pure oxygen was poisonous to the human organism.

Reaching the bottom, I looked upward. The boat now floated like a big cigar high above me; beside it were two flying frogs, each with a match in its front paw—Joerg and Alfred, swimming back to the boat. They waved down to me and I waved up to them. Then I looked around. The sea floor was a good deal more cleft and a good deal less flat than it looked from above. This is often the case; as the light comes perpendicularly from above, the landscape from a bird's-eye view loses its perspective. I had hit bottom directly beside one of the pinna mussels, and the vague bustle was diagonally to one side below me. There were in fact the fragments of two sunken ships, and above them floated tiny fish in a dense cloud. I swam closer. The wrecks were, on the whole, disappointing. They were two small, completely decayed wooden cutters, partly sunk into the bottom; the jutting knee timbers reminded you of the ribs of half-decayed fish.

Like a magic cloud approached by a wizard's wand, the swarms of fish gave way before me. I turned over on my back and forced my way under one of the ship's sides, heavily encrusted with barnacles. In the dark hollow behind a few bream were tumbling about; further forward was a huge crayfish among sea urchins with blue spines. Here, too, I saw no big fish. Having inspected the wreck from all sides, I swam once more, quite vigorously, through the clouds of fish, then dashed some distance across the sea bottom, sometimes so close to the rock that the weeds brushed softly against me.

Uncontrolled delight took possession of me. Never had I felt so free and unhampered under water as I did with this gear. I could take whatever position I pleased. I could sit down or lie down or turn somersaults or stand on my head; here was no clumsy diver groping along the ground, but a new sort of amphibious being swimming as the sea had never seen anything swim.

Really the bottom should have been teeming with fish here. The many clefts and hollows in the rock, the meadows of seaweed between them, and the steady currents across the rock offered ideal living conditions for fish. Nevertheless the place was completely deserted.

Why?

A few small fish lying dead on the bottom told the tale. Here, as along most Greek coasts, dynamite was being used. Of course, it is strictly forbidden; nevertheless this outrageous practice has become universal in the Aegean since the First World War. Everywhere explosions roar in the solitude, and

none of the poaching fishermen bothers to realize that this
bombing kills not only the few fish round about, but also destroys
the small fry and the plankton, the basic food of the sea, over
a far greater area. A catastrophic decline in the fish population
of the Aegean is the result. Whereas once upon a time the
Greek sea was famous for its abundance of fish, there are some
coasts now where the few fishermen who have remained self-
respecting are obliged to go hunting for individual fish by
tracking them down with glass-bottomed boxes and then
surrounding them with hand nets.

"What about the police?" we had asked Xenophon.

"Oh, hell, the police! What can they do in all these islands?
Of course patrol ships go about but the poachers know their
beat and their schedules by this time."

"And what if somebody does get caught?"

"Well, he gets locked up for a while, and when he gets out
he does it again. There's a nervous excitement to it that never
lets you go once you've started. I'm an old hand at it and I
know!"

I had swum another 500 yards when I noticed a small white
object that kept dancing up and down in the same spot among
the rocks like an irresolute butterfly. As I drew closer an unusual
spectacle met my eye. Under a big stone slab, half hidden in
the shadow, sat an octopus, staring with gleaming eyes at
something that danced just under its nose. An upward glance
told me the story. On silvery heights far above floated the
silhouette of a boat, and beside it a gleaming circle: the glass-
bottomed box through which the fisherman was looking down.
I was below one of the strange octopus fishermen, and the
dancing butterfly was nothing more than a bit of meat dangling
on a line, with which the man was trying to lure the octopus
from its hiding place.

Neither the fisherman nor the creature had noticed my
arrival. Pressing close to a rock, I watched to see what would
happen next. The octopus's excitement was visibly mounting.
One of the tentacles separated from the oozing mass and curled

forward avidly yet hesitantly through the water. Immediately
the bait danced back a little. It was astonishing how clearly
the fisherman above could follow the movements of the almost
completely hidden creature.

Then the polyp, oozing rather than moving, left its hiding
place. Only now did I see how big it was. I estimated that it
must weigh a dozen pounds. As it moved, the pattern of its
skin kept changing colour, probably with excitement. Its gaze
fixed unwaveringly on the hypnotic dance of the bait, it glided
along on seven of its tentacles with their innumerable suction
cups, always stretching the eighth out ahead, so that it seemed
to point like a cane through the water. Only the tip curled and
twisted, like an earthworm impaled on a hook, to seize the bait.

Suddenly—the octopus had now come some distance from
its hide-out—greed overcame it. Shooting forward, it snatched
the bait with several of its arms and crushed it to its beaked
mouth. At the same moment the yank came from above and
the hooks hidden in the bait pierced the gelatinous flesh. I
barely saw the octopus fling two of its arms downward, and
then it disappeared in a cloud of ink that it ejected to conceal
itself. The line now led taut into the cloud, and when the current
finally cleared the water I could see it disappearing straight
under the stone slab. The fisherman had been a trifle too slow.
The octopus had managed to catch the rock with one of its
tentacles after all, and had pulled itself back into its retreat.

I was sorry for the man up above. I left my hiding place,
swam over to the slab, seized the line, and tugged at it as hard
as I could. The result, however, was failure. The hook tore
loose. Blast! Only now did I remember what Xenophon had
told us. If the polyp succeeds in regaining its hide-out the fisherman lets down some acrid herb or a piece of copper vitriol
on a long pole and holds it in front of the hole until the octopus's
eyes begin to sting and it rushes out of the cave. And in fact
the fisherman above was in the very act of lowering into the
water a pole with a bundle of herbs fastened to the end. My
over-eagerness had cost him his catch.

Suddenly the pole stopped. The glass-bottomed box was moved excitedly to and fro, and I could see two heads appearing alternately in the bright opening. The fishermen had noticed me, and obviously considered me a sea ghost.

I waved up to them, but their excitement only mounted. Then it occurred to me that perhaps I could make up for my mistake after all. The octopus was still in its hole; possibly I might manage to fasten the hook in it again. I swam directly back to the stone slab and forced my way into the hollow. At first I could see nothing whatever—only sand and rock. Then I discovered the slit eyes in the very farthermost corner. The polyp had adapted itself so amazingly to the coloration of the stone that its body was quite invisible. Only the eyes betrayed it. I strove to reach it with the hook, but my arms were too short. Immobile, like an evil demon, the mollusc surveyed me with its cold, slit eyes—almost as if the stone itself were looking at me.

To try my luck from the other side, I swam round the rock slab, and there to my surprise I discovered a second, almost equally large, octopus lying motionless on the sand under a jutting rock. Its eyes were closed, and when I cautiously brought my hand near, it did not move. Could this be a 'cuffio'?

In July, Xenophon had maintained, the male polyp goes in search of a suitable female, and when he has found one there is first a bitter struggle before he succeeds in penetrating the virginal chamber. After the mating he is devoured by the female, which is to be taken only figuratively, for he remains intact and sometimes even lives for a while, but is only a "cuffio, an empty pouch consisting of nothing but skin and water".

This cuffio, or whatever it was, came at just the right moment. I quickly attached the hook to it. The blot on my escutcheon was erased, even if the people up above were even more puzzled. I waved up at them again, then glided down with hasty fin strokes; down over slopes growing ever more colourful: into a twilight that took on a marvellous, rich, blue tinge.

21

AT a depth of seventy or eighty feet you begin to feel physically the endless extent of the ocean. What you feel down there is the same kind of reverent shudder as when you go in alone about dusk to the mighty vaulting of a Gothic cathedral and the silent chamber seems in the vague twilight to spread into infinity. Where are the boundaries of this greatest continent? As if the sea were a monstrous animal whose very whisker tips you could barely tickle, you look into a gaping maw big enough to swallow up our whole ant-like humanity. What do we know of life in the depths? What do we know of the mysteries still hidden down below? Tiny nets have been lowered like thimbles into the yawning space—are we rashly to deduce from the contents of those thimbles a knowledge of life below? One should mount a headlight and an automatic film camera on the back of a sperm whale, and then one might get a glimpse of that other world that is no less strange to us than the land-scapes on Mars or Venus. The sperm whale is the only surface creature that dives to those awful abysses in its hunting. Fragments of cuttlefish tentacles found in its stomach lead to the conclusion that the molluscs living below are of imposing size. But what other beings, not included in its diet, may it meet besides? Does every sperm whale that vanishes in those icy depths come back to daylight from its tempestuous expedition? Might it not be that, after all, those mythical sea monsters do exist which formerly used to be seen often, and frequently by several people at once, whereas today the noises of ships' motors seem to have scared them away from the upper regions? When Sir Charles Lyell asked the American Colonel T. H. Perkins whether he had ever heard of the sea serpent, the answer was, "Unfortunately I have seen it!"

Unfortunately because he had made himself ridiculous
telling about it. In 1848 H.M. Corvette *Daedalus*, between the
Cape of Good Hope and St. Helena, sighted a ninety-foot
snake-like creature so close that Captain McQuae declared
in his official report to the Admiralty that if it had been an
acquaintance he could have recognized its features with the
naked eye. Baron von Forster, commanding a German U-boat
in the First World War, and five members of his crew saw a
sixty-foot sea monster that was flung seventy or eighty feet
in the air by the underwater explosion of a sunken ship. It
was crocodile-like in shape, had two front and two hind legs
with powerful fins, a long pointed head, and a figure like the
Mosasaurus of the primeval chalk seas. Scholars could not
agree upon the origin of a twenty-four foot corpse of similar
shape that was washed ashore in 1934 near Cherbourg. The
famous Loch Ness monster was seen in 118 cases, sometimes
by no fewer than seventy people simultaneously.

I stood on a rock seventy feet down, gazing into the far
distance, unable to see my fill of this blue that grew ever
darker and richer as it went downward, while above me it
vanished in a boundless silver sky. Little woolly-lamb clouds
floated on high as if in a spring heaven—the waves.

I glided farther down, and a dreamlike mood took possession
of me. The poison of oxygen under high pressure gradually
steals away the power of logical thought. A glorious state!
As if intoxicated, you perceive life in itself, lose every mis-
giving, every hesitation, every fear; you swim, see, experience,
and are amazed—and glide on, ever onward as if you belonged
here and nowhere else. A hairy worm is wriggling in the
branches of a seaweed—I sit placidly there observing it, perhaps as vacantly as a fish would do. All colours seem doubly
intense. Fish flash past, or float along. And time, too, flies and
floats onward, and I am nothing but part of it, a process inter-
woven a thousand ways with the world around, working upon
me.

The farther I penetrated, the more life there was round

Alfred caught a peculiar sea snail which had a little
umbrella on top

I was as interested in the sheer cliffs of Giura as Joerg was in the
ibex which were said to live there

No aerial photo of Africa, but algae on the sandy sea bottom about me. Pressed against a cliff were ten or twenty dark green shadow fish with soft, swaying fins; when I swam past them they retreated as slowly and steadily before me as if they had been painted on a transparent curtain, swaying in the current. Farther down the slope, past great cup-shaped sponges, moved two mighty dentexes. Calmly and majestically the dark blue bodies slid through the water; who knows whence they came and whither they were going? There were any number of sea bream, too, some with blunt lips, others with pointed mouths. Unquestionably these creatures, who usually prefer shallow water, had retired to this deeper region because of the dynamiting. Here, below the sixty-five foot line, ended the sway of the dynamite fishermen. But even here the creatures were still conspicuously nervous.

Before the altar of the sea god I paused. This niche in the cliff looked like a madonna decked out for a high holiday— only that these colourful garlands were not twined of roses and daisies and lilies, but were all animals to which nature had given the form of blossoms. Coral polyps with luminous yellow and red goblets; long-stemmed tubular worms with double aster blossoms; blue and red sponges dangling in cone-like umbels, synascidiae cushioning the rock like bunches of violets; mussels between whose opened shells red flesh bulged out as if in fat petals; sea urchins with black and deep violet spines; a dark red starfish, and two shaggy fish that remained fixed and immobile as if they belonged to the décor.

Not far from the niche two pop-eyes gleamed from a cleft: they belonged to a red grouper weighing a good twenty-five or thirty pounds. If I had had a spear with me the fellow would have been at my mercy. I need only to have thrust the spear into the hole, crowded the fish so far back that he could go no farther, and then impaled him at my leisure.

No! This kind of hunting we would not even begin. It was no longer fair. Here the advantage was too much on our side. That way we could simply butcher the fish one after another, like birds driven helplessly before the beaters.

F

No!

At the altar of the sea god I took a solemn vow that the diving gear should serve only for collecting, photography, and observation; I alone would use it. This red grouper and all the other fish that had fled to these deeper regions should be left in peace at least down here below!

I looked around again. Downward, into the monstrous maw of the ocean; sideways, across the blossom-twined cliffs; upward, to the endless silvery sky. Then I took off from the bottom with a gentle motion. And immediately the water seized me, the buoyancy, and carried me upward as if on gentle hands. Back, upward, towards daylight.

No feeling can be compared with the one you experience when you float back from a great depth to the upper world. Under the swiftly dwindling pressure the body expands, and with it the soul seems, as it were, to expand also, as though one were transported to higher spheres. Free as a bird, without the slightest exertion, you fly upward with growing speed, and as your breathing air expands with each foot you rise you keep spouting bubbles, as if the forces within you would no longer be contained. Faster, ever faster, you mount. It grows brighter, ever more radiant. Your ears start to sing. In a church nave you may know a similar feeling of remoteness as the chorale approaches its mightiest and most brilliant peak. An inner feeling seems to be trying to burst you apart. With a real organ roar you fly through the last few feet, then pierce the gleaming mirror of the surface, diving back into the air.

I looked about me, somewhat dazed. As my breathing pouch was swollen to bursting point I hung as though laced into a life-belt, bobbing like a cork on the waves. The bright light was disagreeably dazzling, as if I had emerged prematurely from anaesthesia on the operating table. At one blow the world I had been in seemed far away in the distance. Had I really seen all that, or was it only imagination? Some colourful dream spectacle brought on by oxygen poisoning? My power of coherent thought returned and quickly measured what I had experienced by a normal scale.

Well, come on, come on! I swam clumsily towards the boat. The mouthpiece tasted sour, and the straps hurt under my armpits. But there was Xenophon, bending down helpfully to pull me into the boat. The straps were unbuckled; at last I was rid of the wet, bloated gear. Only now did I realize the cold, feel how acutely I had been shivering the whole time, how icy it had been down below, and how it was mainly this very cold that had caused my inner warmth and excitement. Quick, into a wrapper and then up forward in the glaring sun! Words and questions passed me by, remaining misunderstood and unanswered. No, for the moment I alone would use the diving gear. Amid the jumble of blossoms hung the dentex. Beyond, the ribs of half-decayed fish; the two wrecks with their fishy clouds. It was an immoderate sensual pleasure to feel the sunbeams gradually penetrating my frozen body. Here, give me a sandwich, Xenophon, and get the gear ready again. I'll sleep half an hour, then I'll take another dive——

We sat mute round the campfire. Joerg and Alfred were annoyed because I wanted to keep the diving gear to myself. Why did I insist? Because of the dentex? Certainly not. Perhaps I would yet spear him myself. More likely it was the sense of being sole monarch in a realm no other man could penetrate. Indeed it was surely that. Not a praiseworthy trait, I know; a weakness, I know. And, anyhow, as soon as the second set of gear we had ordered got there everyone could dive.

Xenophon had bought four big octopi from his fisherman friend, and was busy giving them a thorough cleaning. He looked at us in turn, smiling.

"Well, friends, how shall I do them? They're awfully good simply roasted over the coals, on a grill——"

"For all I care you can throw them back into the water," said Alfred. "I have an awful headache, and I'm not going to eat anything at all."

"Or you can put them into a pot and cook them in their
own fluid, without salt and with a little oil. Then when they're
partly soft you put in some rice and cook it at the same time,
still without water, so it'll absorb the flavour——"

"If you don't mind," said Joerg to me, getting up, "I'm
going to try to shoot a couple of pigeons tomorrow. After all,
a person has to do something constructive. And just swimming
in vacant water with a pointed stick, or looking down at you
playing about with the fish, doesn't make any sense!"

"Or we can cook them with a lot of little onions, with some
oil, garlic, and paprika. Then we can roast the ink sac and the
eggs at the same time over the coals——"

"Oh, yes, I'm sure it will be good," cried Dr. Beckh, who
had worked up an appetite from drawing and watching the
Petermaennchen. Nobody objected.

So we ate them with a lot of little onions.

22

In a disgruntled frame of mind we wandered along the hot
quay of Volos. To the right, dusty houses; to the left, the milky
sea with a lot of ships lying as if paralysed; ahead of us, a little
lop-eared dog of no known breed, which for some reason
regarded itself as our guide. Really, it was enough to drive one
to drink! The expedition was certainly not under a lucky star.

Of course the *Universitas* did not come on the second day,
by a long shot. On the other hand, Alfred's headache developed
into a so-called papadaci fever and he was out of action for
the next few days. Joerg shot all the pigeons in the neighbourhood, numbering two, spent a furious half-day on the
outboard motor, which simply would not start, and finally
vented his temper on poor Dr. Beckh. On an entomological
walk the latter had caught a creature as long as one's finger,
which seemed most remarkable both to him and to me. It

was obviously one of those interesting butterflies with transparent wings that the scientist calls Sesiidae; only which one of the Sesiidae it was we could not quite decide. Joerg happened to come by, and when he saw the creature he burst into such fearful laughter that poor Dr. Beckh turned quite white. Sad but true our Sesiid was nothing more than an ordinary cricket.

This was really not too bad. Dr. Beckh was a specialist in freshwater fisheries, and as for me, anyone knows that the university teaches details only of those animals ranking below worms in the scale of life. But there was no doing anything with Joerg. The first moment a cricket began to chirp he would promptly cry, "Dr. Beckh, do you hear the privet moth?"

So our frame of mind could have been better. And it got still worse as our provisions grew noticeably scarcer, and on the third day it began to rain.

All the same I went out every day with Xenophon and dived six or eight times more at the same spot, where I soon had my established walks along the sea floor; but without sun I could not take pictures, and, besides, on one dive water got into the camera, so that I had to take it apart entirely and clean it. When finally, on the fourth day, mastheads appeared over the cape I bet Xenophon a box on the ear that it was the *Universitas*. It was not the *Universitas*. In a word, those days were a failure.

Then at last the ship came and we learned what had caused the delay. An enemy submarine had penetrated the straits, and there had been a preliminary attack warning, with all departures embargoed. The mate maintained he had seen a submarine going directly by the ship in the twilight; Heinz interpreted the same phenomenon as a coal sack drifting past in the current. A glorious feeling to be back on board. Regular meals, white beds, and firm planking under your feet again!

We set out forthwith in order to reach Skiathos before dark, but once again we did not get far. Barely three sea miles, and then the radio brought a new ban on departures, and our mate, truly blissful, steered our ship here to Volos, in which, for once, he was backed up by Xenophon, who has an old sweet-heart here whom he wants to call on. Furthermore, he is determined to talk us into a trip to Pelion, where he led his notorious pirate fishing life; but on that point I am immovable. Let him talk all he likes about shady woods, romantic mountain gorges, and the mysterious ruined city of Micella—we are going to get out of here at the first possible moment. And, indeed, that is why we are now walking along the hot quay. Now that we have been hung up in this dump for two days I want to talk to the port captain myself. Xenophon and the mate go with me; once again they are not speaking. There was a violent scene at noon because the galley is really a pigsty. I have now divided up the cooking. The crew are to cook for themselves and the mate, while Xenophon takes over our cuisine. Dr. Beckh was fired on yesterday by Italians when he tried to fish for plankton in the harbour; Alfred is still in bed; Joerg has the outboard motor at Pirama, two miles from here, for repair; the radio man is at the port office to get the battery recharged. Also, it turns out that we have nowhere near enough water, but the necessary electricity for pumping goes on here only in the evening. So for that reason, too, we must wait.

Our lop-eared guide remains disconsolately behind. We are announced and are immediately given a cordial welcome by the port captain. He listens to our troubles, then immediately says we can perfectly well leave in spite of the embargo. "Though, of course, if there should be trouble"—he turns to the mate—"you realize that you'll be shot?"

Although the mate is not at all inclined to be shot we decide to risk it. In addition, the port captain is willing to supply us with a small ship for voyages among the various islands. The suggestion was Xenophon's, who believes we can reach the outermost Sporades—particularly Psathura, where the sunken city is—neither with the *Universitas*, since there is no proper anchorage, nor with the motorboat, because the seas run too high. So the *Universitas* is to anchor in the natural harbour of

Planit at the island of Pelagos, while we go on the separate excursions to the islands aboard the *Bosporus*, a two-ton motor tug. This, too, edifies the mate but little; still, in the last analysis he is there for our benefit, not we for his.

On board, our news is greeted with delight. So tomorrow before daybreak we start, even if we have to man the wheel ourselves! Joerg is back again, too: the outboard motor is now alleged to be in order again.

"Hey, what's this? Where's Xenophon running to?"

"Oh, let him go. We're sailing tonight, and he probably wants to make use of the hours in between."

23

THE sea lay endlessly smooth and oily as we passed the mine barrier near Trikkeri. At last the straits of Euboea were behind us. We sat at the bowsprit, gazing into the depths. Thousands of jellyfish, gleaming red, drifted past below us, and among them a steady stream of bunched sunbeams poured into the bottomless abyss.

What are sunbeams?

They come through the vastness of interplanetary space; light is said to be oscillation; what oscillates, since interplanetary space is perfectly empty? People used to make do with the excuse that it was 'an ether' that oscillated, but it soon turned out that this 'ether' was nothing more than a pretty word. Only if what the sun hurls at us are not oscillations but tiny pellets—this is the second possibility—how then explain the phenomenon of refraction, and how explain that light can be split into its colour components by a prism?

What says modern science?

Modern science neatly extricates itself from the predicament by declaring that light is both—oscillation and pellets too. And this monstrosity it calls a 'quantum'.

And, it continues, everything in the world is made up of
quanta. We and the earth and the sea and everything in it
consist of this monstrosity—vibration and pellets in one.
Quanta whirl about one another, producing atoms; atoms form
marriages and companies, producing molecules; and certain
molecules are so especially adroit that they can seize
and hold the power of the sun, producing living matter,
which is expressed in a whimsical transformation of this
energy.

It is the green elements of the plants that perform this
feat of holding fast the sun's energy, and the animals, eating
the plants, steal this stored-up treasure. That is the difference.
That is why the plants stand still, whereas the animals have
eyes, noses, and legs. The plants draw their strength from the
sun, and they need not run after it; the animals, on the contrary, are all parasites, eating the plants or one another, and
therefore they must be mobile. They have to see and hear and
smell, in order to track their prey; they need muscles to attack
and to escape when attacked; teeth to seize and defend themselves when seized, and a belly to digest what they have
successfully eaten.

In the sea, however—and here we are back where we belong
—life is easier to the extent that food actually swims into open
mouths. The corals and sponges, the sea squirts and many
others do it that way—sit as fat and comfortable as the plants
do up in the air, and gulp the sea just as the others do the sunshine. But it is always light—the energy of the sun, in other
words—that is ultimately drunk and pursued and defended;
this is the deeper meaning of the everlasting eating and being
eaten. And hence it comes about that even in the blackness
of the deepest sea the sun still shines. The seaweed on the surface grabs the light rays and holds on to their force; then fish
come and eat the weed with its stored-up energy, eat one
another, and thus the energy that has been eaten; and swim
down into the everlasting darkness, themselves nothing but
concentrated light.

24

DURING our voyage through the Sporades an astonishing transformation took place in the mate. It was as if an aspen leaf had suddenly turned into a sturdy cactus. Scarcely had we left the protecting mine barrier behind us when his body grew firmer. When he mentioned the submarines at all now, it was with disdain. Let them come—his gestures said plainly that he meant to send them to the bottom, every one.

We rounded the gently swelling island of Skiathos, covered with olive groves, and pitched anchor off the little town of the same name. Here Xenophon had a fisherman friend who, in his opinion, could be useful to us on the expedition. Since he added that the man was the owner of a number of excellent vineyards we agreed to visit him.

As soon as we set foot on the wharf Xenophon was joyfully surrounded by young and old. Men, women, greybeards and children came streaming over; it looked like the prodigal son's return. We went up through the tiny, twisting lanes and promptly found ourselves in a delightful, ancient kitchen, where we were most cordially welcomed with black bread and olives by the mother of Vasil, as the fisherman was called. Vasil himself (an agreeable, rather thick-set young man) and Xenophon immediately retired for some private conversation or other; but as one of the vineyards was turned over to us meanwhile we gladly left the two to their secrets. Later Xenophon told me that Vasil would follow us with his little ship and nets, and that several other Greek fishermen would also join us with their boats. I could not quite see what we needed so many people for, all the less since we had already acquired the *Bosporus* with a two-man Greek crew; but as all this would cost us only a few provisions and motor fuel I agreed nevertheless. After all, the Greeks could not help being useful to us in our work and picture-taking.

At three in the afternoon we came back on board. When we told the mate that in spite of the advanced hour we were still going on to Pelagos he agreed immediately. Under his crisp, unerring orders the anchor was raised, the engine started, and the big pennant of the expedition hoisted. The crew grumbled again, because they would rather have spent the night in Skiathos, but one glance from the mate was sufficient to nip this mutiny in the bud. We sailed past Skopelos, among the islands of Steno (Xenophon told us that the bones of former forced labourers were still to be found chained to the rocks in some old silver mines there), and as darkness was falling reached the island of Pelagos.

The sea now lay as quiet as an endless reddish-brown dance floor. While the horizon had a silvery gleam the strip of sky above it was as black as pitch, blending upward into a luminous blue red. We stood in the bows, looking ahead, and an uncertain sense of tension lay upon us all. Gradually the colours died away and the silhouette of Pelagos rose like a stage setting. The sky now looked almost darker than the sea, which still gleamed oilily.

Suddenly Alfred pointed diagonally ahead. Plainly visible in that direction a broad strip came out of the open sea, turning with a sweeping curve in the same direction in which we were travelling past the island. No doubt about it, a ship had gone by just ahead of us! Here, in the solitude of the Northern Sporades, where there were no settlements and normally no ships travelled.

We clambered upon the deckhouse to get a better view.

"If it's a submarine we're in a fine fix!"

"Hand over the harpoons!"

"This is no time for kidding! We'd better get the rubber boat ready."

"Ha, ha! Rubber boat! How about zwieback in a waterproof bag?"

The mate was the only one who remained calm. He pushed his cap to the back of his head, and gave orders to throttle the engine to half speed. Chuffing softly, we went along the black, jagged coast, exactly in the wake of the strange vessel.

At the entrance to the natural harbour of Planit, on the east side of the island, our excitement rose to its peak. On the one hand, this entrance, which led like a canal to the enclosed body of water, was so narrow according to the chart that it could not have been easy for our mate to get through even by day, let alone in complete darkness and without any knowledge of the terrain. On the other hand, the strange ship's wake likewise led into this blind gut—that is, it swerved and vanished in the black façade, for of the entrance itself there was nothing whatever to be seen.

The crew, knowing the navigation of their mate, sent the boatswain to me begging us for heaven's sake not to insist on this foolhardy risk. Heinz, usually so daring, shook his head uncomfortably. Xenophon, who seemed to have risen above the situation, smiled expectantly. Joerg, on the contrary, said at worst we could only be shipwrecked, and this would undoubtedly be very useful for our expeditionary film.

"Let's skip it," I said to the mate. "The sea is calm enough, anyway, so let's stay outside and wait a couple of hours until daylight."

"I'm going in," replied the mate.

He described a great circle and then followed approximately upon the strange track, which now vanished in the darkness, almost head-on at the monotonously black coast. With bated breath we saw the first contours forming out of the shadows. The cliffs of the coast stood out more plainly; a notch deepened before us in the façade; big black caves in the banks, looking like missing teeth in the mountain, glided close past us; then the channel broadened and we arrived safe in the inland lake.

Now we saw the strange ship as well. She was a good-sized sailing cutter. As soon as we had anchored, the mate and

Xenophon went over in a boat to pay a visit. The ship had a cargo of olives, and had chosen this out-of-the-way port for some reason I have now forgotten.

25

In the morning sun the neighbourhood lost every trace of ghostliness. We were in the midst of bare rock slopes, upon which scattered goats plucked the sparse leaves from the low bushes. On the cutter the captain was just in the act of thoroughly washing his feet.

I waited until everyone was assembled for breakfast, then I delivered a formal address that I had long had on my mind. I expounded that our expedition had now properly begun, and that I therefore now required the most zealous co-operation from each member, independent co-operation, with personal initiative and responsibility. If we were here aboard a fine, big ship in the Sporades, I declared, this was by no means a matter of course but a great stroke of personal good fortune, and it was only right and proper that each member should express this great personal good fortune by helping to the limit of his ability. It would not do for our valuable equipment to continue in such disorder. Each member had been assigned his own special tasks and must accordingly work independently to clean and keep everything in order. Nor would it do for everyone to go on appearing at breakfast so unkempt and unclothed; after all, we had a scientific job, in fact a mission, to accomplish, and what would the crew think of us? Nor would it do for people to go on spending their time in bed with detective stories.

I could see plainly that these well-considered words had not failed in their intended effect. Dr. Beckh looked earnest and resolute; Xenophon stared fixedly into the distance; Heinz, blushing slightly, was studying a crack in the planking between his legs.

But I had reckoned without my hosts.

"I knew you were going to make a speech," said Alfred almost before I had finished. "I knew just from the way you combed your hair so carefully beforehand, and even washed."

"But it was an excellent speech," Joerg added. "Maybe a bit too fast, and you swallowed the final syllables here and there, but at least the emotional delivery was beyond praise."

And everyone burst out laughing, and the breakfast went off just like all other breakfasts before and afterwards.

At nine o'clock our first trip was to begin. We wanted to visit the island of Giura, whose abrupt cliffs seemed as interesting to me as the ibexes that were alleged to live there did to Joerg. Since we could not know beforehand what we might find there, and wanted to lose no opportunity, we piled half our equipment aboard the *Bosporus*. Five cameras for surface and underwater shots, with appropriate rolls of film, black-and-white and colour; the diving gear, with all six spare flasks and as many potassium cartridges; the diving helmet with the pump and the 100-foot air hose; fins, spears, nets, rope; also a whole chest of provisions, medicines, and all kinds of spare parts. That Joerg took along his gun goes without saying.

The passage was a stormy one. As soon as we approached the coast we caught sight of diving ducks, swimming in swarms near the cliffs. Joerg fired at them several times, but the distance was too great; besides, the ducks always dived too soon.

We put into a steep cove and made the *Bosporus* fast to an overhanging rock. The region looked most tempting. To explore the area systematically, we formed two groups, one of which swam to the left and one to the right along the shore. When we all met again an hour later, unfortunately we had little to tell. The bottom of the cove was abrupt or sandy; on it grew seaweed or sponges, and crayfish or sea anemones moved about among them, but this was practically all there was to see. Of large fish, at any rate, there were none. And yet we were in the heart of the Sporades, in the most remote and romantic region one could imagine.

"All right, Xenophon," I said, "come on and show us
your rays and tuna fish and seals and stuff. There's nothing!
Not a whisker. Nothing whatever!"

"You can't expect to see everything right away," he retorted
grumpily. "After all, I know the neighbourhood only as a
fisherman, from on top, from a boat. And, anyhow, we came
here mostly because Joerg wanted to see the ibex."

"Well, let's go," said Joerg. "There's nothing to be seen
here under water, anyhow, so let's climb up and have a look
at the ibexes."

Dr. Beckh seconded this motion. "There are sure to be
interesting lizards here."

The ascent of the mountain however, was no trifle. Five
or six hundred yards of steep slope, covered with round, rolling
stones, was the only access to the high part of the island.
We scrambled up, perspiring. Heinz, a true seaman who had
never been higher than a masthead, kept us all amused in the
process.

On reaching the top we found a hut with two women whom
Xenophon had known well from previous visits, and who
received us most cordially with goat's-milk and sheep's-milk
cheese. They were the only inhabitants of the island, and had
a lot to tell Xenophon. Joerg, meanwhile, went stalking about the
countryside with his shooting iron. An hour later he was back,
furious. But Xenophon soothed him. He said there positively
were ibexes here, we need have no doubt of that, but of course
they were not so easy to find. That would take a several days'
stay.

To put us back in a good humour, he led us to a near-by
cave full of stalactites and stalagmites, which actually existed.
Through a very small opening hidden in the bushes we gained
access to a fairly spacious vault whose walls were adorned
with grotesque dripstone formations. With improvised torches
we peered in all directions. The fairly slippery rock sloped
away in the middle; here the cave went on downward. I
leaned forward to light it up better—and the ground slid away

under my feet, and I coasted most ungently into the darkness, ending my journey some yards farther down in a cold puddle.

"Hey! Here I am! Here!"

With a badly twisted leg I was pulled up on a stick. The two women looked after us again, and then we started down to the ship. Alfred, who was still not quite recovered, and had therefore stayed aboard, had swum along another piece of coast meanwhile. But apart from a most remarkably large snail with a little umbrella on top, which he brought back, he had seen only a few large fish in the distance.

In the evening, lying in my bunk with my strained leg, I tried to learn this day's lesson. What a lot of equipment, how little work done! Of course it was the fault of the sea and its yawning fishlessness, but another reason was that I had been too easily persuaded into undertakings that brought the expedition no real profit. We had already wasted a lot of time; our work really must get started. Instead of climbing the mountain we should have tried other spots in the sea. And in that clear water we could perfectly well have taken various swimming shots that had to be taken anyway.

No, things must be different!

26

OFF to Psathura! Off to the outermost isle of the Sporades, by whose shore lies the sunken city! We will camp there in tents for a week; everything necessary is already aboard the *Bosporus*. The mate and crew stay behind aboard the *Universitas*, waving. Waving sadly, for Planit has been a regular stewpot. We steam through the channel, and a sharp wind suddenly comes to meet us. The high waves far around are crowned with white-caps, and the *Bosporus* pounds heavily on the combers. No, in this weather the trip to Psathura is not possible. But no matter; instead, we will go right round Pelagos to the sheltered waters

among the isles of Steno, and Xenophon will take us to his
hole in the ocean floor.

What kind of hole can it be? It is supposed to be a scant
fifteen feet wide and go 200 feet straight down. Alfred guesses
a drowned limestone cave, Joerg and I believe it must be volcanic. The most daring hypothesis is Heinz's. He says it is a
prehistoric well, which sank into the sea along with the city
on Psathura.

"A 200-foot prehistoric well——?"

Arriving on the scene, we sail about for half an hour in a
cove, and Xenophon stares downward through the glass-
bottomed box. But there seems to be a curse on it. He himself
cannot imagine how it happens, but the opening, which he
has seen at least a dozen times with his own eyes, is suddenly
not there any more. Still, this is not so bad because near by
there are fishermen who, he believes, know the place well.
They live in a picturesque settlement on a hill, of course not
anywhere nearly so high as the women on Giura. Just a bit
of a climb; we certainly won't regret it, the less so since one of
the fishermen has an enchanting young daughter, very rightly
called Fair Helen.

All right, let's climb this mountain, too.

The fishermen, however, are absent. Only their wives and
daughters are there, evidently delighted to see Xenophon
again. Here, too, we are most cordially treated to milk and
sheep's cheese. Unfortunately the women know nothing about
the hole in the sea floor. Most dramatically they recount to
Xenophon the cruelties of passing soldiers, and as Xenophon
is most anxious to inspect the scene of the atrocities in person
he promptly vanishes with Fair Helen into the bushes.

This is really going too far!

Leaving Xenophon with his Helen, we clamber back down
the mountain. On the way up we saw a cave that seemed
promising; now we make a trial dive there and before long
there is a shout of triumph. Heinz has seen a fish! We swim over
and gape at this marvel. No doubt about it, down yonder,

"Tell the lazy lout to pump a little harder!" Alfred called to me from inside his helmet

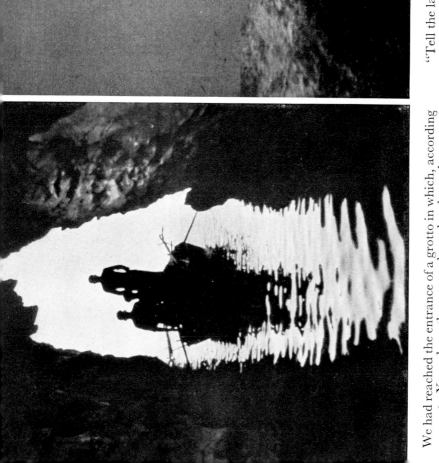

We had reached the entrance of a grotto in which, according to Xenophon, there were bound to be seals

The grotto at the entrance to Planit harbour

Under the microscope the artful
network looks bewildering

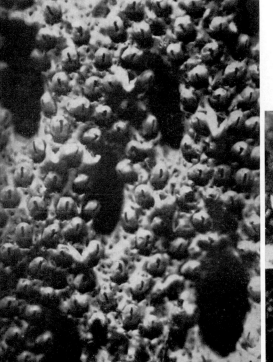

Grotesquely shaped sponges and
yellow coral stars covered the
walls

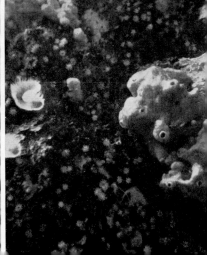

thirty-five feet deep, a red grouper hangs before the entrance
to his cave, studying us as critically as we him.

Joerg starts to dive at once but I stop him. This rare
opportunity must certainly be made use of for our film. After
all, we aren't here for pleasure.

While Joerg and Heinz stay behind on guard over the
red grouper Alfred and I hurry ashore to fetch the diving gear
and a second film camera. As we swim we make our plan
of campaign. I will go to the bottom in the diving gear and
take close-ups of the fish; Alfred will take long shots, first of
Joerg diving and spearing the grouper, then of me crouching
there and taking pictures of the scene. In other words, first shot:
landscape and grouper alone. Second shot: me diving, creep-
ing up, then I raise the camera and the scene shifts to the fish.
Third shot: Joerg on the surface with the spear, approaching
impatiently and making signs. Fourth shot: down below, I
return the signals in slow motion, to avoid scaring the fish.
Fifth shot: Joerg dives, creeps up, and drives home the harpoon.
Sixth shot: I take pictures, swim over, and look at the flapping
fish. Seventh shot: I shake Joerg's hand. Eighth shot: I pat
him on the back congratulating him. Ninth shot: camera
moves in on grouper until it is huge— Then fades into tenth
shot: grouper sizzling over the fire, then the trip home and
a travelling shot of the various members of the expedition as
they start to eat.

We are on the shore. Xenophon is also back by now, and
I hastily acquaint him with the situation. He is to follow with
the boat, rowing softly and holding ready the spare camera
with a new film. We hasten back to the scene of events.

The fish is still there. Joerg however, is extremely nervous.

"If you go swimming round in circles with five cameras
you'll scare the brute away from me," is his welcome to us.

But he is wrong. The fish stays.

Everything goes on exactly as the scenario calls for. At
some distance from the fish I slip down in the diving gear to
the bottom. As I do so, the moment Alfred starts grinding I look

G

inquiringly around as if there were a number of red groupers
in the neighbourhood and I must pick out the proper one.
Alfred signals that the shot has turned out well. While he swims
up again I reach the bottom, which is cluttered with rocks and
seaweed. From here I cannot see the fish. Signs from above
indicate that he is still staying quiet. Excellent! Sliding
cautiously through the seaweed, I stalk closer.

Aha, there he is! A fairly fat fellow with bulbous lips and
a melancholy eye, as if suspecting the misfortunes in store for
him. I cover the last few feet so cautiously that I take a good
two minutes about it. Then, quite slowly, I raise the camera and
press the button. Luckily the fairly noisy buzzing does not startle
the fish. He merely fans his pectoral fins with a certain surprise
as he looks at me. Since he has the sheltering cave behind him,
he obviously feels safe from me.

Promptly I hear Alfred's camera, too, whirring—that shot
is taken, then. He surfaces, then comes back with a fresh
lungful, and I make the agreed signal towards the surface.
Once again I hear his camera, and again he swims upward.
Now it's up to Joerg. This time Alfred takes an extra long time
drawing breath, goes into position, and Joerg is on his way
down. Calmly and confidently, as in our best West Indian days,
he comes oozing down like a snake, holding the spear by its
rear third, so that it shall bear a harmonious relationship to
the body. His legs kick splendidly from the hip. The whole
browned figure with the glittering pane of the mask in front,
hair floating back, and resolutely tight lips is a symbol of concentrated power, waiting only for the right moment to discharge like a thunderbolt at the red grouper.

My camera whirs, Alfred's camera whirs, Joerg's motions
grow slower. The bow of his strength draws ever tauter.
Then his arm whips forward—I sweep the camera along with
it—Ouch!

After all, it is two years since our West Indian days. Neat
as the thrust was, it indubitably missed.

With a startled flip of the fins the grouper has vanished in his hole, and now he reappears, races down the slope, and vanishes in another hole some fifteen feet lower down.

"That's what comes of your blasted cameras," says Joerg as we reappear on the surface. "If you hadn't got him so nervous it would have been child's play."

Nevertheless we have reason to be satisfied. Alfred was able to swing the camera back and forth twice between me and the fish in a most beautiful fashion. Or, I wonder—the film in Alfred's camera, which Xenophon has opened meanwhile, is exactly as it was put in. The perforations were torn at the start; not a single foot has been exposed!

"I'm just glad I didn't catch him," says Joerg casually. "The second time, the scoundrel won't get away from me!"

"Oh, dear, it's a crying shame," Alfred groans. "When you were looking inquiringly around you you had such a magnificently dopey expression. The effect would have been wonderful!"

While we sit in the boat, eating sandwiches, the red grouper has time to calm down. As he is now forty-five feet below, Alfred is going down this time in the diving helmet. For that purpose the boat must be moored exactly above the spot. When we have had a rest I take the anchor down myself, to avoid scaring the fish, and wedge it cautiously among the rocks. At the surface, meanwhile, a glass diving helmet is put over Alfred's head. Xenophon hands him the camera, and Heinz starts pumping. But only fifteen feet down Alfred stops.

"Tell the lazy lout to pump a little harder!" he shouts to me in the helmet when I go to visit him. His face looks strangely distorted lengthwise through the curved glass. I hurry upward and deliver the message.

"Tell him not to breathe so greedily," Heinz grumbles back, and condescends to move a little faster.

Something else is not in order. The camera jams. I bring it up, Xenophon takes it apart, Heinz pumps, Joerg grits his teeth with impatience. Then at last the shots can be repeated.

Two causes for excitement. Joerg declares the grouper

has vanished; I dive, and sure enough he's gone. Hunting, I
find him once more outside the very same hole as at first.
That grouper is priceless! But what's wrong with Alfred? He
is looking upward, tugging vigorously at the hose. I reach the
surface just in time to see Heinz leisurely lighting a cigarette.

Serpent-like, Joerg glides down again.

This time his movements are not quite so pictorial; on
the other hand, he drives home such a fierce thrust that not
only the grouper but a sponge behind it is impaled. As he can't
manage alone I rush to help him, and together we manage to
free the flapping creature from the sponge, and the latter from
the rock. Then we swim over to Alfred, hold the grouper in
front of his camera, nod complacently at one another, shake
hands on the ocean floor, pat each other on the back—and
shoot upward with a sigh of relief.

Of the hundred-odd scenes we need for our picture we
have now shot one more.

27

ON our return trip we once more encountered the wake of a ship,
running straight and mysterious through the sea. The ship
itself was out of sight; the waves had crossed its track for perhaps an hour yet it had remained mysteriously visible. It went
clear and straight across the sea— What was it, actually, that
went clear and straight across the sea here?

If two men hold a rope and swing it so that a wave runs
along the rope only the wave goes on; the rope and the two
men stay where they were. Exactly the same is true of the ocean
surface when the wind stirs it. The individual particles of
water oscillate harmonically up and down, producing the waves.
The water particles, in other words, stay where they are;
only the wave, the harmonic motion, moves on. If it encounters
some irregularity, say a ship's wake, it passes invisibly through

it and reappears on the other side exactly as regular and harmonic as before. The wave remains, the irregularity remains;
oscillations of different kinds do not interfere with one another.

It is much the same when we telephone. Electro-magnetic
oscillations run along the wire, and it is perfectly possible
to carry on several conversations at once over a single wire
without one disturbing the other. Radio waves, too, intersect
and criss-cross one another a thousand times in the air, and yet
one never disturbs another.

And what about oscillations in ourselves?

When we observe anything with the eye, electro-magnetic
waves run from the light-sensitive cells of the retina along the
optic nerve to the brain. There we first grasp what our eye
sees, and there what we see and grasp is stored as memory.
And again: memory—what is it? Whence comes this marvellous gift with which nature has endowed us?

Science speaks of molecular changes in our cortex. But
might it not be something different?

A thousand waves pass across the sea, and yet the ship's
wake is faithfully preserved. A thousand impressions and
thoughts criss-cross the field of force in our brain, and yet the
trails, memories, are only gradually erased——

28

"Hey, Xenophon," Alfred asked, "did you really actually
murder him?"

"Which one?" asked Xenophon.

"Why, that fierce old fisherman whose slave you were.
You know, Psarathanas.... I'm just reading the book about the
pirate fishermen."

Xenophon considered for a while, and then said nothing.

"Oh, and something else," Joerg asked again. "That time
when you were in Porto Coufo and the three strangers in

white wolfskins came in and asked you what you had gained
in the seven years of your fishing——"

"I replied, I've gained *gnosis*. That was the twentieth of
February, nine years ago."

"All well and good—gnosis is knowledge, but what kind
of gnosis did you really gain?"

Xenophon reflected again for a while.

"You're bound to laugh because you're still too young,"
he said at length slowly, "but I recognized that every moment
of my life is equally painful."

As he had correctly predicted, we laughed until we cried.

"I was in Mitilini at Christmas of 1928," he went on,
unperturbed, "and I got hold of Plato in a little edition,
you know, like a pony. I began reading it, and then I shut the
book again because I said to myself, 'If I read that, I don't
need to live at all. If I can acquire so much knowledge and
insight in a short time,' I asked myself, 'what am I to do with
the rest of my days?' I think all true knowledge is deadly. To
me the main thing is to be conscious of my being. To tell
myself every day, I am!"

"But—but—" cried Alfred when we had somewhat
recovered from our new outburst of laughter. "Any sensible
person would have to commit suicide! Whereas people usually
kill themselves because they're crossed in love, and that's no
insight!"

"It certainly is an insight," Joerg contradicted.

"I've never stopped to think," said Xenophon.

"Anybody can see that!" cried Heinz.

"Somehow ideas have always come to me of their own
accord. Whether it was the place or the time, sometimes I
would wait for days, and suddenly the idea would be there.
I've never had any chance to talk to educated people, and that's
why I can't find the words. My secondary school education
was very much interrupted; I played truant a lot, and ran
away at fourteen. So I entered upon life perfectly unspoiled
and unprejudiced."

We pestered him to tell us about his life and wanderings. But he kept silent. He sat among us like a strangely shaped tree, and none of us could imagine what was going on behind that knotty brow.

"I went swimming once when the water was thirty-four degrees," he abruptly said at length. "It's less than two years ago. I jumped overboard with a life-belt; I'd had enough, I didn't want to go on, in short I wanted to commit suicide."

"Then why did you take the life-belt?" Alfred inquired.

Xenophon looked at him thoughtfully. "Yes, I've wondered that myself," he said. "But I don't know. Well, I jumped into the icy water, and when I came to I saw the ship already far off. Then a great calm came over me. I thought about how I had two hours at most to live, but I didn't feel anything. I held myself automatically in the middle of the life-belt so as not to sink in too deep, and tried to pull my knees up to my body to keep the icy water away from my stomach. Gradually I got stiff. And I had really ceased to be, when about midnight a ship came in sight. I wanted to shout, but in a way so that they couldn't tell I was scared. Believe me, I was surprised at myself. I was outside myself, watching my body try to make use of its insight and experience. This was how it clung to life. And still there was this vanity—I was afraid the ship might notice I was afraid."

He laughed briefly, then rose and vanished in the galley.

29

FROM my diary:

July 28. Only brief stay in Planit. The crew is trying to get away, the machinist is sick, the mate has swapped ship's oil for goats, and presents us with one. We hastily pack everything we need aboard the *Bosporus*, then set off for Psathura in a fine, calm sea. On our way bonitos jump out of the water and a lot of jellyfish drift by, including another tube with red and blue spots. In contrast to the other Sporades, Psathura is quite low and small, a flat strip with a tall, thin lighthouse, like a ship with a mast. Lots of reefs; we have to lug everything through the shallow water—chests, bags, acquarium, and other odds and ends. It looks like the entry of the Jews into the promised land. But we like Psathura. We promptly find a pretty camping spot among tall hemlock shrubs and settle down. The fat lighthouse keeper, a colossus; his wife, with a distaff in her hand, a colossess. Some fishermen help us, and Alfred takes films of us from all sides. Marvellous shots. Then, when everything is set up, I take a walk round the island with Joerg. Very lovely. Round stones, very thorny brush, but a good path. The sun has gone down blood red, and the moon rises a radiant orange, splendid in the dark blue. At the lighthouse the colossess treats us to a watermelon and bread, and then we go up the lighthouse. A bomber crashed here recently. It flew round the island for an hour, then landed in the sea and sank in 150 feet of water. They say you can see the plane. In the evening we sit at our wonderful spot and eat the goat meat, which is delicious. Great argument over the question, why is sheep's wool curly? Alfred and Dr. Beckh argue in such a way that neither will accept what the other says. Especially Alfred. So Joerg turns on the radio. Now everyone is asleep, I have finished writing, and go to sleep myself. Xenophon will wake me tomorrow at sunrise as always; I'm already looking forward to it, much excited to see the sunken city.

July 29. Well, there doesn't seem to be much to this sunken city. Vasil, who is back, showed us the way there, but at such a deep place that you couldn't even see bottom. A good hundred feet. Xenophon, however, maintains that it is in a shallower place. Anyhow, both declare it is true that there really was an ancient city here by the name of Psathira, which then sank under the sea along with the island. Apparently the sponge divers know the spot well, since very fine sponges form on the masonry below. The island actually is volcanic, and in the

shallow water we did find a lot of old potsherds, cemented
to the bottom with a thick layer of limestone. Joerg and I got
ourselves put down near the little neighbouring island, and
went hunting there. Clear water, a lot of rocks and sea urchins,
the bottom covered with green in spots. We soon find a wonderful cave for pictures. Joerg vanishes at the bottom and reappears
somewhere else. Then we find a duck, which I follow for a long
time, and it leads me to a good place where shadow-fish are
hanging under a rock. Joerg harpoons two, and I get several
good pictures. Later the water grows muddy because a current
sets in. Hard work getting into the boat with a bag full of
potsherds. Joerg slips, sits down on several sea urchins, and
loses a fin. Heinz saw a turtle seven feet long—quite incredible.
Alfred discovered a rock cliff with a good landscape for diving-
helmet shots. Dr. Beckh, meanwhile, has been collecting lizards.

July 30. Big filming programme discussed. First we want
to take shots near the small island, then at noon tent scenes,
and in the afternoon the diving-helmet sequence. We set off,
but the motor fails, greatly annoying us. At last it does start;
we go over, descend into the strong current and hunt for the
hole in the cliff where we wanted to shoot the scenes. But when
we finally do find it, it turns out that Joerg has forgotten
the bathing trunks he wore in the other scenes, and we have
to go back. Very much annoyed.

July 31. Wanted to go straight to the sunken city in the
morning but Xenophon thought the waves were too high.
Gloriously clear weather. In the west we see Pelion and Euboea,
in the north the steep silhouette of Mount Athos, in the east
Lymnos, and in the south Skyros. Picturesque cloud banks
overhead. Busy taking films; unfortunately the gaskets in the
diving gear don't work, and this robs me of all confidence. At
noon I'm really exhausted and have to rest for some time,
which the others do also. Only Alfred still has energy, and takes
shots of small fish among the reefs.

In the afternoon we walk beyond the lighthouse to the
final cape of the island, the outermost point of the Sporades.

Unfortunately very little stirring there, either, although it looks good enough to eat. Am still unusually tired. Perhaps too little sleep or too much exertion; anyway, the day seems unbearably hot to me, and still I shiver the moment I go into the water.

August 1. A quiet day. High waves, muddy water; once more we can't go to the sunken city. Argument with Xenophon. Yesterday he asserted grandly that a clear sunset and a light east wind were certain to bring good weather. And today? Today he says nature had made a mistake. On the hooks he put out last night were a big dentex, several rays, and a moray, which last we ate with great relish for lunch. We take tent shots, then Joerg says he would like to go for one day to Giura with Xenophon on account of the ibexes. Now Xenophon suddenly maintains the weather will stay bad. Giura is supposed to have been called Polyphemus, and to have been the same island where Odysseus had his battle with the Cyclops. All right, so it was. Accordingly the two leave after lunch. Quiet afternoon; we hunt for sponges and corals. Peaceful evening together. Break apart coral, which teems with creatures inside.

August 2. Another quiet day. We take pictures and go collecting. The surf caves contain the most amazing sponges. Some of them cover the rock like a thick rug; when you pull them off they are an exact impression of the rock. We also find a small formation like tiny trees, which has a strong aromatic smell, and a lot of new crustaceans and starfish. Our collection now includes more than a hundred jars. The setting sun turns the bushes red and yellow. In the evening Heinz comes back from Planit, reporting that the crew is already mutinying wildly. He shot a goat with the revolver. Still no sign of Joerg and Xenophon.

August 3. Late at night the two finally come back. Did not get any ibex. Great goings on. Also, met two fishermen; one of them had only one arm. Offered to lead them. Joerg gave him the shotgun and they went stalking over incredibly steep mountains. Suddenly there's a big buck standing right near. Alas, not an ibex, though, but a special kind of wild goat with gigantic horns. The one-armed fellow peppered away after the fleeing goats with shot, and nicked one. At least Joerg did bring two ducks with him. There are supposed to be three kinds of wild goats in Giura and also real ibexes. And then a cave where the animals go to die. But I'm fed up.

August 4. Once more no sort of weather for the sunken city. Dr. Beckh finds old ruins in the thick underbrush. An ancient watch-tower, he believes. I think to myself, 'All right, if it isn't under water then it'll just have to be above water,' and I set my crew to cleaning the water-tower, which is full of gigantic stones. Lively resentment against Dr. Beckh. We work for several hours in the heat, after which the watch-tower is cleared and we have had enough of matters archaeological. What a lot of nonsense! Joerg and Alfred kept making remarks until Dr. Beckh agreed to give an evening lecture about carp, his special subject. But they were fooled. Dr. Beckh spoke for a good hour and a half; it was incredibly tiresome, but everybody had to listen.

August 5. Joerg was gushing to me today about the antiquities on the little island of Ktamanios; later I heard the place is teeming with rabbits. Of course it was too rough for the sunken city again. By now I've honestly had enough of Psathura. Let the city stay sunken; tomorrow we sail on to Piperi.

30

BUT our departure was to be delayed again after all. It was getting on for evening when we suddenly heard a dull boom close by, promptly followed by a second. We rushed out of our tents and hurried across the island.

It was dynamite fishermen. They had surrounded a school of fish scarcely five hundred yards from our camp, and destroyed it by dropping two bombs. The water between the two boats

glinted with countless dead fish floating on the surface. Whoop-
ing and laughing, the poachers scooped them up with nets,
like cream off milk. The sight of this lawless party enraged us,
Joerg most of all. So these were the scoundrels who had the
gaping fishlessness of the coast on their consciences! People
who would destroy all the young fry of the meighbourhood
just for a few pounds of fish. After a brief, excited argument
we decided to put a spoke in these rascals' wheel forthwith.

"What are you talking about?" cried Xenophon when he
learned of our intention. "You should be grateful that some
have turned up! You wanted to take pictures of sharks, didn't
you? Or have you lost your nerve?"

"What do you mean, sharks?"

"But I've told you—the moment anyone drops dynamite
sharks start coming. It attracts them. Instead of arguing we
ought to be getting the boat ready to go over and see these
people. I'll be surprised if they aren't my old pals."

And so we did. That is, I myself did not join this excursion.
After all, it was a pretty dubious matter to be associating with
dynamiters who had the authorities after them. And I was the
responsible leader of the expedition. What would the officials
say if this ever got out? It was beyond imagining. But, on the
other hand, sharks were the purpose of our expedition, and
after all, observing the sharks and what went on under water
after such explosions would undoubtedly be of considerable
interest. With a certain amount of goodwill you could see the
affair from that angle. And, anyhow, we had no commission
to interfere in the practice.

Before long I heard two more loud explosions, and after
an hour and a half or so my crew came back all excited and
in the best of spirits. They brought the evil-doers along with
them (of course they turned out to be friends of good old
Xenophon), as well as two heaping baskets full of the
dynamited fish, which were fried in oil over the camp fire and
consumed with Samos wine and merry toasts.

"It's terrific," declared Alfred, red with excitement.

"Just imagine! The boats creep very carefully through the water; the oars have to be moved absolutely silently. Up forward in a hole of his own stands Mitcho"—he nodded in the direction of the fiercest-looking character, who promptly grinned broadly—"hanging half overboard, down into the glass box, on the look-out."

"For gopes and melanuri," Joerg added, transferring one fried specimen of each variety to his mouth.

"And you simply can't believe how these fellows see the fish sixty or seventy feet down!" Alfred went on. "We looked down, too, and couldn't see a thing, nothing but seaweed. Well, and when they find a school the boats separate quietly and they get out the bombs——"

"They're regular whoppers," Joerg explained. "They have the effect of two or three hand grenades. The fuse is less than four inches long, and they just calmly light it from their cigarettes, and then wait a couple of seconds because the bomb has to explode just a split second after it hits the water or the fish are gone. And that's why every second or third dynamiter only has one arm or half a face."

"How about sharks?" I asked.

"Yes, there was a shark there, too. I didn't see him myself, only Xenophon and Heinz did. But the fishermen do say sharks almost always turn up. They're trained to react to the explosions."

"All the sharks you please," Xenophon agreed fiercely. "I've often seen five and six at once after a shot."

"I saw him plainly," Heinz assured us. "He was a good twelve feet long, but he just whipped through."

"Of course we'd have to do the thing systematically," Alfred remarked.

"Unfortunately these fellows have to go on tomorrow morning," Joerg continued, "but they'll be dropping some in a week in the Straits of Skopelos, where they say it's particularly good. So we arranged to meet them there——"

That evening I lay awake for a long time. Sharks! During

our whole voyage so far we had scarcely seen a dozen good-
sized fish, and now we were supposed to see as many sharks
as we pleased. And with the diving gear we could simply
go swimming about among them——

"Look, are those fellows still about?" I asked Xenophon
in the morning.

"No, they've gone."

"Too bad——"

"Why?"

"Oh, nothing; it was just an idea."

"Speak up, speak up!"

"Well, I would have sort of liked to see for myself——"

Xenophon grinned from ear to ear. "You forget you have
Xenophon in the crew!" he said with a crafty twinkle. He
went over to his chest, dug deeply, and out came—dynamite.

"Where did you get the stuff?" I asked, astounded.

"I exchanged cigarettes for it yesterday. But seeing it was
me they'd have given it for nothing when they heard I hadn't
any. After all, we need a little supply with us."

"Xenophon," I said, "I don't care if it costs me my immortal
soul, we're going straight to the place where you saw the shark
yesterday, and you're going to heave that bomb!"

We quickly made ready. Of course Joerg, Alfred and Heinz
came along. Reaching the spot, we tossed two charges from
shore and swam out to the spot immediately after the explosions.

At first we saw nothing but swirling mud. The bombs had
not exploded until they hit the bottom, and had torn the seaweed from the rock for some distance around. As we had tossed
at random only an occasional chance fish was flapping in
the mud clouds. I looked in all directions—and suddenly,
close before me, I saw a shark. It was a blue shark. A fat,
muscular, shapely, supple fellow about ten feet long. He paid
me no attention. His interest was obviously concentrated on
dead fish, and of those there were very few. Fifteen feet from
me he snapped up a small wrasse that hung twitching in the

water, then he turned with inimitable grace and in an instant was gone.

I remained under water as if turned to stone. He had looked exactly like the blue sharks in the Caribbean. I remembered the last one we had seen in Curaçao—true, that one had been thirteen feet long and considerably stouter, and yet there was the same motion, the same suppleness, the same crafty look about the pointed nose. Only after a long while did it occur to me that I must surface again and take breath. I was full of a tumultuous delight. The unlucky spell that had hitherto lain upon our expedition now seemed broken. Now things would really start—I could feel it. I had no doubts left about our success.

"Do you know, Dr. Beckh," I said as we went back to camp, "I have a definite feeling that those dynamite fishermen are going to bring us some unusually interesting observations?"

Dr. Beckh knew his duty. "Yes, yes, indeed," he agreed. "Both ecologically and physiologically most interesting."

31

"I AM wearing myself out more than a human being ever did. Alone and without help, my health is no longer good, and I over-exert myself. My body has grown crooked, my beard drips with paint. For months I've been lying on my back on the scaffolding. Joylessly, breathing hard, I am finishing my work——"

Thus wrote the great Michelangelo as he created his titanic work in the dark of the Sistine Chapel. A similar situation, though a thoroughly cheerful one, awaited me when we went seal hunting on the island of Piperi.

Piperi is by far the most inaccessible island of the Northern Sporades, which the Greeks call 'Eremo,' the 'Lonely Ones.' Nowhere along the abrupt coasts is there an anchorage;

only at one spot is there a slanting rock slab, slid half into the
water, up which a boat can be drawn out of the water if a
storm threatens. Probably because of this inaccessibility the
thick evergreen woods on the heights have survived. Half-way
up the island are remains of a former pirate settlement;
scarcely fifty yards below the peak, astonishingly enough, a
spring spurts a strong jet out of the rock. If you approach from
the west, Piperi looks like a sleeping lion; as we came from the
north, however, all we saw was the extreme angular posterior.

We went on an expedition to the wooded heights, which
struck us as remarkably like home; then we wanted to see the
promised seals. Xenophon guided us along the coast in the
boat, talking as we went: "Off Cape Agrelios near Zagora I
saw a seal fighting with an octopus in the summer eight years
ago——"

"What day was this?" asked Alfred.

"It was the sixteenth of July, at twelve o'clock noon,
fifty yards off-shore," replied Xenophon promptly. "You
must know that the seal is the worst foe of the octopus. And
do you know how the seal sets about getting the polyp out
of its cave? Of course you'll start laughing when I tell
you——"

"Probably tickles it with its whiskers."

"Maybe tells about a sunken city."

"No, much better than that. It simply sits down in the
hole and starts stinking so terribly that the octopus can't
stand it any longer and comes out. Then the seal grabs it by
the head, and a battle begins, because the polyp immediately
clutches the seal's nose with its tenacles and the seal tries to
shake it off. To do that the seal comes to the surface, and you
can plainly see it shaking its head to and fro to get rid of the
clutch. And once it succeeds, it gulps down the octopus with
relish."

"Xenophon," said Joerg very gravely, "you saw all this
yourself?"

"I've seen it at least ten times myself," came the firm

With hammer and chisel we pry fragments from the rock wall

In his diving helmet Alfred clambers over the mast of the sunken ship

Beneath the wreck lay a chasm the walls of which resembled a tropical flower garden

answer. "In fact that time off Cape Agrelios it was hardly fifty feet away. When the seal saw me it was scared and dropped the half-dead octopus. I picked it up and dressed it well and took a glass of red wine with it—to the health of the seal!"

Meanwhile we had reached the entrance to a rock cavern where, in Xenophon's opinion, there must certainly be seals. It was a deep cave, leading quite far into the rock. We made the following plan of campaign:

Alfred and I, each equipped with a camera, would take up our positions under water outside the entrance to the cavern; the others would go the length of the cavern in the boat and drive the seal out with shouts. In that way it would have to swim right past our cameras. As seals are well known for their good teeth we were much excited as we went into the water. But nobody bit us. We only heard the shouts of the others, echoing terribly from the depths of the cavern, but of seals there was no sign. Not even fish or crabs or anything else passed by. Since Xenophon's last visit the seals had either died or emigrated. To get at least some good out of the situation I took films of Alfred waiting, and he took pictures of me taking pictures of him, but that was absolutely the only yield of our excursion.

We searched a few more caves, some of them with entrances below the water level, and this brought me the experience where my situation was like that of the great Michelangelo. I groped cautiously into the darkness of one cavern—cautiously, because I was still thinking of a possible angry mother seal defending her young—when I saw that instead of deeper darkness ahead of me it was getting lighter. The passage in which I was must obviously be drawing light from the other side as well. So there must be another exit. I groped curiously onward. And suddenly the passage opened, and before me lay a tremendous vault whose appearance was simply beyond description.

Yes, beyond any description.

I was in an undersea chamber, some fifty feet high and

H

about sixty-five feet wide at its broadest part, recalling the dark vaulting of the Sistine Chapel. Just as Michelangelo had expended his whole art gloriously adorning walls and ceiling, here nature had lavished a profusion of brightly coloured living creatures to give a naked crypt in the rock the magic splendour of an Indian temple. The broad dome of the vault was sprinkled with a thousand yellow stars—coral blossoms spreading their dainty tentacles in the water. The walls, going downward, displayed such a multi-coloured and bewildering confusion that shapes and colours blended in the oddest combinations. Ghostly pale sponges hung as if by cobwebs from jutting side platforms, or stretched clumsy, curved fingers into the water. Amid a cascade of reddish-purple limestone seaweed appeared the face of a kobold with twinkling eye and a long, waving green beard. At another spot a spider-like creature seemed to be crawling through the gorgeous fur, but I could not see where it began and where it ended. Despite the comparative darkness, a fairy-tale blue coloured the spacious chamber. The light shone dimly in at the lower end of the vault through two other holes, which, like the passage I had come in by, led out again into the sea.

I swam hesitantly closer to the walls. Now that I could get a nearer look, the bewildering multiplicity dissolved into a no less bewildering number of individual beings. That yonder was unquestionably a coral—but when I reached for it, it jumped back. How could that be? It was perched on a big shellfish, and the shell had closed at my approach. Or here, this brown pennant of seaweed—it ran away! How so? A large crab had planted this weed on its back by way of disguise, and now turned about in order to threaten me more effectively with its claws. Or that spotted sponge; with a hasty flip of the fins it vanished, a shaggy fish in the broad expanse of the mausoleum. Crabs, fish, corals, sponges, mussels, tubular worms, moss creatures, starfish, bristly worms, limestone seaweed—all lived here, entangled into thick, colourful bunches. In the dome overhead, among the yellow coral stars, I saw glittering pearls. What could they be? When I tried to take hold of them, they flipped away like quicksilver. It was some time before I understood. They were air bubbles that had got caught. Drops of air here below in the treasure house of the sea.

At one elevated spot enough air had collected to make a silvery mirror. When I approached and looked upward, I jumped. A horrible creature with a single big, gleaming Cyclops eye and a corrugated double snout was coming down upon me—myself, reflected! Endless ages ago a worm had crawled ashore, and from it the land animals had gradually developed, and finally man as well; and now this creature was swimming with fins in the sea again, with artificial gills, and entering even this remote cathedral——

Sitting on the floor of the grotto, I wondered whether it would not be possible to reproduce such an ocean cathedral in a museum. Yes, it was perfectly possible, but if it were true to nature it would be gaudy and in the worst possible taste. A really magnificent sunset cannot be painted. A really passionate emotion cannot be recounted. Only nature herself can transmit the strongest effects.

We spent the night beside the rock slab that had slid into the sea, and next day I dived into my cathedral again. To permit a careful examination of these astonishing life communities on the cavern walls, I went to work with hammer and chisel, chipping off good-sized stone fragments with all the organisms upon them, which were then received by Joerg and Alfred at the cave entrance, taken up to the *Bosporus*, and there photographed in colour.

Floating on my back, close under the yellow-starred ceiling, I chiselled away, and starfish, worms, and water ticks fell on my face. This was the situation when Michelangelo's letter came to my mind. Yet my activity was the very opposite. While he created beauty I, with the rude hand of science, was knocking gaps in the perfect beauty of my Sistine Chapel.

32

A RATHER choleric dowager crab, crawling about her business, chanced to stumble over a sponge she had not noticed.

"Oh, do watch what you're doing!" she cried in exasperation. "Another old sponge! I really would like to know what sponges are good for, anyway! Why do they exist? Just to get tripped over!"

"Excuse me," replied the sponge, but——"

"Yes, yes, I know what you're going to say," the dowager crab interrupted, angrily rubbing her bruised leg with her claw. "Human beings sometimes wash with your sort—but they could do it just as well, if not better, with a flannel. No, no, don't tell me. You're a thoroughly useless and unnecessary set of plants."

"I'm an animal like yourself, madam!" said the sponge in a pleasantly serene voice.

"You, an animal?" said the dowager crab, amazed.

"Certainly, madam. You'll find it confirmed in any textbook."

"I never read anything but novels," replied the dowager crab. "Why, it's almost unbelievable—an animal? No eyes, no legs, no claws—what are you living for, anyway?"

"May I, too, make so bold as to ask a question?" the sponge inquired civilly.

"Well, all right, though I'm in rather a hurry."

"If you don't mind my asking, what are you living for yourself?"

The dowager crab laughed aloud. Really, this sponge was quite a character.

"What am I living for?" she repeated. "Gosh, a person just lives, enjoys life, passes the time, has various duties——"

"Good food, you mean?"

"Yes, of course, good food, too."

"And then possibly love?"

The dowager crab blushed slightly, but could not deny that love did play a certain part in her life. Everything to do with it—the little ones, and so on.

"And you see," said the sponge, "that's exactly how I look at life, so I've simply dropped everything else. If you'll take the trouble to look closely at me you'll see I'm nothing but a stomach that reproduces itself."

"A stomach that reproduces itself?" cried the dowager crab in great astonishment.

"Yes, that's right, a stomach that reproduces itself. Of course not a simple stomach like yours, madam. You see, I'm a gourmet! I have a thousand little hollows, and I savour what I eat in each hollow."

"Well, I never!" cried the dowager crab, most impressed.

"Yes, that's how it is. What good do your eyes do you, may I ask? All they really do is distract your attention from your food. And your legs? They get tired and you trip over things. To say nothing of those huge claws, which have to be polished all over again every evening. I just sit here peacefully without any of those garnishments, and grow fat doing it, as you see. Long ago Lao-tse said, 'He that has little shall receive; he that has much shall grow bewildered; hence the wise man stays in a state of Wu-Wei.' "

"Wu-Wei?"

"Yes, persist in inactivity, and there will be nothing you can't accomplish——"

"I must say one wouldn't know it to look at you," said the dowager crab, shaking her head. "And tell me—you have some experience of love, too?"

"Yes, indeed," said the sponge, "though naturally on the same moderate scale as the rest of my life. In our early youth there comes a time when we float impetuously in the ocean, yearning for the wide, romantic world——"

"Ah!" said the dowager crab, sentimentally.

"Well, yes, but it doesn't last long. Then we see reason, settle down, and grow up into stomachs. Don't you agree that it's the ideal answer? No annoyances, no quarrelling, fat, dumb, and happy. How did Lao-tse put it——"

"All right, all right," she hastily interrupted him. "You know, I can't really make head or tail out of your Mr. Lousy, but I truly did enjoy meeting you. You really quite deserve a person's respect. Au revoir, Mr. Sponge!"

"Your humble servant, Madame Crab!"

33

WE worked for three days in the shore caverns, then bad weather came on and we went back to Planit. Our mate and the crew were fairly fried in the heat. They said this was all well and good, only for heaven's sake let's get away from here. But to the general regret we found another and almost lovelier grotto near the entrance to Planit, and so we stayed two days more.

In the blue darkness of this grotto I was to make a discovery of great significance for me. It carried me into studies that almost monopolized my attention for two years. I was swimming down a colourful wall when, to my amazement, in a luxuriantly overgrown alcove I discovered red roses! Yes, red roses, blossoming here on the rock or mounted on gorgonia. Roses, but whose petals were not soft and full but made of a dainty, fragile calcareous fabric. The petals looked like fine tulle.

With the pounding heart of an orchid collector I carefully separated these strange marvels from the rock, bedded them down on shipboard with the greatest solicitude, and allowed no one to come within a yard of them. It was love at first sight. Later, when we were diving about the wreck at Elephteri, I found similar forms, but nowhere near so dainty, and in the region of the current by Lita Donisia we were to discover an area where the whole bottom was covered with these 'Neptune's Cuffs,' as a scientist has called them. These, however, were rugged in form, stout, and as tightly curled as a bushy aster.

What sort of beings were these? Were they corals? And did the various forms belong to the same species?

Before I knew it I was lost in a jungle of scientific problems. Under the microscope my orchid presented an uncommonly bewildering spectacle. Many hundreds of tiny animals had created this lacy work of art, each one building itself a tiny house, and each house rising above and beside the others, according to some mysterious law. The animals themselves had the shape of dainty polyps; they groped eagerly through the water with eight tentacles for yet tinier animals. When scared they would vanish like lightning into their shells and a dainty little door would shut behind them.

No, corals they were not; this was fairly easy to determine. Coral branches are also built up by tiny polyps, and each of these, too, has its own retreat—but these holes are nothing like so artfully constructed as my tiny houses were. Furthermore, my orchid petal displayed a whole series of altogether differently shaped individuals, scattered at large among the normal shells. There were some that looked like beaks—obviously these specimens defended the colony. Others formed a spherical chamber—these were the incubators for embryos. Others, again, climbed up the rock like roots; they anchored the branch.

They were sea moss, bryozoans—a group of animals including some thousands of species, often incredibly bizarre in shape, which the layman scarcely ever hears of. Only, which one of these thousands of species did my orchid belong to? Or was it a new kind? My orchid left me no peace; and before I knew it I was deep in the morasses of so-called systematics, compared to which stamp collecting is a kindergarten game. For in order to classify a stamp you have only to look in the catalogue, but where was a catalogue for my bryozoans?

Cat, dog, bear and wolf may be easy enough to distinguish, but what about the fish, let alone the insects, of which there are no fewer than three quarters of a million known species? You have to start by burrowing among the faded leaves of scientific journals the world over, tracing, examining, and comparing hundreds of species before you finally come to the right category.

And then? Then you know where you are even less than ever, because there are no fewer different opinions among scholars than among politicians. Is the tiny arch at the bottom of the little door to the animal's dwelling a typical characteristic? One scholar says yes; another says certainly not! One man calls the animal *Retepora aureacea,* and appends his own name because he believes it is a new discovery; the next man smiles as he reads this, writes in his own monograph: '. . . and it therefore seems justifiable to discard this alleged species . . .' and arranges it with five others in a new unit, to be called *Retepora cellulosa* and bear the name of a naturalist some fifty years dead.

Let no one say that this is a dullard's pastime. On the contrary, if anyone has lost his zest for life he should turn to biology and his cares will vanish. What an immeasurable field! What countless mysteries and marvels in every crumb of earth, every drop of water, every last scrap of skin!

But back to my orchid. For two years I studied it, examining every hidden recess of its tiny chambers by microscopic section; I even pored over Swedish, South African and Japanj ese journals in search of it, and, by the sweat of many months, reduced its marvellous state organization to mathematical terms. And did I know it? Heavens, I had scarcely begun to know it! I was just gradually starting to get a perspective of the abounding mysteries in its life. And this orchid of mine was just one among over a hundred Reteporidae hitherto described. And the Reteporidae were only one of the three hundred known groups of bryozoans.

And what did the bryozoans themselves amount to in the

whole animal kingdom? What indeed, compared to the fish with their twenty thousand species, the butterflies with their eighty thousand fluttering representatives, and the two hundred and fifty thousand different beetles that scrabble busily all over the globe?

No, he who once gets tangled in the jungle of biology will not break out of it in a hurry.

Nor will he be in any hurry to do so.

34

THE hot summer air flickers over the sluggish waves. The isle of Skopelos stands grey-green against the sun-drenched sky. Yonder on the slopes insects whir, snakes crawl, lizards bask in the sun, withered leaves rustle in the faint breeze. The olive trees sag under the burden of the fruit. Summer has brought ripeness, fulfilment. If only it will bring fulfilment to our own fervent desires as well!

Exactly at the agreed time we reach the straits between Skiathos and Skopelos, and the dynamite fishermen, too, are punctual to the minute. Their boat comes towards us from abeam. They are savage- and evil-looking fellows indeed. One has a face quite black with beard stubble; the second, our friend Mitcho, wears a pirate's red shirt; a third waves to us with hands that could easily break a piano apart. We greet each other cordially, and as the weather is so fine we start work at once.

We take the poacher's boat in tow, and as we pass other poachers we take them also in tow. It is a gay procession moving across the sea—though anything but a religious procession, it must be confessed.

What, do you want to drop here? Here, where the sea has no bottom?

No, of course we're not afraid! Afraid? We don't care if it's three hundred feet deep; all we've got to have is sharks, and then everything'll be all right!

A dull blow echoes through the water, and the ocean brandishes an accusing arm of foam at the sky. Like a fountain the spray splashes down on us. In an instant we are overboard, floating in the midst of the cloud of spray, diving to get below the white foam, peering downward.

Boundlessly deep and vast the blue abyss spreads below us. In this yawning space some hundreds of blasted fish twitch. A moderately good shot.

But there is a shark. A small, in fact a very small, shark, only five or six feet long, but all the saucier for that. Like an angry hornet he rushes up, circling us twice at such speed that there is no chance to photograph him. Now he rushes at Joerg, straight from the front, so that Joerg almost snubs his nose with the harpoon. Another lightning circle, two of the fish are snapped up, then a vanishing tail fin and the show is over.

We wait, but nothing more comes. The little shark was the only guest. Laughing at Heinz, who had kept rather too close to the boat, we clamber out of the water.

Xenophon, meanwhile, has been most strikingly transformed. For the first time I see him lose his detachment. He talks excitedly with the poachers, who also look fairly excited. I tell him to his face that he has never believed a word we have told him, which he admits without further ado. The shark, he says, is the most fearful of monsters for every fisherman and no fisherman would ever venture into the water when a shark is near by. As for himself, everything is different now. He will take personal charge of things, and we can be sure of getting an eyeful. This place where the boys dropped their dynamite is a bungling choice. Let the fishermen begin by making some drops over yonder along the coast, just beyond the little cape. Suppose we go over to the Elephteri beacon, where there's a sunken ship that will certainly be interesting for us? By the time we rejoin the fishermen in the afternoon some sharks, or at least some big rays, will have turned up. The fishermen's dynamite, however, we'll have to pay for.

We're glad to do this. And they can keep any fish they kill. Cordial farewells. We watch the poachers waving behind us for some time, then their boat turns away. We steer at top speed for the beacon.

"Won't there be some ibexes swimming about there?" asks Joerg sarcastically.

"Maybe a Fair Helen will be sitting by the beacon."

But this time Xenophon is quite certain. No, we needn't worry; this wreck can't have evaporated. The ship is the *Volos,* and sank one stormy February night eleven years ago. At carnival season it went straight at the beacon. Furthermore, we can see the mast from here.

He is right. Next to the beacon, which stands quite alone on a reef in the middle of the sea, a slanting pole sticks out of the water. We are soon there, making our vessel fast to the masthead. Like Munchausen tethering his horse to the steeple.

Donning the diving gear, I float downward. The wide-reaching contours of the ship's hull loom vaguely up at me. In the middle, the cargo hatch, like a great gaping maw; forward, the second stump of a mast, like an ugly broken nose. And there are two eyes, too. One triangular and wide open, the other slitted and leering scornfully. Involuntarily I keep closer to the mast; in this ghostly atmosphere it is the only real and solid element. It is decently covered with all sorts of mussels and seaweed; long green beards hang from the cables. The water is a grisly green, not very clear. Now I float down through the tremendous masses of snow to the silent, sleeping village.

It grows noticeably cooler. A green twilight veil descends upon everything. On the middle platform of the mast I pause. Once the look-out stood here gazing at screeching gulls; now I stand gazing at swarms of little fish floating motionless in the water. They're the same kind I saw near the ship's ribs in the straits next to the pirates' isle. And they are the same as in

France, at the wreck where I had the battle with the octopus. They are what you might call wreck fish, creatures obviously created for no purpose but to symbolize black mourning banners for the remnants of former human glory.

Close forward of the ship's gaping maw I reach the deck. The water here is as full of little green algae as a soup of farina. Farther forward stands the winch that once hoisted the anchor; now the whole ship is one solid anchor, and the rust slowly eats its way through the iron. Matted algae like little icicles hang from the erstwhile rail. Here people once strolled, standing laughing by the rail. It's getting abominably cold here! As if with frog hands the cold trickles down my back. A jellyfish drifts by and I photograph it. But the release button works only hard and reluctantly. Down here the water pressure is so heavy that the metal walls of the case have bulged inwards.

Frightening as the big square ship's maw (the former cargo hatch) looks, it is irresistibly tempting to dive into its blackness and inspect the hold. I slide cautiously down. The hold is gigantic and empty and dark, like the stomach of an enormous whale, lying in wait, tired and hungry on the bottom. Only a long way forward light comes dimly in—that might easily be the mouth through which Jonah entered his strange prison.

To one side below me, among a lot of indefinite objects, there is motion. It is perfectly possible that they are some sort of quite harmless fish playing about; nevertheless I decide against taking a closer look. There is a squirming, twisting motion, and it all seems most uncanny. Luckily I am alone, and thus not required to show excessive courage. Through a crack in the side I leave the hold. And heave a sigh of relief now that I have the open water before me and the plain, straightforward iron side at my back.

Since I cannot see the wave sky I must be sixty-five or seventy feet down. The ship's side, like a castle wall, falls away behind me. Do I feel somehow ill at ease? No, I feel fine. Even the cold is nowhere nearly so distressing as it was. The bottom on which the wreck lies is sandy, sinking away at an angle.

Following it, I come to a spot where a cleft in the floor, a gully with perpendicular walls, leads downward. An unusually colourful scene. The walls of the gully look like a luxuriant tropical garden. There are even some of my orchids here. Scarcely has my eye made out the first one when they appear everywhere from the confusion. Their delicate, gauzy lace adorns mussels and sponges.

On a gorgonia grows a dainty little rose, so tiny that my fingers— Damn!

I am just able to snatch my hand back in time. What a vile brute! From amid the luxuriant garden, directly beside the tiny rose, appear the slavering jaws of a moray. And in fact a fairly big moray, whose open mouth plainly shows the sharp little teeth. It stays motionless in a posture of attack. This is an enchanted garden, with a witch guarding it, and every knight is bitten who tries to pick the rose and free the enchanted princess.

With the camera I chase the moray back into its hole and pick the tiny rose. Unfortunately no rescued princess falls upon my neck. Not even a thunderclap. With the rose in my hand I float back to the wreck, reaching the huge propeller a hundred feet down. Its massive blades, too, are overgrown with my orchids on the shadowed lower side. Several dozen blossoms have been welded here into a complete circle. With great care I remove this large piece. As it is known how long the wreck has lain on the bottom, this specimen allows us to calculate the speed of the animals' growth. That carnival night eleven years ago, at earliest, some of the first larvae fixed upon the iron, formed the first little house, the ancestrula; and then above this there grew up first a little funnel, whose edges wrinkled more and more until finally it turned into a rosette, which fused with others in this ring-like formation——

I glide up over the screw and back to the deck. From afar I can see Alfred, who is just clambering down the last bit by the mast in his diver's helmet. I swim over and show him my wreath.

"Come on, get on the other side," comes his voice hollowly from inside the helmet. "Then we can get the schools of fish between us."

So we separate, but just as we have the fish well between us a heavy blow strikes through the water. All of us, Alfred, I, and the fish, sway sideways as if in a gust of wind. The very idea! They must have gone stark crazy up top! Throwing dynamite while we're in the water! It's the merest chance if our eardrums are still whole! Alfred and I hurry upward in great indignation.

Above, however, we find only amazed shaking of heads. No, nobody threw any dynamite. Of course not. What could give us that idea?

As the reef of Elephteri is perfectly alone in the open sea we are able to ascertain that only one boat is within sight, and thus must be responsible for the bomb. This boat is a good mile and a quarter away from us. A mile and a quarter——

Then that is how far those nefarious bombs can reach.

And the day goes on. We rest on board, gather warmth, wrangle a little because Joerg and Alfred are determined to use the diving gear, we dive again, eat up a huge dish of Austrian *Schmarrn* with stewed plums, bandage a wound that Alfred has got from a piece of sharp ironwork, and are back at three o'clock with the poachers, who welcome us boisterously. Yes, they say, several sharks have already been there, but by now they're gone. There are rays, though, more than enough, swimming back and forth down below, picking up the dead fish off the bottom. They say we have only to dive and keep our eyes open and we shall be sure to see one.

Good! As the depth here is ten fathoms and the diving helmet can't be used because the pump is out of order, I am the only one to reach the bottom. It is an oddly dead landscape in which I find myself. Rock slabs and patches of sand, occasional pinna mussels in a disagreeable, chalky light. Nowhere a seaweed or a moving animal, nothing but dead fish everywhere, the sad aftermath of the explosions. The bottom looks like a deserted battlefield.

I sit down on a stool of rock and wait like a huntsman at a standstill. But gradually, since nothing appears, I grow bored. Besides, the chalky, lunar light gets on my nerves. I stare upward, but nothing is to be seen either of the boat or of any swimmer. In this unpleasant illumination I cannot see even the waves. I feel as if I were in a whitewashed hospital room under a radiation lamp.

To pass the time somehow, I get one of the pinna mussels and open it with my knife. The moment blood drops into the water little fish appear, greedily and impudently approaching and even nibbling at the knife. When I have cut the two occlusive muscles, and the eighteen-inch shells open, a banquet begins—and I cannot stop a tragedy from taking place. In this pinna mussel, as in almost every one, are two little crabs, a couple, and scarcely is the mussel open when one of the impudent fish is on hand and one of the crabs vanishes down its gullet.

But here comes a ray!

Instantly I have aimed the camera and am shooting. But this ray is a most sensitive type. Although he is still a good fifty feet from me he jumps at the whir of my camera, wheels about, and swims hastily off in another direction. He looks like a flapping bird with wings much too big and clumsy. He trails a long, thin mouse tail behind him, straight as a string. It is not a particularly large ray, not more than twenty pounds or so. I follow him with the camera as long as he is in sight.

Meanwhile the second of the little crabs has gone to its doom. The fish at my feet squabble over the remains of the pinna mussel.

Scarcely have I rewound my camera when another ray appears, this time a considerably larger dignitary a good five feet across, who, to my delight, is not in the least disturbed by the whir of the camera. Flapping leisurely, he approaches, snaps up a fish from the bottom not thirty feet from me, turns to and fro with relish, and then, without the slightest sign of fear, swims past me at a distance of twelve or thirteen feet. In the white, sharp light the two spines on his whip-like tail are plainly visible; the larger, main spine is forward, the smaller, spare spine close behind it. The creature's head is pointed, its forehead high and angular. While I am shooting I pray to heaven that I have set the distance and aperture right. Later, when the ray is out of sight, I find both were correct. For a moment this disagreeable landscape seems positively attractive.

Where can Joerg and Alfred be? We could have taken some splendid spearing shots with that ray. Gradually the solitude gets on my nerves. I wait a little longer, and then my vision begins to go funny. I can't see clearly. First I think the fault is with the mask, that it has fogged, and I lean forward to rinse the inside of the glass with the little bit of water that always penetrates the mask. But it is not the mask. My view is perfectly clear, and yet I can no longer sharply distinguish various things within my field of vision. When I try to concentrate my gaze on one of these spots it blurs as if there were hot air between it and me. And at the same time my aversion to this dead, lunar landscape and the ugly, cold light increases to a feeling of downright fear. I'm sitting in a cemetery down here—funny that I hadn't noticed it before! The hospital room is white-tiled, the medico has not yet come to turn off the disagreeable radiation lamp. A funny thing that I don't swim up. Why not? Why do I stick here on the rock like a weather vane on a steeple? Should I call? Will he come and turn off the lamp then? Is it too late? Well, all right, in a cemetery, an echoing, tiled, white cemetery— With a last effort of will I pull myself together and shoot upward.

The boat is fairly far off when I break the surface of the waves. I shout, but it is some time before it finally deigns to approach. Joerg and Alfred have followed the big ray, which has now come quietly to rest on the sand, and they bring

Red roses! The highly fragile colonies of retepora look
like delicate lace

The dragon-headed scorpaenoid is feared because of the poisonous
spine on his dorsal fin

The ray wallowed back and forth, so that he disappeared in a constantly growing cloud of sand

Suddenly I saw Joerg. He came rushing down with determination

me the harpoon, with a rope attached, saying I should hurry up and dive and spear the brute. With some difficulty, supported by Xenophon, I get safely into the boat. Is something wrong? Joerg asks. No, nothing particular, I insist. Only a strange feeling of uncertainty that came over me down below. All right, he says, if I don't want to dive any more myself, let me give him the gear. They have already tried diving free, but the place is nearly seventy feet deep. No, I say, something is wrong with the gear; I have just had peculiar troubles with seeing. Oh, go on, troubles with seeing—the thing will be done in a moment, and it would really be a shame for that ray to go unspeared——

No.

Why I'm so set against it I don't know myself; anyhow, I feel wretched, and disinclined for any further argument. No, and that's all there is to it.

As I lie flat on the ship's bottom and Xenophon is looking after me, I hear Joerg and Alfred making one more attempt to get at the ray with a free dive. They fasten the harpoon to a long fork, such as the poachers use to fetch up the dead fish, and from Joerg's shouts one gathers that Alfred comes awfully close to him this time. But he doesn't quite reach him.

Later, in my half sleep, the voices come closer again. It is Joerg's voice I hear above the others, and he says something derogatory about an expedition leader who considers himself the principal of a kindergarten. But by this time I am already asleep.

35

SINCE Knut Hamsun wrote his *Viktoria* there is nothing much more to say about love and the strange motives behind it. One motive, indeed, was not touched upon there—the most remarkable and perhaps the most underlying of all.

I

Joerg was, as has been remarked, in a bad humour, and this grew worse next day when it began to rain. One of Vasil's vineyards did help us to give some meaning to the otherwise useless day, but Joerg's annoyance could not be appeased by grapes. And so it happened that Xenophon began to feel the effects of Joerg's surplus energies.

The immediate cause was one of Xenophon's peculiar observations upon nature. From the rain we got on to the subject of dew, and he boldly asserted that dew could see, as if it had eyes. He backed this up with the statement that notoriously more dew fell upon green than upon yellow; he said he had observed it a hundred times aboard his ship, which was painted part yellow and part green. And on the island of Malta, for this reason the gigantic pans to catch the dew were painted green, whereas the ripe grain was yellow, and being already ripe, no longer needed any dew. The watermelons in Palestine, on the other hand, were of course green since, as it never rains there, they were entirely dependent on the dew. When he soon afterwards remarked that work was an "opiate for empty shells," Joerg got up and took off his bathrobe.

Now Xenophon had lost much of his self-assurance since our encounter with the sharks. Although Joerg's movements were quite inconspicuous he immediately suspected that evil things were in store for him, and sought safety in flight. Joerg followed him like a flash, and promptly pitiful cries of woe came from the beach, and Vasil's sailboat, upon which Xenophon had taken refuge, rocked as if in a hurricane.

When we came up Xenophon was completely inside the tiny cabin and Joerg was sitting with all his weight on his head.

"Well?" he asked, giving the poor wretch air for a brief moment. "Is every moment of life equally painful?"

"Yes, very painful!" cried Xenophon, twisting and writhing.

"And the ibexes, my good man?"

"Oh, ouch—the ibexes!"

"And what about the dew, my friend? Can it see?"

"No, no! I take it all back and assert the contrary!"

When Xenophon was released he looked like a cream-puff bakery after a storm. Anyone who supposes, however, that he bore Joerg a grudge for this will be as mistaken as we were. The very opposite was the case. From that day onward Xenophon showed such unlimited devotion to Joerg that it sometimes bordered on the comical. No matter what Joerg commanded, it was done promptly and without question. If Joerg said, "I notice my harpoon has not been sharpened," Xenophon was on the spot in an instant, sharpening as if his salvation depended on it. And if Joerg said for pure amusement, "Xenophon, go up that cliff and jump off!" and the cliff was a dozen feet high, Xenophon would, it is true, groan and wail loudly but still he would crawl up and jump, and his love only grew so much more devoted.

36

I AWAKENED as if from under an anaesthetic. There were echoing sounds about me as if in broad corridors. Through a thick fog I saw Joerg leaning over me.

"He's coming to," I heard him say, and some other heads joined his.

They tried to stick something into my mouth, but it was so tightly closed that all my teeth ached. I tried to open it but could not. This tired me so much that I shut my eyes again. Strange how I could not remember anything, nothing at all!

When I woke up a second time I felt considerably better. It was afternoon, and I was lying under a fig tree. Xenophon, sitting beside me, was chasing the flies from my face.

"Well, returning to life?"

"What went on?" I asked, dazedly. "Has anything happened?"

"No, no, everything's all right," he said. "Just you lie

quiet. Hungry? Or do you want something to drink? You
gave us a fine fright!"

I tried to remember. Something must have happened, but
what it was I had not the slightest idea. Xenophon summoned
the others, and I now learned that I had dived and come to
grief. All well and good: dived and come to grief—but how?
I knew what the words diving and coming to grief meant, but
every recollection connected with it was gone. I—who was I,
anyway? And Greece—how did I come to be in Greece? In
my head was a yawning emptiness, where I groped like a
blind man in a completely strange neighbourhood. And yet
I could feel that I was within arm's reach of the answer to
every question. I had only to catch hold of a corner somewhere.

"But surely you must remember," said Alfred. "You're a
Greek diver, married for the second time. She's ten years older,
and rather fat."

Everyone laughed, and I did not know whether to laugh
too. After all, it was possible. Anything was possible.

"A retrograde amnesia, nothing more," Joerg observed.

"And it will pass off?" I asked.

"Oh, it may easily pass off," he replied cheerfully. "But
it may equally well last for some while. There have been cases
where it went on for years."

A fine prospect!

I ate a little, then fell asleep again. When I woke up the
stars shone bright above me. Then suddenly memory began to
dawn. Of course! At the last moment I had pushed off! What
foolhardiness! How could I have experimented on myself?

What had happened?

Early in the morning we had sailed out into the straits
and had divided up. While Joerg and Alfred tagged along
with the dynamite fishermen the rest of us went to the wreck,
where I meant to collect orchids in the underwater gully.
For this purpose I used a mesh basket hanging on a rope, and
every time I filled it it was hauled up at a signal, and came down
again empty. This had been done twice, and I was fairly tired

from dragging the big basket after me, when suddenly the same troubles with my vision began as at the spot where I had taken pictures of the ray. My first impulse was to swim up, but then I had a better idea. Or, rather, a worse one, as was soon to appear. It occurred to me that other people would go under water with this diving gear, so it was my duty to determine its weaknesses. Obviously the spots before my eyes were symptoms of the oxygen poisoning we had been warned against. But what would happen next? How long would you have after the first signs appeared?

So I stayed below, observing myself. I was, so to speak, my own guinea pig. It would have been more sensible to surface, tell my friends, tie a rope round my waist, and then make the experiment. But, as I say, the first sign of oxygen poisoning is precisely that one loses one's normal hesitations—as in the altitude sickness of aviators. Why shouldn't I study these disturbances of vision for a while?

So I went back to the bottom, sat down within reach of the rope on which the basket hung, and waited to see what would happen next.

Quite a good deal did, and soon. With every passing second my vision grew worse. Objects near by, such as the net full of orchids, I could still distinguish plainly. The side of the wreck, however, as well as the rocks and the gully, blurred into vague spots, as if I were looking at an old, spoiled film. And the faster the whirling before my eyes, the more oppressive was my sense of anxiety. I began to tremble. My thoughts slipped away from me. An awful echoing began inside my head. I was barely able to push off from the bottom with one last motion, then I was paralysed and lost consciousness.

If I was still alive at all, I owed this to the fact that I had pushed off—and to some passing gulls. Usually I kept the contents of my air pouch so adjusted on my back that I was a trifle heavier than water. When I rose somewhat and the air expanded accordingly, I grew lighter, and thus moved on upward of my own accord. Here I floated on the surface, with only the air pouch sticking a little above the waves—and this attracted the attention of the passing gulls, who circled the strange object to see if it might not be edible; and as Heinz had been shooting at gulls with a carbine, he noticed the birds' behaviour and fetched me out.

"I got films of it all, too," he told me the next morning proudly. "In fact I even got a colour picture of you being taken aboard, blue and stiff."

I also learned something else on this occasion. As soon as Joerg and Alfred had convinced themselves after my mishap that nothing fatal had befallen me they had left me in Xenophon's care and each of them had made several descents with the diving gear that very afternoon.

"I take it we did as you would have wished," Joerg declared cheerfully. "We were just interested in seeing that nothing interrupted the diving work——"

After that, there was no possible retort to this. So I gave in, and from that day on we used the diving gear in common.

37

Why is pure oxygen poisonous to the body under high pressure?

A doctor who had studied the subject gave me the following plausible explanation: As is well known, the red corpuscles do the transporting of the oxygen in the blood. They take it from the air breathed into the lungs and carry it to the tissues and cells, where it is consumed in the combustion on which animal life is based. On the return trip they pick up the waste of the combustion process, carbonic acid, and transport this to the lung capillaries, whence the poisonous gas is exhaled. Further, it is well known that every liquid under increased pressure absorbs gas in solution. If, then, breathing pure oxygen you dive to a great depth, in other words into higher pressure, the blood itself absorbs so much oxygen that the red corpuscles are unemployed, as it were, and can no longer 'sell' their oxygen anywhere. And what is the result? As they remain charged with oxygen they can no longer carry back the carbon dioxide. This would mean that oxygen poisoning was ultimately a poisoning of the tissue with carbon dioxide.

Against this theory, however, it must be said that ordinary carbon dioxide poisoning, which easily happens in a diving helmet if the pump is not worked hard enough, produces by no means the same symptoms.

38

"Just a minute. You say animal life is a process of combustion? What do you mean?"

"That's right, Xenophon. I say combustion processes are the basis of animal life, and so they are. The plants take in the sun's energy and store it up; the animals, on the other hand, eat the plants and their stored-up energy, and transform it into motion and that process is called combustion.

"It's the same with a locomotive. We stoke it with coal, but coal is no more than petrified plants; these in turn still contain the solar energy they once stored up; solar energy drives the locomotive. And cars are the same. Petrol comes from crude oil; crude oil is the final product of decayed animal bodies; these bodies in their day ate plants and the solar energy they had stored up; solar energy drives our cars, too. In other words, the energy question is extremely difficult. All energy of any importance comes from the sun; the plants are the only ones that can chain this energy; animals, men, locomotives, and automobiles alike ultimately consume plants and the energy they have stored up, and transform it into motion—by the process of combustion.

"Combustion hasn't necessarily anything to do with flames. We and the animals don't burn like stoves. On the other hand, all combustion needs oxygen. That's why we breathe."

"All well and good, but where does the oxygen come from? If breathing has been going on for millions of years the stuff is bound to run out some time."

"Well, Xenophon, then you've got the plants again. They're so obliging that they not only store up for us the energy we consume in the form of vegetables and fattened pigs, but also supply the oxygen needed to burn them. A unique degree of selflessness, when you stop to think about it. Like someone sitting on a pyre and handing you a match to light it.

"The plants produce oxygen, and with this oxygen the animals burn the plants in their stomachs—this is the state of affairs that has prevailed since the beginning of creation. But how about the sea? Plants need sunshine; this never penetrates more than thirteen hundred feet below the waves; consequently there can't be any plants deeper down; consequently nobody produces oxygen there; but where do the animals get it that have been drawn up from thirteen thousand feet?

"This again is by special courtesy of the water. Whereas usually warm substances are lighter than cold substances, water at 40 degrees Fahrenheit is heavier than at freezing point. Therefore the ice floats on the surface, and consequently also—as the celebrated *Meteor* expedition discovered—the surface water, warmed by the sun, sinks at the poles into the deep sea, while at the equator icy water from the depths streams to the surface in compensation. Thus we have in the deep sea a current running from the poles to the equator. And so it comes about that fresh water, rich in oxygen, keeps constantly pouring from the upper levels into the deep, permitting, even down there, an almost unlimited swimming, loving and eating—which is combustion; which is living."

39

Two days had passed since the mishap, and I was feeling quite hearty again. Nevertheless, Joerg still thought a rest was called for, and he and Alfred left me behind on board, taking along the diving gear and a lot of spare flasks and potassium cartridges. Four hours later they were back. Even from a distance I could see they had been successful. Laughing and shouting, they laid the boat alongside and tossed at my feet several slimy serpent bodies a good four feet long.

"Well, what about that?" cried Joerg.

This time Xenophon had guided them to a different wreck, which had been a lot longer on the bottom and was completely chewed up by the swell. Among these old ruins they had dropped two bombs, whereupon not, indeed, sharks and rays but over a dozen morays had appeared, scenting blood; they had emerged through the wreck and gone wriggling hither and thither to clean up the dead fish. Joerg had harpooned no fewer than six of these wily creatures, and Alfred had been able to take pictures of no fewer than four spearing scenes from beginning to end. Both were beaming with pride and joy. And as Joerg beamed, Xenophon beamed too.

Unfortunately the weather turned bad again. By afternoon the sky was completely overcast. Dr. Beckh and I worked at arranging and storing the collections; the others amused themselves by observing rock fragments under the microscope. When it started drizzling towards evening, we went back to Skiathos and spent the following day trading with Vasil for several cans of olive oil. As the pre-arranged date of our return to the Piraeus was approaching, we decided to spend the last days once more in the Straits of Euboea. According to Xenophon's tale, the phase of the moon was just right, in the next two days, so that there would be no current; we hoped to profit by this for a thorough study of the sea in the region, once investigated by Aristotle.

We bade farewell to Skiathos and sailed the next morning to Trikkeri, where the *Universitas* with Dr. Beckh as super-cargo turned off towards Volos to fetch water and more fuel, while the rest of us went ashore from the *Bosporus* to visit the village of Trikkeri, high on the mountain, the home of the Greek divers.

Here, too, the delight of the Greeks at seeing Xenophon was quite touching. We were surrounded everywhere, and one diver invited us to his house and presented us with peculiarly shaped sponges and a black gorgonida that he had brought up from two hundred feet. Next we were led to the little church in the village, where there was a hand-carved altar well worth seeing. From the churchyard we had a glorious view of the sea. The rain had stopped while we were climbing, the sun had come out again, and so the air was clear and glittering. We could see far beyond Euboea. A few spherical clouds were grouped over the island.

By noon we were back aboard the ship, and about three we reached the straits. For once Xenophon had not been wrong. There really was no current. We dived not far from the site of our first expedition, and discovered in the middle of the channel a seascape that made plain the strong influence of currents upon the dwellers on the ocean floor. Since current water is rich in oxygen and always carries fresh food particles with it, living conditions for the immobile animals were highly favourable. Some fifty large stone fragments lying on the flat, sandy bottom of the straits were so lavishly overgrown with sponges, corals, sea squirts, bryozoans, and other animal and vegetable organisms that almost nothing could be seen of the stone underneath. These fragments stood up like blossoming islands. As this lavish, rank growth was simply teeming with worms, crabs, snails, echinodermata and small fish, the absence of large, predatory fish could be attributed only to the iniquitous dynamiting, whose traces were visible here as elsewhere.

I was delighted to discover that my orchids also grew in their thousands on the mushroom-like chunks. As I have mentioned, the specimens we found here were smaller, coarser, and bushier than those I had gathered in the cave and at the Elephteri wreck, raising the interesting question whether this was some other species or group, or whether the difference in shape was merely an adaptation to the strong current. As I had decided meanwhile to make a more careful study of these interesting animal commonwealths I organized a large-scale enterprise such as we had never attempted before.

Taking turns, Joerg, Alfred, Heinz, and I went successively to the bottom with the diving gear and the helmet, and sent up to the boat in a constant succession of raised and lowered nets an endless stream of the luminous red animal-plants; Dr. Beckh and the mate received them and carefully boxed them in sawdust. We did our best to record exact data on the location and numbers of the ones we found. The creatures abounded on the sides of the mushroom-shaped rocks, obviously because here they were protected from direct sunlight.

When the current set in again on the third day I declared two days off. At Heinz's suggestion we went to Jaltra, on the other side of the channel, where there is a radio-active warm spring. The big hotel there proved to be entirely vacant; we found the spring at the back in a rocky niche. We bathed longer than was good for us, and then, to recoup our strength, went back through the arm of sea to the coast of Euboea, where the vines in the endless vineyards hung full of the most magnificent grapes. For want of transportation a good share of them dried on the vine and fell off. We did our very best to remedy this, then travelled a few coves farther to a spot where the Government had recently put up a net barrier to catch tuna fish. The manager of the weir gave us a cordial welcome, and said he was most willing for us to take pictures of the tunas, only unfortunately none had turned up yet. We swam around with the cameras among the completely empty nets, and would probably have taken a quick departure but that a daughter of the manager turned up who was strikingly reminiscent of Dorothy Lamour. Our interest in the weir immediately revived, and we decided to wait another day for the tuna fish. That evening we invited the manager and his daughter on board, and this was the first occasion during the entire expedition when all the members arrived properly dressed and groomed. Next day, with not so much as a tuna fin to be seen far and wide, Alfred instructed Dorothy Lamour in swimming with the fins, while Joerg applied massage to her ankle, which she had wrenched in the process. I showed her our collections, Heinz displayed the nautical instruments for her, Dr. Beckh photographed her from all sides, and Xenophon talked Greek to her. Then, after having sung melancholy songs that evening under a starry sky, we went back to work the next day with renewed strength.

Here in the straits, too, there were supposed to be sunken houses. A fisherman, to whom at Xenophon's request we made an appropriate payment, guided us to the spot in question. I dived and at sixty-five feet hit a muddy bottom, which, however, had neither temples, steeples, nor anything else to show. As the visibility was extremely poor I swam round in a circle; finally, I noticed a round handle sticking out of the mud. I pulled at it, and a jug made its appearance. It was encrusted with various limestone animals, and looked exactly as if some fisherman had tossed it overboard twenty years before, on noticing that it was cracked. The fisherman above, however, raised a great cry of triumph when I surfaced with this booty. He assured us it was a most valuable antique piece, and with this he considered his job to be done.

On the way back to Chalcis we passed the wreck of a ship that had been sunk by a bombing attack during the war. As it was scarcely forty feet down, we dived without gear. The wheel at which the helmsman had stood during the attack would still turn. Down on the promenade deck, where the passengers had rushed to the lifeboats, there was now a greenish-blue twilight. Diving through a bomb hole, we reached the dining saloon. Where people had sat and eaten, now fish swam across broken dishes and over tables covered with a grey, compact slime.

In Chalcis I parted with the ship and my companions. While they were to go back round Cape Sounion to the Piraeus I drove ahead to Athens, in order to launch the preparations necessary for the continuance of the expedition. From the ever-rising curves of the serpentine highway I looked back mournfully at the ship, growing ever smaller. How fine it was to be in the midst of a job, and how depressing to have reached its conclusion!

Out of the iridescent uncertainty, which one always decorates with the most colourful expectations, comes something definite, final, past. The spark of sunlight on the waves has finished one of its circles, its prescribed course has been made plain, and hope and imagination, those most faithful of companions, have to wing ahead again in order once more to gild reality (which always has the bitter after-taste of the ephemeral) with gleaming new expectations.

40

THE *Universitas* did not come until the second day. The weather had been stormy, and, besides, the mate had insisted on delaying until they could join company with a coastguard vessel again. I waited for the first uproar to die down somewhat, then explained the new situation to my associates.

The *Universitas* was no longer at our disposal; unfortunately I had not been able to do anything about that. Instead, we were to have a ship called the *Sultana*, a small iron motor ship so narrow in the beam that she was simply bound to capsize even in a wind of force four. This had, in fact, already occurred twice, but each time the *Sultana* had been raised and put in shape again. The present condition of the vessel was unusually bad. Bunks had to be built in the cabins; so far as I could discover, the sailing gear was completely inadequate; as to the motor, one of the cylinder heads had cracked, and required recasting. So that was the situation.

In addition, I told the assemblage that the second part of our voyage would not take us, as intended, to Crete and the Cyclades but back to the same region we had come from. I had recognized that it was a mistake to keep rushing to new islands. In the old days when we were still working from a tent we had been tied to one place, and thus compelled to exploit all its possibilities. This time, on the other hand, the ship and our whole great apparatus had driven us, and we had made the mistake of letting ourselves be driven. No, we would go back to the same region, and this time only to three places that had proved rewarding; and there we would do a thorough job. First we would make a still more careful examination of the straits near Lita Donisia; then do nothing but take films for a week or ten days at the place where there were the sharks and rays; and finally we would make extensive collections again in the sea cavern of Planit.

At the conclusion of my speech I amazed all those present by resigning my office and appointing Joerg the new leader of the expedition. He was now to organize the practical running of the enterprise as he thought best; I reserved to myself only the establishment of general aims.

"In short, all you want to be is honorary president?" Joerg asked me, sucking thoughtfully at his pipe.

"Yes, that's about how I see it," I said.

Joerg placidly smoked his pipe out, then fetched a big book in which he entered everything, and set immediately to work. First of all, Xenophon was relieved of his office as chef. His love for Greece and his affection for his old friends were all very admirable, Joerg said, but feeding not only them but their entire circle of friends on the q.t. at our expense was really going a little bit too far. Henceforth Heinz would have charge of the provisions; he, Xenophon, would in future be responsible for the perfect order of our entire equipment; he, Joerg, would make a careful inspection of the cameras, diving gear, and so forth every morning, and if everything were not clean, bright, and shining, then Xenophon would look upon the time when he had been the slave of the wicked Psarathanas as a delightful vacation. Then he turned to Dr. Beckh and advised him to spend his time at the Piraeus investigating the scientific literature that was undoubtedly available at the university, possibly with particular attention to the cicadas and sesiidae. And so far as Alfred and I were concerned, the way we tried to make films was simply preposterous. Nobody could possibly expect any useful work to be done if we never made up our minds until the last moment. We were to start work immediately on a detailed scenario, listing all the scenes to be shot and all the properties needed.

In short, Joerg did the job better than I had. He told everyone what he thought, worried about no hurt feelings, and got his way in what he wanted done. And so everything would have been simply fine if only constant new and almost insuperable difficulties had not kept rising up before us.

August 23-31. The carpenters are working fairly fast, but the motor is always up to new tricks. One bearing is gone, and the cylinder head is supposed to be welded, then a new one is cast and promptly cracks. We go out several times to the mole, where, since nobody uses dynamite here, there are more fish than in the entire Sporades; marbled bream, mullet, even dorado, branzinos and mackerel. A school of salpas grows highly confidential when I sit down among them. Several telephone calls to Berlin. Some of the test films are underexposed, and a number are out of focus. We've got to pull ourselves together.

September 1. The motor is still not ready. There are difficulties of all kinds. I go over with Alfred to the *Mary Word,* an eight-thousand-ton tanker that is being raised in Skaramanga, and we take pictures of professional divers at work with underwater cutting torches. Then we have lunch and go over to the other side, where there is a better wreck. We waste a lot of time before the diver is finally ready; then we go down with him. He's as crazy as a coot. Every time I want to shoot him he stands still, and then he runs. Afterwards I go swimming about, and encounter a strange diver, who is at work on an anchor. For the fun of it I swim round him like a fish. Most impressive! He turns and runs without looking back.

September 2. We sail first to Salamis, but I find no dynamite there. Unfortunately there is a high wind, so we can't dive until afternoon. More and more difficulties with the *Sultana*. We work the night through, Joerg and Heinz standing guard.

September 3. Trial voyage a failure.

September 9. Still at the Piraeus. It's enough to drive you mad. The cylinder head was supposed to be ready on Wednesday. On Tuesday a general strike began and work was stopped. After long parleying we finally persuaded the workmen to go on, and so the cylinder head was ready today. No dynamite to be found anywhere. I go from pillar to post, then happen to meet a diver who tells me about sharks at the southern tip of the Peloponnesus. He refers me to the port construction office, where I deliver a long lecture and get what I want. Four hundred and fifty instead of three hundred cartridges, in fact.

September 10. Today the motor ran for the first time, and once more something was not right. This time the bearing. Also, they say the connecting rod has been switched. At this I rise up in righteous wrath and set off for Athens, where the strike is still going on. Here I happen to meet the port captain of Volos and achieve the following: we will get everything ready by tomorrow morning, and at eleven o'clock a truck will pick us up and take us to Chalcis. There we will take a ship that will carry us to Lita Donisia, and there the *Bosporus* will pick us up on the fifteenth and be at our disposal until the arrival of the *Sultana*.

The gigantic animal continued swimming along, and we were able
to film him from both sides

He seemed to be in a merry mood, twisted and turned, and cut
graceful capers with his tail

The promenade deck, along which the passengers had raced for the lifeboats

The wheel at which the helmsman had stood during the attack

September 11. We pack and just to make sure I phone again, but no car comes. Then it does and we load up and drive off. A terrible road. It rattles and bangs fit to wake the dead; and we have a whole case of dynamite in the car! Alfred, however sits placidly on the case, declaring it is the best seat. "If it goes off, I'll be dead on the spot and you'll just be crippled for life——"

41

THIS time there was a strong current in the straits. Except for a brief period about noon, when the current turned from one direction to the other and the water stood still for a few minutes, the sweep was so strong that only the motor boat could make headway against it. Nevertheless we carried out our programme. We anchored the boat in the middle of the stream and made ourselves fast to it with a long line. Once we were in the water, the current would carry us off until the line was taut. Then we had only to tilt our bodies downward and the current would automatically carry us to the bottom. There we would work within the radius of the taut line, and when we wanted to rise again we had only to push off and we would be carried up. With the helmet or a diving suit this manœuvre would have been impossible.

Once the line broke and the water swept me along over the rocks. I tried to cling to a sponge but it broke off and on I bounced. The bottom grew flat; I tried to push off, and then an eddy caught me and swept me over a seven-foot underwater threshold lying athwart the current. And to my astonishment I was suddenly in perfectly calm water!

Just as there is often a spot under a waterfall where you can stand without getting wet, I had tumbled into a sheltered spot where I could adjust my diving gear at leisure and study the threshold with its hollows.

K

Here, too, we later made extensive collections. The process was quite complicated. We anchored the boat so that it was exactly above the sill, went down hand over hand to the anchor, let go, were washed across the sill by the eddy, put into a net what we had collected, surrendered ourselves once more to the current, were carried upward, and on the surface we were hauled back to the boat. This performance, too, would scarcely have been possible with any other diving gear.

42

"I REALLY don't understand you," said Xenophon in the evening as we were bandaging each other's wounds. "You go diving the whole blessed day, get broken heads, and all for what? Just to fetch up some grass and sponges like those every fisherman here gets in his net by the pound and throws overboard for junk!"

"But a man like you who has found gnosis ought to understand," I told him. "To a fisherman that stuff is junk, of course, but to the man who knows everything about it it brings insight."

"But you don't know anything about it!" said Xenophon. "What do you do with all the sponges? You put them in alcohol, and then what price insight?"

"Quite apart from the fact that we *really* do know something about it," I replied, "that isn't what matters. Our main job is to preserve the material properly and record exact data on where we find it; the rest is up to the various specialists in the museums, anyway. Have you the slightest idea how many creatures there are in the sea? You'll never find any one man who knows them all. Why, just take the sponges and corals alone. There's only maybe a single specialist, and even he would need a whole library to identify them all."

"And what good does it do one of these specialists? What good does it do him to keep studying new sponges?"

"He gains insight," I said. "Real gnosis, my dear Xenophon! All the animals and plants and everything else in the world are somehow inter-connected. So even a sponge specialist might easily make discoveries of general importance."

Xenophon said nothing, but chewed pensively at a fish head. Since Joerg's trouncing we had come closer to one another. He was nothing like so brusque any more, and felt himself more as one of us.

"You know, it's like standing in a cesspool," he said after a brief pause. "If you look up out of a cesspool you can see the stars in broad daylight through the little opening, that's true. But what good does it do you? You're still standing in a cesspool! What good are the two or three stars when you can't see the rest of the world?"

"One up for Xenophon!" cried Alfred. "I can't accept specialists with their blinkers, either."

"All I'm getting at is," Xenophon went on, "that I shouldn't want to exchange a single day of my life, not even one of those when I was wretched and desperate, for the kind of insights a sponge can bring me."

"Where were you ever in a cesspool?" Joerg asked.

"In Jerusalem. The summer of seventeen years ago. I cleaned cesspools professionally there for two months."

Heinz laughed until he almost choked on a fishbone. The rest of us pestered Xenophon to tell us how he had hit upon this occupation.

"Hell, nothing to it," he replied. "I had a sort of little gardener's cottage I was living in, and once when I cleaned up the garden I used the manure to start a compost heap. Then I thought how nice it would be if you could put some wet muck on it. So I hit on the idea of cleaning a cesspool. Well, the land we lived on was covered with hundreds of feet of rubbish before you came to bedrock. The cesspool was down below, and it looked like a church carved out of the rock, heaven knows how many thousands of years old, with pillars all round, and eight inches of mud because it hadn't been cleaned for

years. Afterwards I cleaned a bunch of other cisterns, but I
couldn't stand it for long."

He laughed, broke open the fish head, and fetched out
the brain. Putting the fish aside, he went on, "I could never
stand it long anywhere. It would be all right for a while, then
I'd have the urge to move on. I had to hunt for a long time
before I found what I was hunting, because I simply didn't
know what it was. I've vagabonded all round the whole
Mediterranean, through Italy, France, Spain, Tunis, Egypt,
Palestine, almost all on foot, more than eight years altogether,
until finally I found my fishing boat—the ideal answer to
the question, 'How can I live without money and without
being tied to one place?' "

"Tell us, Xenophon," I said, "tell us how you came to
be a vagabond."

All the wisecracking we usually cultivated had suddenly
dried up. We gathered curiously round our knotty tree.

"I didn't turn into a real vagabond until I ran away from
home the second time," he said after a brief consideration.
"I was just sixteen. I changed my money at Tarvis on the morning of March first, the year of the inflation; I kept one hundred
thousand crowns, big beautiful bank notes. I went to Venice,
picked out a grand hotel, went to bed, and said to myself,
'How long shall I stay here?' Actually, all my cash was just
enough to pay for that one night. But I spent that whole night
with the feeling that I should be enjoying life for some time.
In the morning the dream was over and I had to fork over
everything down to the last solitary lira. So I tramped through
northern Italy, acquiring a few phrases like *'sono povero!'* I
never begged from poor people; mostly I went into delicatessen
shops, and they'd cut off the fat from the ham for me, or anything they couldn't sell to their customers.

"But I still had certain habits, like brushing my teeth,
eating breakfast, and undressing at night. When I slept under
a lemon tree, I would put on my pyjamas. It was only afterwards when I thought things out, that I realized how ridi-

culous and unnecessary this was. I also discovered that, just as my childhood habits had been a hindrance in my life as a tramp, my school learning prevented me from getting ahead. In spite of all my playing truant, I knew too much—about the idea of honour, for instance, and that sort of thing. I finally got on the right path because one night my clothes were stolen. That left me with no shoes and no trousers, so I swapped the rest of my outfit for a real tramp's uniform. Barefoot, long trousers halfway down my calves, a striped jacket, much too short— it was spring by now, May—that was how I wandered, pretty aimlessly, into the blind alley of the western Riviera. I still didn't like certain things, but my desire for freedom won, so I just accepted that I would have to do what I had found embarrassing in other people only a few months before. I often wondered whether I would have been happy with ten lire a day to buy bread, and I think I would. But even without the ten lire it was all right. Well, that was how I turned into a vagabond."

43

Two days later we were back in the Elephteri region. When the poachers saw us coming they gave such spontaneous cries of joy that it properly warmed our hearts. And when we showed them our case of dynamite they were quite beside themselves. Savage Mitcho simply couldn't imagine such riches. This time we should be satisfied! They would parade all the sharks from far and wide past our cameras!

As it was still early, and a specially beautiful day at that, they took us straight to a spot where there were gopes. There, by way of introduction, we threw a particularly big bomb, ducked down in the boat, and I started the camera to film the mounting column of water—but nothing happened. White and glimmering, the bomb went to the bottom, and the fish whose deaths we had plotted cheerfully went on living.

"Shame to waste the good dynamite," remarked Xenophon, who still had, from his poaching days, the habit of economy in such matters.

A yell made him spin round. Joerg, who was peering into the depths through the glass-bottomed box, gave signs of extreme excitement.

"Quick, look here!" he cried. "Well, I never—look at the size of the fellow! This is for me!"

Instantly we all squeezed our heads together over the glass-bottomed box and the boat tilted alarmingly. Diagonally below us, right beside the bomb, which lay on the bottom like a neatly wrapped package of sandwiches, something was moving that looked at first glance like an open blanket swinging with the motion of the sea. It was a ray, a really gigantic creature, whose like I had never seen before. It was sniffing at the bomb.

"He'll eat it! He'll eat it!" cried Heinz beside himself with delight. "If it would only go off!"

"Quick, Alfred!" cried Xenophon. "Let's have another bomb! This time I'll put the fuse in myself!"

"Are you plumb nuts?" yelled Joerg. "I'm going to harpoon him, obviously! Where's the long rope?"

"You're out of your mind!" I said. "But of course I'm going to take films first!"

This was not much to Joerg's liking. "You're sure to scare him away," he groaned. "I can tell you right now you'll scare him away again. Damn your silly films, anyway."

Luckily I had the diving gear already on. I quickly donned the mask, stuck the breathing tube into my mouth, and clambered over the gunwale. Xenophon handed me the camera and I fastened it to my neck strap by the snap hook. Alfred and Heinz also scrambled overboard. Everyone was in a state of great excitement.

To avoid startling the ray I went a little way off before

descending to the bottom. The water was agreeably refreshing. I trembled with suppressed frenzy. Calm, calm, calm! Scarcely a hundred feet from me was a film subject almost better than anything I could have hoped for. If I succeeded in filming the harpooning of this brute our picture was a sure thing. What a wonderful background to introductory titles that ray would make! And round the harpooning scene we could shoot a detailed story, just as it had really happened, the whole proceedings in the boat, the excitement, Joerg grabbing for the harpoon. Xenophon about to throw a second bomb, the poachers in the next boat delightedly urging us on, and one of them looking dejected because he had not put the fuse in right.

I was on the bottom. The floor was flat and sandy, broken by chest-high bushes of green seaweed, behind which I could easily hide. A glance upward: Alfred was already filming; Heinz, a little to one side, was busy with the still camera; of Joerg only legs and body were to be seen. He was still hanging to the boat, obviously waiting for the harpoon head that Xenophon was filing for him.

I compelled myself calmly to check once more all the settings on the camera. I also ran off a foot or so of film. Everything was in perfect order. I crept cautiously through the shrubbery and reached the creature's immediate neighbourhood unobserved.

It looked as if the ray were actually about to devour the dynamite. He studied it from all sides, and then, just above the bottom, he began rolling to and fro so that he gradually vanished in a growing cloud of sand. The buzz of my camera did not impress him at all. He seemed in a lively and cheerful mood, twisting and turning, so that now the powerful pectoral fin, then the tail, then the whole creature, emerged from the cloud, burrowing, kneading, cutting graceful capers with his tail; he gave me a very fierce and then a very friendly look— in short, he behaved exactly as a cameraman's dream.

All at once I saw Joerg. Between my shooting and the

friendly behaviour of the ray I had quite forgotten the spearing scene. Now Joerg came resolutely plunging down, and I was not in the least prepared. I was much too close to get him and the creature on the film together, and, besides, I had only ten feet left, which of course was nothing like long enough for the whole scene. Joerg's conscience was uneasy, however, about his unauthorized proceeding, and as he dived he looked in my direction. With the most urgent gestures I could command I gave him to understand that he must for heaven's sake have patience. He checked himself reluctantly. With arms and legs, and particularly with his harpoon, he indicated that he was fed up, that he was freezing on the surface, that the ray was bound to swim off, that he was not disposed to wait any longer. With an emphatic flip of the fins he shot up again.

Possibly the ray had grasped the deeper meaning of our pantomime; at any rate he now came out of the cloud and swam leisurely about in the vicinity, which suited me admirably. As Alfred had meanwhile dived from the other side we managed to get the creature between us, so that each of us got the other together with the ray in the picture. With this my fifty-foot film was used up and I shot joyfully to the surface.

"What's the idea? What did you come up for?" cried Joerg, beside himself. He had just been about to dive again with the harpoon.

I said soothingly that I only needed a new film. Then he could go straight to spearing. To hurry Xenophon, who was changing the films, he accompanied me to the boat, which had drifted away a little. Alfred stayed on guard near the ray. Heinz also came over to the boat and told us about the marvellous pictures he had taken.

Xenophon was just in the act of screwing up the watertight case when excited shouts came from Alfred.

"A shark!" he yelled. "He's swimming next to the ray! Quick, quick!"

We saw him dive, obviously to take pictures, but in a

moment his head appeared above water again. This time he was waving his arms in despair. "The scoundrel! The damned brute will end up by driving him away. The ray is getting restless already."

If men should ever succeed in shooting a rocket to the moon it will leave the earth hardly any faster than Joerg left the boat at that crucial moment. With a noise of disappointment such as a dromedary might make if you rode for days through the desert and then started to pass by an oasis, he vanished, fins whirling. If I knew Joerg, nothing in the world could now prevent him from dealing death to the ray at the very slightest opportunity.

Hastily taking over the camera, I followed. I arrived just in time to watch the end of the tragedy. About fifty feet down, Joerg followed the creature as it swam off, and was within ten feet of it when the ray realized he was there, visibly took fright, and started away down the slope with double-quick strokes of its fins. Although it was perfectly senseless, Joerg jabbed after him; his whole rage and despair were expressed in the movement. Then he floated upwards, exhausted.

To avoid coming immediately into his view, I turned round—and saw a shark hanging scarcely ten feet behind me, observing me with ominous interest. I was so surprised that I started involuntarily. And this in turn startled the shark so that he turned in a flash and scattered like a puff of smoke in the distance.

"Boy, what a shark!" Heinz told me when I met him near the boat. "He swam right past me. A twelve-footer, easily!"

"I saw one, too," I said, "though he was only about eight feet long."

They must have been different sharks.

Without a word, like a thundercloud, Joerg climbed into the boat, took off the mask and fins, and lay down full length on the bottom. But he was to be in the water again only too soon. The rest of us had been swimming about scarcely for two minutes when we encountered another ray. He was not so big as the first one, but a good 125 pounds in weight. He lay quite motionless on the sand, with only his eyes rolling.

In a moment I was below again. As I came closer I saw that what was rolling was not the eyes but the two nostrils, whose flaps steadily opened and closed as the breathing water was drawn in. This ray was sleeping soundly and deeply. I got so close to him that I finally had only his head in the view finder. Then, as I was shooting, something most puzzling happened. Suddenly the ray had a little hole in his back, and from it a thread of blood spiralled up. Also a line slanted up from it.

I looked up, and saw Joerg's highly satisfied face. While I had been staring through the view finder he had dived and harpooned the ray. So we had deftly missed for the second time an opportunity to shoot a harpooning scene.

It was some seconds before the ray discovered that his nap was over. Flapping angrily, he lashed about him with his tail and reeled away, dragging Joerg behind him by the rope. I followed, shooting the two of them, until they vanished from my sight. Then I surfaced and filmed the boat, which now also charged off, towed by the ray. Xenophon yelled with delight, the poachers followed hastily and yelled still louder, Heinz, swimming, hauled in on the line and yelled loudest of all. But the ray had the last word. When he came to the surface and Heinz tried to get into the picture with him, there was suddenly a whizz an inch from Heinz's back and the poisonous spine bored into the gunwale beside him.

We killed the creature and pulled it into the boat. Joerg cut the spine out of the wood and started polishing the sharp barbs with his knife. "That'll make a wonderful pipe cleaner," he remarked, in high good humour.

"Do be a good fellow and dive for the dynamite," said Xenophon to me before we departed. "We can perfectly well dry it, and it would be a shame to waste."

Heinz shook his head regretfully. "It's a crime he didn't eat it."

44

WHEN you look in the mirror you look double. In the middle is the projecting nose with the two holes at the bottom, to right and left the eyes, above it the hair, below it the mouth, and farther to the rear the plate-like appendage of the ears— all well and good, but what is it really? Why do we look like that, and not differently? Since we, like all the higher animals, have developed from worm-like ancestors—indeed, from one-cell animals—each part of us must have arisen or been invented at some time in the course of our tribal history. That is why our face is not only handsome or ugly, but is at the same time also a mirror of our past.

Our oldest heirloom, you might suppose, must be the mouth. Since eating is, after all, a basic characteristic of all animals, even our first multi-celled ancestor, living like a coral in the sea, must already have been doing it. True enough. Only this coral mouth later developed into the exactly opposite end of our alimentary canal, and so it is better to pass over this delicate point with a Greek word, and simply observe, with the zoologists, that man belongs to the group of 'Deuterostomians.'

In our worm stage we gained our symmetrical appearance, because as worms we started to crawl in definite directions, and for this purpose you have to be symmetrical. In our round-mouthed stage we acquired the separately articulated head as well as brain, eyes, and nostrils; in our shark stage, our teeth and movable lower jaw; as scaly newts we gained the external tear duct. And our reptile ancestors? Did they leave us nothing? Certainly: the pineal gland and the eyelids. Furthermore, the crocodile presented us with the first model of the ear lobes. From our mammal forefathers we received hair and cheeks, and from the primates the projecting nose and the mobile fingers.

The oddest history, however, lies behind our ear. For with this, when we were still in the round-mouth stage, we used to breathe. It developed from our first gill slit, which then atrophied in the shark stage and turned into the so-called spout hole—the same one I mistook for the eye in the ray, which led to this entire meditation. There are other examples to be found. Our teeth developed from scales that grew over the sharks lips into its mouth (which is why the shark today has several rows of teeth); our lungs sprang from the air bladders of fish when they became unnecessary on coming out of the water, and so, too, the arches of the gills lost their reason for existence, and from them were formed the tongue bones, the cartilage of the epiglottis, and the little bones of the inner ear —which brings me back to the ear again.

It remains only to add that on the night when all this went through my head I was suffering from the most awful earache. It got so bad that I awakened Joerg, but even he could not help me. I had an inflammation both of the outer ear (which we have from the reptiles) and of the middle ear (which I owe to my newt ancestors), and possibly also an irritation of the eardrum (which developed from a skin that grew over the spout holes of the tailless batrachians, and thus represents a further example of change of function). So it happened that I tottered about on deck for several days with a big bandage round my head like a living beehive, and had more than enough time to reflect that pain, that ugliest arrangement in the body, is due to our worm ancestors, while pleasure is our most ancient heirloom—perhaps, indeed, the deepest rooted feature of living matter in general.

45

Since Joerg and Alfred, as good friends, did not want to leave me alone in my anguish, the next morning a wound on Alfred's leg swelled up so much that he, too, could not venture to dive again, and on Joerg's neck a nasty abscess had formed, which put him likewise out of commission. While the sunny Greek sky arched blue and cloudless over us we lay side by side on deck, telling each other about our troubles.

"This is an awful pain," I said. "Like somebody drilling into your head from both sides."

"It's jabbing me all the way up to the knee," said Alfred. "As if there were a clock with a pendulum in my calf, and the pendulum kept banging against the bones."

"As for me," said Joerg, "I feel as if someone had worked a hook under my spinal column and was pulling me up like a butchered ox."

Into this placid atmosphere Xenophon burst with exciting news. To explore new areas for our film he and the poachers had dropped dynamite off a cape on the other side of the island, and three sharks had immediately appeared, one easily ten feet long and very fierce, the other two rather smaller. He said the big one had whizzed right under the boat and had tried to snap at the rudder. It was a very vicious brute.

"Well, Heinz, how about it?" said Joerg. "Don't you want to shoot the sharks? We're invalids."

Heinz looked rather irresolute.

Joerg, meanwhile, was determined to go diving himself, despite his Fujiyama, as his abscess was christened. He could not turn his head, of course, but, after all, this was not essential in diving. Alfred immediately declared that he would accompany him. Even if he wasn't allowed into the water himself, at least he could watch from above and change the films. So I was left alone, on board under six blankets and with bad chills.

The combat team did not come back until late in the afternoon. They'd actually seen sharks, and Joerg had dived at once, but when he got down they were gone again. He then swam about for some time just above the bottom, which was about sixty feet down, and finally encountered a smaller shark, which, however, immediately turned tail also. Only after half an hour did a large blue shark arrive and refuse to be disturbed by Joerg's presence. Now the camera jibbed. Joerg whizzed up in a fury and got the other camera, but before he was down again the shark had taken its leave. He waited patiently for a while longer, and was about to give up when a rather broad shark appeared in the distance—or, rather, a big ray! The creature came fluttering closer, and bedded down in the seaweed not twenty feet from Joerg.

"Believe it or not," Joerg went on, "but I used up all the film and only afterwards thought of getting the harpoon. Meanwhile my oxygen had run clean out. Even so, I raced down—at fifty feet my air is gone for keeps—I fall faster and faster—the pressure in my ears won't even up—I see the ray foggily—stab him—the rope winds round my leg—he rushes off, dragging me after him—I just manage to get loose with one last effort—and come to the top, practically cold."

"We pulled him out with the gaff," Alfred added.

"And the ray?" I asked.

"We pulled that out, too."

"How big?"

"Oh, one hundred and seventy-five pounds."

"And what are you doing with him?"

"We want to sell him in Skiathos. I hear ray meat is in great demand there. We think we may be able to swap it for oil."

As my earache could not stand the voyage to Skiathos I was evacuated ashore and entrusted to the hospitality of the poachers. Big, ungainly Mitcho took me to his house, where an astonishingly clean room was assigned to me. Over a big, old-fashioned bed hung a picture of the Madonna; round a mirror on a bureau a dozen smaller pictures of the Madonna were stuck; to the left of the door hung several yards of first-class fuse, neatly rolled and within easy reach. I had a fairly high fever, and tossed all night in great pain, with disagreeable dreams. Early in the morning two little girls appeared, who took the most touching care of me. I learned from them that Mitcho, the support of the family, had gone to work early in the morning. About noon he came back with Joerg and a considerable bag of dead fish. Joerg examined me and told me he had dived at the same place as yesterday, and this time had got two eagle rays in front of the camera. They had flown past him like great birds, and he had shot a whole fifty feet of them. (These were the only creatures of this kind that we laid eyes on during the entire expedition.)

On the second day I sent the *Bosporus* to the signal station at the mine barrier near Trikkeri. There Heinz was to telephone to Athens and find out what had become of the *Sultana*. But within half an hour the *Bosporus* came back, and following her—the *Sultana*. The two ships had met halfway.

Though the *Sultana* consisted chiefly of drawbacks, she had one advantage—a small elevated deck where we could take our meals with a glorious view. As evening fell, touching the olive groves of Skiathos with a golden gleam, we ate marvellous spaghetti, drank two bottles of wine that we had cooled by letting them down sixty-five feet into the ocean, and felt at peace with ourselves and the world. My ear had improved considerably, Alfred's leg was almost completely healed, and Joerg's Fujiyama was on the verge of eruption. A great spiritual serenity lay upon us all.

It was to be interrupted again next morning.

Voices and loud laughter awakened me. Then Heinz appeared in the cabin to tell me that the fishermen had caught a big turtle in their nets during the night, a splendid specimen weighing more than twenty-five pounds. He looked at me meaningly. This would surely be a splendid opportunity to get some shots of a turtle hunt for our film. We had only to fasten a gut to the creature's hind legs and we could film the act of catching a turtle under water with our bare hands. It would certainly be a most effective scene.

Now this was rather a ticklish matter. Of course there could be no question of our including faked shots in the film, but on the other hand it really wasn't our fault that we had not encountered such a creature so far. That we really could

catch turtles by hand we had amply proved in the West
Indies. If we were now to assist fortune a little, at least it would
not be a hundred per cent fake.

As this was an important matter of principle we held an
expeditionary council on deck round the turtle, which lay on
its back, flapping its legs. After some argument we agreed
that we should at least try the shots 'for fun'. Whether they
should go into the film could always be decided later.

'For fun' is the start of every false move. The road to hell
is paved with good intentions. But fate meant well by us, and
spared us this dangerous temptation.

"Of course that business with the gut line is silly," declared
Joerg. "I'll simply hang on to the hind legs, then let go for a
minute before I 'catch' the turtle."

And so it was done. Joerg and Alfred swam out some
distance into the sea, Joerg with the turtle, Alfred with the
film camera. We heard them discussing details of the scene
on the surface, then they dived and disappeared for a while.

But the turtle would not play. When Joerg let it go it
did not stir. It sank through the water like a sleeping frog—a
pose that was useless for film making.

"You'll have to give him a little poke," said Alfred when
the two came back to the surface, and we saw them vanishing
again as if at a word of command.

This time it was an extremely long time before they surfaced again. To our amazement they reappeared a hundred
feet from the place where they had dived.

"Blast the brute, anyway!" yelled Joerg.

"Quick, quick—there he is!" cried Alfred, and the two
were gone again.

The poke had been enough to restore the turtle's *joie de
vivre*. With a few lightning strokes of its flippers it was well out
of Joerg's reach before he could grab it again.

An exciting pursuit developed. The fishermen, to whom the
turtle belonged, jumped into their boats and rowed off. As
the water was fairly clean, and the turtle, an air-breathing

"I recognized," said Xenophon, "that every moment of my life is equally painful"

One of the divers of Trikkeri presented me with a black gorgonida

He sank down like a sleeping frog—an attitude which could not be exploited photographically

Heinz thought we ought to tie him up with a gut string and film him that way

reptile, had to surface from time to time, it was soon redis-
covered. With loud shouts the fishermen rowed in that direction.
Mitcho, standing in the bow, gesticulated like a soap-box
orator. Joerg and Alfred urged the crew on from the stern.

Luckily I had the film camera handy, and luckily also,
for a change, our outboard motor started at once. The fishing
boat gone wild was a splendid screen subject! When we came
closer the turtle had just disappeared again and the boat was
rowing in circles, hunting. Then it was discovered again, and
immediately the yelling and wild rowing were resumed.
First we went some way along the shore, then the turtle turned
about and swam back over the same stretch. It was visibly
tiring. It appeared on the surface at shorter and shorter in-
tervals. Finally, when the boat was close enough, Joerg and
Alfred jumped overboard, and after a certain amount of
splashing Joerg actually caught it. The fishermen, greatly
delighted, rowed up to receive the creature. But Alfred stopped
Joerg from handing it over.

"Wait, wait!" he cried. "That was no good at all! I can't
take pictures of you from behind, after all! When you're
catching it, you've got to show a little consideration for me!"

"All right, then we'll let him go again!"

That evening we sat together with the fishermen round a
fire, both the fishermen and we in the best of humours. Alfred
had taken the desired scene—and there was no fake about it.
After its third release the turtle had escaped for good—and
we really wished him luck. The fishermen had demanded
twice as much for the creature as they could otherwise have
got anywhere—and they, too, had really earned it.

46

As the weather took a considerable turn for the worse we
decided to leave early for Planit. The whole sky was darkly
overcast, and the seaway was heavy. In Planit we could carry

on our collecting in the cave even with wind and rain, and then we could go back to the shark grounds.

The voyage passed without incident. In Planit, where we arrived about lunch time, we set to work at once. The boat was anchored right in the grotto, and Joerg, Alfred and Heinz took turns at going to the bottom with chisel, hammer and collecting nets. Unluckily, on account of my ears, I still could not venture into the water, and had to be satisfied with helping to sort and preserve the stone fragments they collected. What splendour they brought to light! If you studied under the microscope no matter what part of the growth on these rock fragments you were transported to a landscape with fabulous monsters as fantastic as any fairy tale. Out of a forest whose trees bore red and blue bubbles instead of branches appeared a dreadful dragon, and hurled itself upon a giant woodlouse with innumerable twitching legs. Above a sapphire-green cavern floated a yellowish veil that seemed to be alive. Growing straight out of the rock like an opened blossom towered the claw of a monstrous crab. And all this so small that it took place somewhere within the surface of a bit of stone. Somewhere in a few drops of water.

I thought to myself: showing anyone a picture like this ought to make him think. People today suffer from the fact that the world has become so much a matter of course to them. Once upon a time every corner concealed a mysterious force, a demon, and the fear of the unknown with which everyone had to deal made people stop and ponder. Today you switch on the light, the radio, you spin the telephone dial—nature is conquered, there is no more trace of demons. The world has grown free, free of mysticism and fear, but free also of reverence. How lovely my blue-papered grotto was! In every crevice it hid a mystery: every movement of the tiny dragon bespoke the marvel, life.

In three days we did our stint. We soldered up the cans, packed the collecting jars in cases, and said a final farewell to Planit. Fortunately the weather had improved, and we steamed directly back to Skiathos. As we were passing among the isles of Steno Xenophon astonished us by asking me if he might not have another look for his hole in the bottom of the sea.

"Without Helen?" Joerg asked.

"Without Helen," was the positive reply.

And to our utter amazement he really did find the place. It was exactly as he had insisted. On the left side of the same cove where we had previously hunted in vain there actually was a hole about thirteen feet across in the ocean floor, at about twenty feet down, and when we lowered a sounding line into this abyss it really did go to about a hundred and seventy feet.

We anchored the *Bosporus* directly above the spot; I proposed to descend into the hole in the diving helmet, which would keep my ears dry. With a strange feeling I let myself slide down along a rope into the dark opening. I could not help thinking of the times when as a boy I had devoured Jules Verne's *Journey to the Centre of the Earth*. Like that shaft in the crater of Stromboli, as it were, this black abyss yawned below me.

What creature might be hiding there?

The least agreeable moment was when my legs were dangling in the unknown while my head was still up in sunlight. Then I plunged completely into the shadow and my eyes grew accustomed to the darkness. Of monsters there was nothing to be seen. The upper region of the shaft was overgrown with sedentary organisms in the usual fashion; below, the walls of the abyss dropped off perpendicularly, as if lit by pale moonlight. To get a view of everything, I kept revolving as I let myself down on the rope. The lower I went, the sparser were the growths. In all probability this was due to the poorer supply of oxygen in the water and the higher proportion of the gases produced by decay. In the Black Sea, closed on every side like a tub, all life comes to an end at six hundred and fifty feet. Here in this shaft was a chance to study in a small space the dependency of the various organisms upon these factors, so vital to life in the water. Like a spider on its thread, I dangled in the middle of this peculiar well. To get closer to one wall I clamped the rope between my legs and paddled over with my arms. But when I tried to get a handhold there I slipped and swung back like a pendulum to the opposite side, where I pushed off with my feet and thus returned safely to the spot I wanted. Alfred, who had followed me in the diving gear, danced about me with malicious glee. The advantage of the diving gear was plain here.

I let myself down still farther. Gradually the last trace of life disappeared. The walls, which widened perceptibly downward, were now completely bare, sprinkled with fine sand as if with dust. Suddenly my head plunged into water! I got a fright such as I seldom have had. The diving helmet had simply stayed above me! Quickly I pulled myself up along the rope and dived into the air inside the helmet.

This, then, was the end of the tube. So I was already a hundred feet down. The tube went tautly upward. I felt below me with my feet—and got a second fright. The rope, too, ended just below me! What would have happened if I had suddenly clutched at nothingness, fallen, and lost the helmet would not bear thinking of. And how easily the weight of the helmet might have torn it free from the tube!

Before I started to climb I looked into the depths and upwards once more. From down here the entrance to the shaft looked like a small chimney, and below me I could now see to the bottom. The lower .end opened out like a bottle; the floor led diagonally to one side, where a tremendous black shadow gate opened. Perhaps the cavern went down into the depths there—perhaps really to the centre of the earth.

47

"Come on, tell us a story," said Alfred to Xenophon. Evening had fallen, and we were sitting over a bottle of Samos wine.

"What's the use?" replied Xenophon. "You live your

lives, I live mine; what do you want with mine, or I with yours?"

"Then you don't want to tell us?" asked Joerg, getting up meaningly.

"Oh, yes, Joerg, anything you want, I'll tell you," cried Xenophon, now most zealous. "What shall I tell you?"

"Whatever you like. Tell us about your vagabond days," said Joerg, sitting down again. "But just don't try keeping one of the girls from us!"

"Well, then," said Xenophon, "I'd better begin at the beginning. As you know, I'm from Styria; my father's a trader. First I was put in a high school, a *realgymnasium,* and had to remain in the third form because I played truant all the time. At first just a class or a day at a time, then once it was three weeks. Our class teacher was a stiff-necked scoundrel. He said, 'No, my friend, I'm not giving you your report card; I'm sending it direct to your father.' Then the old man put me in a Catholic institution, and there I put on a sleepwalking act. I climbed from the second to the third floor, then through the toilet window across the gutter and down to the chapel entrance, and from there over the fence. Not that I had anything to do out at night; I was satisfied to be free. They'd drag me out of bed at six o'clock, and then I'd get another half-hour's sleep at Mass. But once, just as I was climbing over the gutter, I heard yelling down below, and saw the big hats of the nuns. 'Quiet! Quiet!' they cried. 'Or he'll wake up and fall off!' So then I knew what was what and began balancing crazily and finally let them wake me up. I don't know how it ended; anyhow, they asked me in the morning and I said I couldn't remember anything, and that was all.

"At the end of the year, at the exam for promotion, I had to translate the life of Miltiades by Cornelius Nepos. As it happened I knew that piece well, because Miltiades was a great old faker who impressed me very much. So a man read aloud to me in German, and I had to translate it into Latin, without any book. I surprised hell out of him. Further exams were at the end of June, but I thought to myself, 'I don't care much; I'll just stay away over the holidays, and then I'll say good-bye,' I had a thousand crowns in my savings account for a christening present, and our bookkeeper gave me something, and I'd saved up some, so that I had a very nice little sum, fifteen hundred crowns, and with that I set off. I lived very simply, but the small change ran out in Bad Gastein and I had to break into the thousand. I went into a grand shop where there happened to be no customers. Not having any experience, I put down the thousand first, but the salesman, in proper business fashion, didn't take it; he began by giving it back, and I pocketed it. The man counted out the change, and probably thought he had the thousand. Anyhow, I went to the station as fast as I could go. I'm not sure whether I ever gave it back to him afterwards—I suppose I must have, ha, ha, ha! I was fifteen and a half years old, and now, Joerg, take note that I'm not keeping any girl from you: I knew one in Salzburg who was so beautiful that I can't even tell you how beautiful she was. 'Take off your shoes,' she said to me, 'and I'll give you a new pair.' I took them off, but I had such a dirty pair of socks on that she ran off in a fright.

"I went down the Salzach as far as Golling and got into Germany over a bridge, but not through the customs barrier. I footed it as far as Ingolstadt, then I got sick of it, and I earned some money as a day labourer on a building site— I'd never changed the thousand—and then I went by train straight to Heidelberg, on account of the student songs. That was when I found out that you destroy the aura if you really go to a place you've dreamed about. Then I went in a rather round about way to Karlsruhe. I hadn't brought any papers with me so I wrote to the town hall in Judenburg, where I was born, for a baptismal certificate. But they knew I'd run off, and that certificate was my ruin. I was living in Karlsruhe at No. 8 Moltke Strasse, right up under the roof, and looking out of the window I saw a big lightning conductor; it branched off in all directions, and in the middle was something big and golden. It was easily fifteen feet high. I clambered up that night and finally I had all the tools I needed together. But first I went to the post office for the baptismal certificate, and then I was going to get out immediately. The postal clerk reached for a letter, and fooled about, and suddenly there was somebody behind me saying, 'Come with me, young man.' My old man had finally got sick of it, and they had got out a warrant for me. So I was deported to Austria, and I had to leave that lightning conductor in place, too.

"A cousin of mine is married to a doctor in Vienna, and she took me in. She's a cousin of my father's, Hilde is, and Alfred reminds me of her terribly, because she had the same saucy way about her. Her husband gave me two wonderful suits, and was even nice enough to say, 'If you happen to need money you can just sell them.' And I really did sell them to a second-hand man for a hundred thousand marks. Well, so one morning early I landed back at home, and promptly told my father that I wasn't staying there, not under any conditions. And in February—it was abominably cold—he got a passport for me, and fitted me out besides. He gave me three hundred thousand crowns, the cook gave me a hundred and a kiss, and so I was off to Italy, and you already know how I turned into a tramp there. Then I wandered along the Riviera, tackling all the food shops, till one day I found the road blocked off—the French border.

"I didn't really want to go to France at all; I just didn't want to go back the same way to Genoa. Well, on one side was the sea, on the other the high mountains, behind me Genoa, so I had to get across the border. I went back a little, and up into the mountains, and the Italian frontier guards brought me back down. Well, vagrancy below the age of eighteen isn't subject to any penalty. So they let me loose, and I went right up again, calculating that the Italian sentries, who had had an excuse to get out of their mountains and down to Ventimiglia, wouldn't be back yet. Only I went a little higher, and again I was caught by an Italian guard, and it was the same one.

They were very nice, even gave me macaroni, and were all
delighted with an excuse to go down to town. I was released
again, and I went straight to the sector I had cleared of sentries,
and so I got across the watershed without being bothered,
and passed the French sentry, who had a dog. Regular
Fenimore Cooper stuff, against the wind. In Menton I cleaned
out a confectioner's. I said I was hungry, and they gave me
ten fritters; but apart from that there wasn't much doing in
France. I walked by forced marches to Cannes and Fréjus.
The countryside is very beautiful, but for a tramp it's the least
desirable thing you can imagine. I can still remember the
incredible lack of understanding shown by the French when
I went and said I was hungry: '*J'ai faim, donnez-moi quelque
chose à manger!*' The most inconceivable things were set before
me. Early in the morning, wine, chocolate, white bread,
without any friendliness at all; not like in Italy, where they're
glad to help a vagabond along, but as humiliating charity.
That wasn't to my taste, and I could feel that you had to travel
in a different sort of style in France.

"I got to Marseilles, and there I had the idea of working,
saving up, and then travelling on my savings. So one day I
went down to the harbour; there's a regular slave market
there. Hundreds of men are standing about, and the foremen
that handle the discharge of ships and jobs of heavy work
pick out their people. I joined the crowd, and was practically
left among the dregs when a Negro came up to me, an educated
fellow, and asked if I really wanted to work, and that kind of
thing; I said yes, and told him my situation—make some
money and then go on. He said he could use me somehow.
He had a room somewhere, and he gave me a place to sleep
there. I went out to eat with him, and in the evening I had to
accompany him to regular seaport dives—you'll see why in
a minute. I didn't understand why at first myself, but in his
company I was still a fairly decent-looking character, and the
man did nothing but get people drunk, very drunk, and then
probably rob them. A few nights later I actually saw him

taking ten-franc notes from the pocket of a Frenchman who had just landed from North Africa.

"Now I knew what kind of spot I was in, and so one afternoon I simply packed up and left Marseilles not knowing where, just anywhere to get out. Once, beyond Arles, I bedded down very badly in a roadside ditch and covered myself with spruce branches that had been cut off. By now I had nothing but the suit I was wearing and a bundle hanging round my neck by a string, with a few odds and ends and some chow in a handkerchief. Of course I was barefoot. And then I had a necklace and a ring with a red stone that I lost a year later on the promenade at Valladolid, and the passport where they had once written in: *Pas admis en France, il faut le visa Français.* This page annoyed me, and so I took it out of the passport. But something kept me from destroying it, and I hid it in a song book that I also had. Well, after that night under the spruce branches I was terribly tired, and when the sun came up I picked out a sunny spot and just lay and stretched, and when I suddenly woke up there was a French gendarme in front of me, who took me off to the station. I was thoroughly searched, and sure enough they found in the song book the page where I was expelled from France. I had really been in a pretty hopeless frame of mind, even before; I was not doing well in France, and I was glad enough that evening to get some warm water with a few scraps of bread. In the morning they pulled me out of the cell and two mounted policemen took me between them and rushed me as far as the boundary of their precinct. Here there were two more policemen, on bicycles, and I had to run between them to a bigger town. They really drove me pretty hard. We passed by a big Roman arena, and then came to a police barracks, and when we marched into the courtyard a French officer came up and immediately said they were to untie me. Then he asked me something, and I stammered something about being hungry. He brought me a piece of quince cheese; it wasn't bad, but there was very little of it; I'd rather have had a piece of bread. The day wasn't very far advanced, and the policemen were sent away and others took me over. Next I was led to the Palais de Justice, to the *juge d'instruction*, the examining magistrate, and he said, 'You have no money, no residence, no work; that's vagrancy, and the penalty for it in France is three months in jail. But don't you want to work?' Of course I said yes, I'd work. It was just about lunch time, when the examining magistrate usually left the building, and he said to me word for word, in German, that I must swear to him not to leave my work without letting him know. I promptly raised three fingers and swore, and he took me in through the back entrance of a big café, where he got a job for me, but I'll tell you about that another time, because I'm tired now and the bottle is empty—but I swear to you, Joerg, that I haven't kept any girl from you—or perhaps just one, and you'll have to forgive me that much!"

48

It's morning, the sun is smiling, and I'm well again. Possibly Xenophon's story was good for my ears; anyhow the inflammation is gone and I'm a new man, or, rather, the old one. I feel as if the world were my oyster today; all the energy dammed up during ten idle days positively cries out to be put into useful endeavour.

We have been out for an hour. Unfortunately the coast has been full of wild ducks since yesterday, and Joerg is peppering away early and late. And yet yesterday we discovered a new spot near Skopelos where three sharks appeared at the first drop. But before Joerg put away his gun and condescended to enter the water (currents make it rather cold there) the sharks had already devoured the few fish that had been killed there and had taken their leave. Dynamiting is no use at all unless enough fish are killed. The sharks come, and if they see there is nothing to eat they go right off. Alfred has a headache today—tomorrow is his birthday—and Joerg said he wasn't in a diving mood either, and loaded himself up with some fifty shotgun cartridges. To combine his ambitions with our film work, we started by going to a cove, where I tried under water to get at some diving ducks that were swimming about. We left the boat out of sight behind a cape, and I swam into the cove under water with the diving gear; the boat was to follow in ten minutes, and Joerg was to scare the birds under water by shooting. Diving, after ten long days, was pure pleasure to me; only unfortunately the ducks flew up in the air instead of diving.

By now it is almost nine o'clock, the sun is fairly high, and as Joerg already has five ducks, a good basis for tomorrow's birthday banquet, we head for the spot where the sharks are. To right and left, cliffs rising steeply from the water—luckily nowhere another duck that might distract us. I have the diving gear on, Xenophon is hanging with his head overboard, looking for gopes or melanuri, and Joerg is preparing the bombs, an art in which he has become a master.

The double beat of two bombs echoes away; in a moment I am overboard with the camera. As luck will have it, we have hit upon a large school of gopes, and so the water all around is full of dead and stunned fish floating in a silvery, twitching rain. Doubtless an unmitigated villainy that we are perpetrating here, but we are thinking only of our film; we want as many sharks as we can get, and we are willing to stoop even to this means. And, anyhow, how many depth bombs are being dropped every day in the war? And every second or third fisherman hereabouts has been dynamiting for twenty years. What do our few puny bombings amount to?

As I sink deeper, Xenophon's face follows me through the glass-bottomed box. He looks tense and very grave. Yesterday, when the sharks arrived, Joerg and Alfred threw him overboard out of pure devilry. Of course it was a perfectly harmless affair; the sharks moved only a couple of feet in his direction, but even so he yelled and screamed as if cannibals had him in the pot. With the current carrying him away from us, he had

trouble in getting back to the ship. And we watched at the rail
and laughed until we cried.

But the first shark has appeared! Close upon him follows
a second. They are both ground sharks, eight or ten feet long,
dark-coloured, both of them fairly clumsy and rather tiresome
in their movements. While I swim down to them, filming as
I go, they neatly pick up one fish after another from the bottom
—but here is another, a third, quite different shark with a
pointed nose, who shoots straight at me like a devil. Aperture
f 4, distance twenty-five feet, slow-motion— Like a torpedo
the plump body swerves past me. To avoid being attacked
from behind I keep revolving. Two tuna fish have now also
turned up, behaving even fiercer, and looking scarcely like
animals at all, but rather like metallic machines. Without
pausing for a moment, without a hint of the casual grace
peculiar to sharks, they shoot hither and thither, snapping
up one fish after another. I film the sharks first, then go after
the tunas. I get some good shots of the first one, and then
suddenly the camera goes wrong. Every time! I pound on it
with my fist, but it simply will not work. The eyelet on the
case of my own camera has broken off, so I have to use Alfred's,
and it consistently fails me at great depths. Somehow the
pressure squeezes the steel case against the housing, so that the
film won't run. There is nothing for it but to go up again and
to get the still camera, at least. I pop upwards like a cork.

Just at the moment when Xenophon is handing me the still
camera the film camera begins buzzing again of its own
accord. All right, then I'll take both along. How is it below
today? Joerg asks. He is sitting in the bow, cleaning his gun.
It's wonderful below! And in an instant I am on my way down
again.

When I come up there are five sharks and three tunas
darting hither and thither in the silver rain; meanwhile,
however, all except the one shark with the pointed nose have
gone. He comes at me very nicely and I get a splendid sequence
of him. Danger? As I am rewinding the spring I see his ominous

little eyes. Then he turns carelessly away. The party is over. The stricken fish have either floated to the surface or are sprinkling the sandy bottom with silver. Only twitching fish, floating free in the water, really give sharks any satisfaction. Those that are dead on the bottom merely get picked up more or less condescendingly. The same as a cat takes real pleasure only in a squirming mouse. My film is used up, so I let myself float to the surface. Most rewarding. At least six long shark scenes, and one short one of tuna fish, on this reel. And the day has only begun!

In the boat there is great excitement. A tuna fish has repeatedly appeared in the vicinity, snapping for floating fish on the surface. I swim hastily to the indicated spot, but there is nothing to be seen of a tuna fish now. Having described a few more circles, I climb back into the boat. We have to go back to the *Bosporus* because we have forgotten spare oxygen flasks, and we haven't enough dynamite. Looking back, we see the tuna leaping again. All right, just wait! We'll be back!

Alfred hands us the things we require; he still has a head-ache and no inclination to come with us. Our next step is to go a little farther along the coast and drop dynamite in shallower water; but although enough fish are killed no shark appears. As other fishermen are dynamiting on the other side of the island, presumably they are luring the sharks away from us. I sit down on the bottom and wait, but the water remains vacant. In vain the blasted fish twitch; only a fat moray that is rippling along not far from me takes pity on six and devours them. Each time it thrusts its head forward like a snake.

Now we go back to our first spot and drop bombs there, but here, too, only one fleeting shark turns up. Although this is my fifth dive I feel not a trace of fatigue. On the contrary. For the sheer fun of it I swim in a wide circle, and am finally rewarded by a shark of considerable size. When I come to the surface again I am welcomed by general pleased excitement. Lured by the floating fish, numerous *michos* are flapping just above the surface, and since Xenophon maintains that these birds taste almost as good as ducks, and we can still use a number for tomorrow's banquet, Joerg is hard at work again.

On the next, my sixth, dive two rather insignificant sharks first appear, parading up and down like sentries before Buckingham Palace, and then a pretty fat one with a crafty look, who is absolutely a born film star. His every movement is consciously effective, so to speak, and there is not the slightest trace of stage fright. Without batting an eye, you might say, he lets me come within a dozen feet of him—then with the eye that is not looking through the view finder I notice a dark shadow approaching the shark from behind. At that moment the sun goes in and it is as dark as a tomb, but luckily this does not last long and the light comes back. The fluttering shadow is a giant ray! And it swims straight for the spot where the shark is placidly snapping up fish! With intense excitement I swing the camera from shark to ray and from ray back to shark —then the two are so close together that I have them both in the view finder. What a scene! A ten-foot blue shark and a ray just as big peacefully munching fish together. It couldn't be better in a zoo.

Unfortunately, before this dive I replaced only my potassium cartridge, not my oxygen flask, and it is now empty; so I have to surface again. Xenophon hastily replaces the flask, and Joerg asks if I haven't had enough yet. No. Although I am shivering all over, I glide down again. It would be a sin and a shame not to make full use of this day.

There is nothing more to be seen below. The bottom is now covered far and wide with dead fish, a great battlefield, but the only guest at this richly spread table is once more a moray, this time a grass-green specimen. It lies coiled like a cobra among the seaweed, slavering at me, and as I keep drawing closer, shooting as I go, it backs up literally hissing with rage, into a cleft in the rock. I realize afterwards that on account of the sharks I had set the camera for fifteen to twenty-feet, so that this close-up is bound to be out of focus. But after all the other successes that does not matter. As blissfully as if I had won a battle, I swim upwards again. Despite my exhaustion, or perhaps for that very reason, I am filled with a sense of strength difficult to describe, a burning warmth starting from the solar plexus. Only in the boat do I quite realize how cold I have been for some time, and now I realize, too, that I have eaten nothing at all. It is two o'clock, and therefore high time for a lunch break. Then, at Joerg's imperious demand, we go back to the wild ducks; while he misses splendidly twice I dive again, out of pure high spirits, for the eighth time. But I suddenly feel alone and unsure of myself. Now, with no shark in sight far and wide, an oppressive feeling of anxiety comes over me, and so, contenting myself with a few shots of a steep, bizarrely stratified rock wall, I swim back to the boat. We can really afford to be satisfied in every way. Eight dives in one day is a new record. And eleven ducks and two michos is not bad.

49

"We stopped outside the café into whose heart you had just been taken," said Joerg to Xenophon threateningly. A bottle of Samos had been uncorked, and again each of us had a glass before him.

"Yes, that was in Nîmes, in the spring of eighteen years ago," said Xenophon obediently. He thoughtfully drained his glass, lit a cigarette, and went on. "Well, so the *juge d'instruction* took me to the heart of the café—namely, the cashier's desk. On the right, the beer tap; to the left of that, a passage to the kitchen; in front of it, a main room; to the left and right three smaller rooms, and on the boulevard a huge terrace full of armchairs—it was the best café I ever saw in France. Mine host, in a smart black suit, with a red face and flat splay feet, Monsieur Grosse, looked me over from head to foot, and his first step was to send for a blue apron; he planted himself in front of me and tried to put the neck strap of the apron over my head. But his stomach was so fat that he bumped into me.

Naturally I didn't bend my neck, so his hands didn't reach over my head, a scene so cheerfully amusing that I laughed out loud. At that he flew into a real French fury and ran me into the kitchen and started me washing cups. The judge came and looked in on me every day; it was all very humane. I was sixteen now, with the first fuzz of a beard appearing.

In the evening Monsieur Grosse called me to the desk, handed me eleven francs, and told one of his waiters to take me to a pension. There I had a room, all dark, with six perfect strangers. I paid eight francs, so I had three left. I used to get breakfast in the café; I would tuck away a good *café au lait*. I knew just one thing; when you're working like that the only thing to do is to save, because the work itself is not much fun, and so I found the pension too expensive and looked about for another room. When the noon break came Monsieur Grosse would appear punctually at the moment when I was supposed to go, and say '*Allez-vous en!*' But since I didn't want to eat out, for reasons of economy, I would stay in the room for the staff, and that got so tiresome that I soon went back to my work. And apparently the man did think of me—saw I wasn't eating, and had them give me lunch, too. He really looked after me. And I didn't stay long in the kitchen, but was transferred to the taproom, where I grew very skilful at filling beer glasses. So I soon made a financial recovery, and gradually built up my wardrobe again. One of the patrons, a terrifically amusing fellow, spoke German, and was the paid watchman for the shops of Nîmes. At the time I was suffering badly from not having any recreation. I looked terrible, always in the stuffy café atmosphere, saved money like mad, and never allowed myself any of the things a young person really needs. And so this man made me an offer, and I gave up my job at the café—of course I told the *juge d'instruction*, and he didn't mind—and became the night watchman of Nîmes. But I always had just the one thought—to go roving without having to beg, and, believe it or not, the ideal solution was the fishing boat, but that was still a long way off!"

Descent into the perpendicular shaft near Steno

As though illuminated by pale moonlight, the walls of the shaft fell away to the depths

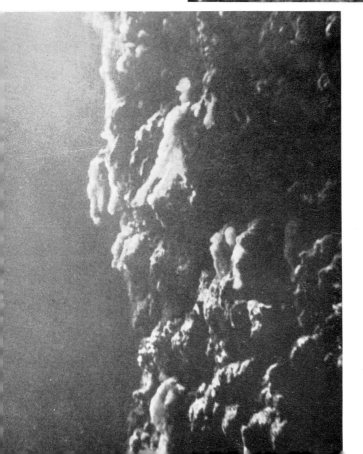

Soaring cliffs—and fortunately nowhere another wild duck

"Are you trying to tell us there were no girls in the café?" asked Joerg.

"Oh, yes," Xenophon hastened to assure us. "I was about to tell you, anyhow: mine host had a young daughter. She came into the restaurant every day through the rear entrance; there was a narrow passage there with an icebox, and I was posted in front of it with a sheet of newspaper spread over my hands, and Monsieur Grosse used to put the daintiest tit-bits there for her. His wife, a little timid person, always waited at the rear entrance, while the boss was carrying on with Mlle Virolait, the cashier. The girl was fifteen or sixteen, and to prevent the paper from giving way she always used to help by reaching under the newspaper, and would stroke my hands so tenderly that I just can't tell you how delightful I found it. Later I had a nice little note from her, and we often used to meet at the Tour Magne—the place I ran past in handcuffs between the two bicyclists. Both of us were still real children; it was really quite idyllic!"

"H'm, very nice," said Joerg. "And was that all?"

"Well, Joerg," sighed Xenophon, going on after a pause, "possibly there's still a word to be said about how the business ran. The Frenchman is very precise in his drinking habits. In the forenoon he drinks his apéritif, at twelve he goes to lunch, and at one o'clock he's back in the café. So there were slack hours; between twelve and one I had almost nothing to do. There were bells for unsatisfied customers: lights would go on on a board, and there was nothing worse for a waiter than having such a thing happen in his section. Monsieur Grosse would always go out himself then. Besides this there was another bell signal, which didn't ring very often, for a locked room that was called *le salon*. Mlle Virolait would fetch the key and hand it over to the waiter; it was the love room. For a long time I didn't know what went on there; the whole thing was most mysterious to me. As I could learn from the fellow who got the key, I soon came to know all the ladies who practised love professionally, and when I knew people by sight

M

from the street who looked highly respectable to me, and then
saw them go into the salon, I used to think my thoughts about
them. There was an absolute rule that these ladies could not
sit on the terrace; in that respect Monsieur Grosse would take
no excuses. He would simply chase them off, and so Monsieur
Grosse, too, served to shape my opinion of the ladies.

"Only I did take an extreme liking to one lady who often
came with her little daughter, an incredibly intelligent child.
She always smiled so nicely at me when she passed, and so of
course in order to approach her I used to take a special interest
in the child. Well, one day just at the slack period—my slack
period, that is, when the place was full of patrons, but they
were all drinking coffee and hence were no business of mine—
she came rather hurriedly and asked me most charmingly if
I could keep an eye on her little girl for a while. Of course I
was glad to, thinking she had some errand to do, and scarcely
was she gone when the bell rang and I heard Mlle Virolait
call, '*On sonneau salon!*' You can imagine that was pretty much
of a let-down for me!

"Now for a strange coincidence. I'm walking along with
a cigarette and no light on a windy day, rather like today, when
a man comes out of one of the bays of the arena, lighting a
cigarette. I speak to him in French, he asks me a question,
and what do you think?—it's a man in leather shorts, a Viennese.
He was a painter, working in Arles, and we got a bit friendly.
He was a regular rascal, I found that out right away, and so
I thought to myself, 'I'll do him a favour and introduce him to
Lucy'. That was the lady with the little girl. Well, what should
I say when, after a while, she told me the fellow wanted to
marry her? Her business was flourishing, he gave her all kinds
of presents, and she took it as a matter of course to let me in
on it. Of course I refused at first, but then I did accept part of
her takings. You can see how easily a person might slip into
something like that without trying at all. At the same time
Lucy was really fond of me, and when we said good-bye she
would sometimes give me a kiss in the dark. Then one day she

asked me if I couldn't help some of her girl friends, too. Hell, I really didn't do it for the sake of money, but as an alert hired hand in a café of course I knew the young lads who had no connections. And then came something that has been repeated over and over in my life: one day the whole thing gave me a pain, and I cleared off. Well, you simply can't imagine how happy I was to go rolling along the highway again—this time in the direction of Spain."

50

ALFRED'S birthdays are a dangerous business. His twenty-fifth ended with an air bubble in his heart. (See *Diving to Adventure*). This time, on his twenty-seventh, he nearly wound up in a shark's belly.

That morning we went out to the same spot as on the day before and ran into a boatload of strange dynamiters, who were already hard at work. Xenophon knew only one of them, but considered the whole lot rather suspicious company. We, too, dropped a bomb, and before long Alfred and I were swimming in the midst of sharks and tuna fish, each of us trying to photograph the other near a shark or a tuna.

Suddenly I noticed Xenophon waving excitedly at us with an oar.

We swam to the surface, and were received with shouts by the strange dynamiters. They gesticulated frantically at us that we should come out of the water at once. A tuna fish was the cause of the excitement. He had appeared several times near the boats and was now to be killed with dynamite. One of the poachers, a particularly savage-looking fellow, already had the bomb ready to throw. While we climbed hastily into the boat Joerg told us the man had been on the verge of throwing the dynamite despite our being in the water.

Scarcely were we in the boat when the tuna fish had the unfortunate idea of coming to the surface right beside us.

Without a moment's hesitation the dynamite fisherman lit
the fuse of his bomb and tossed it over in our direction, so that
it slapped the water right alongside of us.

"Hold up our dynamite!" cried Xenophon, yanking the
boat back with a powerful pull at the oars. There was the explosion! We felt the boat heave up, a crash, everybody tumbled,
then we came down and a waterspout descended on us.

"What a bunch of jackasses!" cried Joerg, whose gun had
nearly gone overboard.

In a moment Alfred and I were back in the water, peering
down. At first we saw only white foam. Then the veil dissolved
and an unforgettable sight met our eyes. The tuna had been
hit. Helpless, robbed of its sense of balance, like a dog trying
to bite its own tail, it went tottering in a circle. And just at
the moment, when the dissolving veil of foam cleared the view,
a gigantic shark, a brute probably fourteen feet long, whipped
with incredibly swift strokes at the tuna fish, straight through
the middle of it, and before we realized what had taken place
before our eyes he was gone again in the distance. But a striking
change had taken place in the tuna. It now hung quite motionless in the water, and a grey cloud spread out. A cloud of
blood——

The shark had bitten off half the tuna's belly.

And the corpse of the tuna fish had not yet reached bottom
when a second, smaller shark whizzed up and took a mouthful.

Slowly the wretched remnants sank into the seaweed.

Alfred, who had put on the diving gear, went down at
once and inspected the corpse of the tuna. It looked very bad
indeed. The bites were marked as if cut with a razor. Even
the backbone of the tuna fish had been neatly severed. No
matter how friendly you get with sharks, when you see the
work of their teeth a cold shiver goes down your spine!

Alfred was still absorbed in his contemplation when the
big shark appeared a second time—obviously to fetch the rest
of the tit-bit. My heart skipped a beat. As the shark was coming
at Alfred from behind he could not see it. And since Alfred

was thus between the shark and the tuna fish the brute was bound to assume that this strange creature was going to fight it for its booty.

Slowly, as if warned by some inner voice, Alfred turned. His composure was admirable. Not the slightest fear or surprise was visible. As quickly as if it were the most natural thing in the world he raised the camera and started filming the shark.

The shark was so amazed at this that he slowed his pace and finally stopped not ten feet from Alfred. At this Alfred put the finishing touch to his impudence by lowering the camera, calmly rewinding it, and shooting again.

Seen from above, the shark, beside little Alfred, looked like a locomotive. The creature was enormously long and fat. I stared down spellbound, at first not even thinking of trying to do anything myself. And indeed what could I have done? Both Alfred and the creature were sixty-five feet down; at best I might distract the shark's attention. Then I wondered, 'Why doesn't Alfred shout?' After all, we had mastered even the most dangerous sharks in the Caribbean with this weapon. But then I remembered. With the best will in the world he could not shout. He had the breathing tube of the diving gear in his mouth!

I now dived forthwith, and gave several shrill yells myself, which would have sufficed to rout all the sharks in the Caribbean. This Greek character, however, showed not the slightest reaction. I yelled again—again without success. Finally I realized: naturally! Naturally I could not frighten by yells sharks that were used to dynamite blasts. Here in the realm of the poachers our weapon was bound to fail.

Alfred mastered the situation by himself. At the psychological moment he suddenly shot forward, straight at the shark, and thrust the camera right in its face. Startled by this, the shark turned about and vanished for ever.

Alfred returned to the surface somewhat pale. "I meant to stick it in his mouth," he said with a rather unsuccessful smile. "He'd certainly have choked on it!"

51

THE birthday was celebrated with great festivity. This time Joerg's birds were admirably prepared under the expert direction of Dr. Beckh; the table was wreathed with flowers, and many solemn toasts were drunk. Afterwards, over the black coffee, Alfred revealed to me that they would all like to go to Skiathos that evening. He said they had lived a monastic life long enough and Xenophon knew his way about.

So we went to Skiathos.

The details of what went on there I do not know, as I myself stayed on board with Dr. Beckh, and the participants in the evening revels had only imperfect recollections next morning. The celebration began in a pub, and by eleven o'clock had made such progress that further action was transferred to private dwellings. This we on board could tell from partly pleased, partly startled, cries that sounded to us, apparently in large part of feminine origin. In this connexion there were differences with the Italian occupying power. If I correctly interpreted the speeches and rejoiners, some in Italian, some in Greek, some in German, there were involved first a violation of curfew, second a girl named Rosita, whom the Italians were reluctant to cede voluntarily, and finally some potatoes the Italians had requisitioned some days before from anchovy fishermen, and that Xenophon now very vocally injected into the debate on behalf of the sufferers.

The following two hours were spent in various parts of the town, which never seemed to quieten down, and then came the rendering of songs that generally belong to the jewels of the Austrian repertory, but that here apparently did not find the appreciation they deserved. Finally, about three in the morning, the main troop of three men gathered on the wharf. The fourth, the missing member, was forcibly pulled out of a house, then we heard the motor starting, renewed merry song, and half-way to the vessel the boat capsized. With incessant shouts and laughter the whole party reached us, riding astride the keel of the boat and paddling with their hands. Heinz yelled for his carbine; he was determined to go back and see that the anchovy fishers got their rights; Joerg tried to soothe him and divert his target to the metal buoy of an Italian sailing cutter that was floating near by; Alfred, scarcely on board, jumped back into the water in all his clothes to dive for apples that had been lost when the boat capsized; Xenophon flung himself full length on the deck, in a fit of hysterical laughter so alarming that Joerg had to take medical steps and join the other three in sitting down with all their might on his stomach.

Anyone who might suppose, however, that the evening in any way impaired the energy and performance of our expedition would be greatly mistaken. When the sun rose the next morning our ship was already moored to the mast of the wreck at Elephteri, and punctually at nine the filming and collecting planned for that day began. This was, indeed, the last organization accomplishment recorded under Joerg's outstanding leadership. As noon approached he confided to me that he was tired of responsibility, and with the best will in the world could not order himself to repair the outboard motor, which had been ruined when the boat capsized.

So it happened that I appointed Alfred our new expeditionary chief.

52

I HAVE already remarked that pleasure is our oldest heritage, if not the most essential element of living matter in general. What does this signify? What, indeed, is the essence of living matter?

Adaptation to purpose, one might suppose, would be the

peculiarity of living creatures. Everything about animals and plants and about ourselves is marvellously adapted to its function, and the more carefully we study organisms, the better adapted they seem. But this adaptation came, so to speak, of itself. As living creatures were in constant competition among themselves only the most suitable and the best adapted forms could hold their own. Even though nature did produce creatures with eyes on the soles of their feet and toes on the top of their heads, these never achieved distribution because in the struggle for existence—in the struggle against the better adapted forms—they were bound to perish. That is why living beings are well adapted. They have to be. It is no miracle, but harsh necessity.

This concept of Lucretius, which Darwin immortalized two thousand years later, struck everyone as being the philosopher's stone. People said hereditary tendencies were different, so individuals were not exactly alike among themselves, so there were always better and worse adapted individuals, so in the struggle for existence the better adapted were bound to survive, thus explaining all forward development. But there is a catch in it.

If you fasten a rubber band to the wall and a stone to the other end, and pull the stone away and then let go, it flies against the wall with exactly that force with which it was pulled out. The more trouble you take, the harder you pull, the greater is the force within—what is called 'potential energy'. It is exactly the same if you pick up a stone and put it on a box. The resistance you have to overcome is the earth's attraction, and here, too, the applied force is stored up in the stone, which at once becomes evident if it falls off—on your toes. The heavier it is and the higher we lift it, then the greater the force within it. The invisible energy content of a body is also increased if you apply heat—for example, to the water in the boiler of a steam engine. For heat is nothing but the rapid motion of the tiniest particles of matter, and the faster the motion, the greater its power to drive the machine.

The characteristic feature of the stone, the water, and all matter is simply that it always falls 'down,' cools off, slows up. That its energy content, in other words, can only grow less. The earth grows cold, mountains are razed, motion is retarded— but life is a stone rolling uphill. From dust, from tiny primeval forms, come million-fold energy: the whole teeming life that populates our earth today. This is the essential and the mysterious element of life, and we perceive the effect of this truly divine spark within us—as pleasure.

We are the stone rolling uphill—are we not to feel within us the force that drives us?

53

ON 29th September we re-entered the familiar harbour of the Piraeus. Here good news awaited us. Thanks to the efforts of the able Mother Explorer, the expedition could be prolonged by four weeks. So we could go to Crete after all! A dance of joy on the deck followed this message. It had to be admitted, though, that the war situation had grown worse meanwhile. Ships were now being sunk constantly in the very area between the Piraeus and Crete. But surely no one would bother our rattletrap——

Once again there were the accustomed difficulties, but by now we were experienced and obstinate enough to clear them all out of the way within a week. With much merriment we put to sea on 4th October, holding a southerly course.

An autumnal chill was in the air. The pleasant part of this was the wonderful distant view we enjoyed of the passing mountains of the Peloponnesus; less pleasant, almost overnight the sea had grown so cold that none of us really felt like going into the water. We dived near Hydra but found nothing there to justify the name, only a few worms of the genus Bonellia, which are indeed of great interest to the zoologist—because their

larvae become male only if they can attach themselves to the
proboscis of a female (almost as preposterous a case as the
worm Ophryotrocha, which is always male at first, and becomes
female only when it reaches a certain length, so that if you cut
a piece off it turns male, to turn back into a female on further
growth)—but this did not satisfy our combat team by way
of plunder, nor could it compensate us for the shivering cold
from which we suffered.

When we approached Monemvasia and our Greek captain
was heading straight for this picturesque town we explained
to him that we wanted to go right on and round Cape Malea
that same evening. Mutiny by the entire crew, Xenophon
included, was the result. Any child could see, they said, that
we were going to have a storm, and Cape Malea— Oh, Cape
Malea! Papa Jorgi, our fat cook, even put on his spectacles in
his distress, and tried by reference to his numerous family to
dissuade us from so suicidal an enterprise. But we were just
in the mood to round the cape, did not think the weather bad
at all, but suspected, rather, that the Greeks and Xenophon
merely wanted to pursue some private business in the town—
in short, Heinz took command and, our crew pale with terror,
we passed the dreaded cape in the best of weather—which,
however, as we later learned, was really a rare piece of luck.

For one day in Neapolis we pursued archaeological studies,
discovering a petrified starfish and a most luxuriant fruit
orchard. Then, to keep from getting out of practice, we dropped
a bomb near Elaphonesos; it did not explode but nevertheless
attracted a number of parrot fish, which surprised us by greatly
resembling the ones we knew in the Caribbean. The evening
was spent at Kythera, and our farewell to the tiny town was
a barrage of tracer bullets because of the unfriendly attitude
of the local girls; later we ourselves, passing Antikythera, were
the target of Italian rockets, and in the excitement our signal
blinker went overboard. Finally, at dawn, we reached Crete
where, being unable to send any signals, we were received
by the coast watch with a well-aimed shot across our bows,

after which a fighter plane circled round us like an angry bee.

We cast anchor by the romantic Cape Gravonsa, and climbed up to the old Venetian fortress, trying to be duly impressed by the historic significance of Cretan soil. Here Zeus, lying new-born in a cave, was saved from his child-eating father only because Rhea, his mother, presented her husband with a rock wrapped in diapers, which he devoured. Hither Zeus, grown to man's estate, carried off the Phoenician king's daughter, Europa, by appearing on the beach in Phoenicia in the shape of such a gentle and amiable bull that she sat upon his back, whereupon he swam off with her to Crete. Here the love-smitten Ariadne gave Theseus the ball of wool with which he penetrated the dreaded labyrinth and freed Greece from the maiden-eating Minotaur.

Unfortunately the coast—despite the fact that Theseus was a sea god by descent and might very properly have shown his gratitude for the ball of wool by doing something to beautify his realm—proved to be perfectly desolate and uninteresting. Owing to a cold current that flows there, the sea floor was overgrown with nothing but tiresome green weeds and, except for some pinna mussels that we fetched up in the bay, it had neither fish nor sponges nor anything else worth mention. We therefore contented ourselves with driving off a swarm of hornets that came to greet our vessel, then we went off lizard hunting with Dr. Beckh.

Next day a wild goat was bagged and a tall, flowering agave was felled—both in honour of Heinz, because it was his birthday. It now began to rain, and the hornets came back with reinforcements, but we once more put them to rout, and the rain, too, stopped during the afternoon. Finally, on the third day, our underwater activites got going again. Joerg and Heinz discovered in the bay a ship that had been sunk by bombing, still boasting a mast in good condition; they reached the conclusion that this mast and the anchor chain were in the public domain and could surely be sold at the Pireaus for high prices. They calculated that this would substantially relieve the expeditionary budget, and therefore founded the "Joerg-Heinz Ship Salvage Company" which spent a day and a half carrying out the purpose for which it was chartered. We then left this hospitable spot and set sail for Canaea.

The only pleasant thing that awaited us there was the news that our longed-for second diving gear had arrived by plane. Here, too, the sea bottom proved barren and uninteresting. Only bath sponges were very plentiful, which we exploited by fetching up as many as each of us thought he could use in the rest of his natural life. Work with two sets of diving gear proved most amusing. We could now swim in pairs across the ocean bottom, pointing out this and that in sign language. We bagged the only good-sized fish we saw in this submarine wilderness by Alfred chasing him out of his hole from behind with a harpoon and my welcoming him from the front with the other harpoon.

As a permanently drunken chief mate was deputy for the port captain at Canaea we had an easy time getting permission to proceed at once to Santorin. Our crew mutinied again, and Papa Jorgi once more put on his spectacles, but we had had enough of Crete and there was not much time left; so Heinz took command again, and exercised it with a heavy hand. At that time the open sea between Crete and Santorin was considerably threatened by submarines, but if we put out at dusk we could easily be beyond the danger zone by dawn. I accepted an invitation to deliver a lecture, for which I was presented with a large bottle of raspberry syrup, and on the second evening we raised anchor.

Xenophon was so furious at our lack of caution that for the first time his invariable restraint left him. While we played cards for a while and then crawled into our bunks without further misgivings, he paced restlessly to and fro on deck. A fortnight later he got a disturbing letter from his mother in Graz, asking what could have happened on that particular night. She said he had appeared to her in her dreams and had bidden her good-bye with great tenderness.

At two in the morning the motor suddenly stopped. There were rumblings, excited voices were heard, and then Xenophon appeared in my cabin. Yes, sir, it served us right. A bearing had burned out, and that was what came of this idea of cruising on the open sea in this leaky tin can. He said we were now exactly at the spot in the Aegean where land was farthest off in every direction; the motor was done for, and tomorrow morning we would offer the submarines a beautiful target— provided we did not capsize in the first morning breeze, because without a motor the ship could not even head into the wind.

To his distress we did not display the proper seriousness even now. Alfred and I seized upon the two sets of diving gear; Heinz ran about with an axe, saying he would chop off the hand of anyone who dared dispute his seat in our rubber boat after the sinking.

"I really don't see what ails you," said Joerg to Xenophon. "After all, two years ago you jumped overboard yourself to put an end to it all, and what more can happen to you now? And if the ship really does sink, well, what the hell? We'll all simply hang on to the mast so prophetically acquired by the Joerg-Heinz Ship Salvage Company!"

We radioed SOSs in all directions, but apparently there was nowhere in the Aegean a vessel that felt inclined to assist us in our distress. Gradually the scattered stars climbed higher and morning dawned. Luckily no wind came up. At seven o'clock the mechanic surprised us by contriving to get the one remaining cylinder going alone. So we started off again, though as slowly as a very tired old man on foot.

Morning brought an incomparable panorama. To the left we could see as far as the Peloponnesus, on the right as far as Rhodes, behind us the mighty mountain massif of Crete sat enthroned, and before us lay the Cyclades, topped with cloud banks that displayed every imaginable shade of brown, wine-red, yellow, and on to pitch-black. In the unanimous opinion of everyone on board with any local knowledge a frightful storm was bound to break before nightfall. So everything depended on whether we succeeded in reaching Santorin on the one cylinder—and whether we were sunk before we got there.

At ten in the morning the motor died for the first time, at twelve o'clock a second time, and at three-thirty a third time. Santorin was now within arm's reach and yet, at our speed, still a good two hours away. As our compressed air would barely turn the crank over once more our fate rested on whether the motor kept going this time as far as the island. The wind freshened, the weather grew ever gloomier. There was an electric tension upon the water.

"It's no use your looking for submarines all the time, Xenophon," said Joerg, who was lying at ease in an armchair. "If you do see one, you can't do anything about it. Come on, sit down here, and since we're all so jolly and sociable together —how about telling us another bit of your adventures? We still don't know how you got to Jerusalem. Let's go!"

Xenophon refused. He said he was not at all in the right mood for telling stories. He really couldn't.

"I'm waiting," said Joerg, and that was all he said.

54

"You're almost worse than Psarathanas," sighed Xenophon, sitting down and strengthening himself with two strong brandies. "He always used to put his cold feet against my calves at night, and I wasn't allowed to stir. But as far as I care, you can have it your way."

He drank a third glass, and then seemed to regain his equanimity.

"Spain is nothing but listing the places on the way," he began. "The Spanish side of the Maladetta is completely pathless. I footed it along rushing brooks that had mule bridges across them; you might say the country is very much like Greece. I was several days getting out of the wild valleys. I had money with me, of course, and I can still remember the tall, two-wheeled carts with a leather pouch that had a little spout, and you held it up, and the wine poured into your mouth in a thin stream. For a long time I couldn't communicate with the people; their long, clean-shaven upper lips and their berets made them so much alike that I completely lost my memory for faces. They all looked the same to me. All I remember now from those days is several considerable drinking bouts, one near a mill that was really idyllically situated among the cliffs. I stayed some time near Barbastro and Huesca, then the heavy autumn rains began and I thought to myself, 'Now you head south.' I'll skip Valladolid, where I lost the ring, and Burgos; that took about three months. Slowly I began to get a feeling for beautiful buildings. I rode long distances by train, too, but I didn't stay anywhere long. I had some odd experiences with hospitality. I'm sitting in a café with a man, start to leave, and say, 'I've got to look for a place to stay.' He says, 'My house is yours!' We'd drunk quite a good number of *usos*—it's a kind of brandy; the friendly waiter pours his agreeable guest so much that there's a lot slopped in the saucer—and I stepped out for a moment, and when I came back the man was gone and I had no place to sleep. That happened to me often. Often they'd take me to some house and say, 'I'll be right back,' and then they'd disappear. And it was in Spain where I rushed into an orange grove for the first time and took a bite from an incredibly bitter *naranzackia*.

"Then from Almería I crossed over to Algiers. I was meaning to board the boat at Carboueras, but they were looking for a fellow that fitted my description, who had got into some kind of trouble, and so that night I walked the fifteen miles to Almería and caught the steamer there. In Algiers I came ashore with one French franc and arrived all covered with soot, but I can't remember why it was. Maybe I shovelled

coal and made less money than I lost on ruined clothes. I had
now reached the point where I had to work. I signed on aboard
a regular coast-wise tub with a French and Algerian crew
that made the run from Algiers to Tunis and back. I was in a
pretty low state at the time. I had a bad tooth, and was always
going to get it attended to but never did so, because whenever
we reached port everything immediately got drunk up. This
went on for seven months—I was just seventeen. It was summer,
in fact the worst heat was over, and I jumped ship in Bône,
because that's about the most wonderful country you can
imagine. Regular beech and pine forests right down to the
coast. And me always wishing to find some beautiful spot with
some way to live there. But what could I do? Then I worked in
copper mines at Philippeville, not right in the town but a dozen
miles inland. My job was with the cheap labour that picked
the metal out of the rock in the open air; I had to supervise
it. I didn't do anything there but go about with a watch and
make bets about what time it was. Once I guessed within ten
seconds. It was an awful time. This went on for several months,
until Christmas. And always that inner urge for freedom and
movement.

"But one day I went on, anyhow, to Malta, where I did
a good bit of drinking to excess and got hauled into court
several times. And there I met an English girl, scrawny and
not particularly pretty: her name was Molly. Once she showed
me a box with four hundred pictures of herself: she had
formerly had a music salon, and her father was a high English
naval officer, but I shan't tell you about that because you won't
believe me, anyhow. The park where we always used to meet
was called Floriana. And when I left, the ship was hardly out
of the harbour when she threw herself into the ocean. Of course
they fished her out again, ha, ha! A lady that was there told
me about it afterwards. I got to Cairo—the passage didn't
cost me anything; without knowing it I smuggled hashish in
a sealed package that I had to give the agent at Cairo—and
lived there fairly grubbily, in Muski, a very notorious quarter,

The sea reared up and raised an accusing arm of spray towards
heaven

Already there came yet another, a third and quite different shark.
Like a torpedo the taut body swished through the glistening fish soup

at the house of a Jewess. During the month of January I was
pretty badly off, but then on the first of February I moved
into a wonderful apartment—two beautiful rooms with bath
and light. The story is rather inglorious, so I will pass over it.
I spent that month as if in a dream, sitting out a lot in the sun
on my balcony, but by the end of February the dream was
dreamed out.

"Then somehow I got a fixed idea that as if to punish
myself I would go clear across the desert to Suez on foot. I
went with the last of my money to one of those Arab bean
kitchens where you got unsalted beans with a little olive oil—
people in Egypt live incredibly simply—and to avoid diluting
my digestive juices I didn't drink anything before I left. It's
quite interesting the way you just stumble into danger like
that. Well, so I started out, went through the Arab town,
which I knew pretty well by then, and right beyond the last
houses the desert begins. There are a few half-starved dogs
running about, and in the holes in the ground a few terribly
poor beggars live, but then you're clear outside. It must have
been about noon when I left the city; I went straight into the
desert, so far as I could tell steadily to the east. Of course I
had nothing with me to eat. And that evening I saw a broad
green valley again, and then two pointed needles appeared,
the two highest minarets in Cairo, and from their position I could
figure out that I had simply gone in a semi-circle half the day.
So I turned round again and went straight out into the night.

"I had a tremendous thirst by then, but I kept on hoofing
it all through the night. Once I slept a little on the way, but
hyenas kept howling round me the whole time. I didn't walk;
I was walked, you might say, perfectly unreasonably, but finally
I got where I was going—not, however, because I wanted it
that way. It was all right in the morning, and then three
Bedouins crossed my path, and one rode over and went through
my pockets, silently and as a matter of course. He didn't
find anything. The only thing I had was an amulet, a scarab,
from the wife of a police officer in Port Said. That's an awfully

sad story. The tragedy of a young Vienna girl who had tied herself to an Arab. She was really beautiful; I can still remember how she appeared in the door—the husband had invited me there, saying he had a surprise for me. We talked, the husband, she, and I, and she was almost irritated, and sided with me against him about the country, the dirt, and so on, and when I mentioned where I was living we looked at one another for a moment, and I knew right away I should find a message from her the next day. So I did; I was really waiting for it. Naturally the husband never caught on—I was clever enough for that; there are ways.

"Well, she had given me the scarab, and when the Arab started to take it away from me I got so energetic and furious that he saw it wouldn't work. Well, so I was standing in the middle of the desert, and I realized plainly that my own strength wouldn't take me the last fifty miles to Suez. Later a rider on a she-camel met me, dismounted, and gave me camel's milk out of a tin can to drink. That strengthened me, and I marched on a couple of hours more. Suddenly behind me I saw three dots coming rapidly closer. They were three cars; I waved, and the third one stopped and took me in.

"But Suez wasn't what I wanted, either. I tried to get aboard a ship that was sailing to India but they threw me off again. I worked for two weeks in an oil refinery, then I cleared out again and walked back to Port Said. But there the ship I wanted to go to Malta in left just as I was arriving. Oh, well, I thought, you can simply walk to Alexandria. A perfectly impossible undertaking, of course. That's where the Nile breaks up into ever so many branches. And I only got over two; that region looks pretty much like a lake, long rows of telephone poles—it simply wasn't possible in that direction. Today I realize it was bound to be so, but at that time I kept deluding myself, simply stalling myself off by running away. A constant flight from daily monotony, an emptiness in myself that I kept running away from. So I went back to Port Said and got ferried across to the east bank, and then on to

Kantara, and there I lay down in a passenger car in the station and fell asleep. About noon I woke up with a dry throat —there was a frightful heat—and without hiding at all, just walking upright, I went through the station and the Customs, along the tracks to the north.

"I spent the night with some Bedouins; they were very hospitable and gave me hard-boiled eggs and brandy. They had German military buttons on their clothes. These Arabs told me the water train went through at ten in the morning, and that there was a place where it went uphill, and you could jump on without being seen. So I did it, and it worked fine. I got into a goods wagon and hid in an empty space. I stayed there all day. At twilight the train stopped out in the open, and twenty men jumped on my wagon and threw off the roof from over my head. I was left on the bottom of the wagon. The train went on, night fell, and I took off my jacket, spread it over me, and fell asleep. Suddenly I was awakened by a railway man's lantern. He said to me, 'Ticket, ticket!' and took me along.

"We jumped from one wagon to another, from roof to roof, and got to a little compartment with two benches, a platform, and a glass door. He was a fairly young Arab, in fact sort of pretty, with thick lips, a leather pouch, and he took his coat off right away. He got out a brandy bottle and eggs, and then he began—well, he began bothering me; you know the way Arabs are. A station came, he took his lamp, gave a signal, whistled, and we went on again, and he started all over again. I kept putting him off pleasantly. I thought to myself, 'every minute is nearly half a mile; let's see how far we get.' But then he began to be very troublesome indeed. The door was open now because it was very hot, and I told him to turn round for a minute. And when he willingly did so I gave him a kick that sent him flying out—as sure as I'm alive, I did, and we were going at least twenty-five miles an hour. At the stations after that I gave the signal myself—ready, off we go! I got as far as El Arish, and from there to Lydda, and then on foot

into the mountains. In the last of the daylight I tramped into
a fairly busy suburb of a good-sized city that lay ahead. At
first I didn't dare ask, but I wanted to know where I was, and
finally I went timidly into a store. They were all talking
Yiddish. I was in Jerusalem!"

"And did you steal his coat?" asked Alfred.
"No," said Xenophon. "His watch, though."

55

SEVERAL times the motor had run more slowly, and
Xenophon's story had lagged noticeably in each case; but we
did get to Santorin. While the thunderclouds gathered ever
more menacingly and the night came nearer with stormy
tread, our motor chuffed its last strength out. And when we
came safely into the inner circle of the crater island it even
speeded up like a horse drawing near the stable. It was unquestionably a well-behaved and praiseworthy motor.

Santorin looks like a sugar loaf from which mice have
gnawed away the point and the whole inside, leaving only a
sketchy ring (which the housewife, understandably annoyed,
has flung out on the street, where it has broken and the pieces
have landed in a large puddle). The outer sides of the island
ring slope gently, and are covered with fertile vineyards; on
the inside, where the volcanic mice have been at work, the
walls drop almost perpendicularly for a thousand feet. Santorin
is the largest crater in the world; it measures more than four
and a third miles in diameter, which makes it even bigger
than that of the fabulous island of Krakatoa. If you sail into
the crater lake through one of the gaping holes you feel as if
you were being transported to the Grand Canyon. The lava
and tufa formations lie in coloured stripes one above another,
and high up on the lava walls villages are enthroned like hawks'
nests, shining like snow on black mountains. In the middle

of the lake, in geologically recent times, a new and still active volcano has formed, a tiny island that changes its shape through eruptions almost every decade. Not a blade of grass grows on these recently cooled lava mountains. Above, from the sharp roof of the island, flies the white smoke flag of the volcano; below, on the wildly indented coast, sulphur-yellow drainage flows into the sea. When storm threatens, one particularly deeply indented bay offers the only sheltered anchorage of Santorin. Into this bay our faithful *Sultana* chugged.

So many ships had already gathered here that we found a free place only with some difficulty. The ships were lashed together so closely that you could easily jump from one to the next. Now this was a pretty bad business. If we didn't want to risk having everything stolen from our decks we had no choice but to take turns in standing watch during the night. In view of the storm that was already beginning, it was not a pleasing prospect. But mightn't there be another way?

As soon as darkness fell and the storm began to howl, Heinz and I armed ourselves with guns loaded with tracer ammunition and posted ourselves one fore and the other aft of the adjoining ships. And immediately we could be heard yelling furiously at each other.

"You scoundrel, you good-for-nothing!" cried Heinz, and a luminous streak whisked past me through the rigging.

"What—? You—? You dare——?" I yelled back, and an equally large cluster of light whammed in the other direction.

After a repeated exchange of shots, which was followed with horrified eyes from the hatches round about—we withdrew to our cabin, laughed ourselves half-sick, and slept the sleep of the just while storm and rain raged.

Nothing whatever was stolen that night.

56

ONE should not speak of the devil. Otherwise he may decide to put in a personal appearance and take a hand in matters——

The weather had remained windy, so we were now working at a spot in the inner circle of the island. Diving gave you a sort of an uncanny feeling. Just as the crater walls rose almost perpendicularly a thousand feet above the surface, they fell off almost perpendicularly another thousand feet into the depths below the water line. So we were swimming over completely black, bottomless water.

I found myself breathing uncommonly fast. But except for the biting cold of the water I felt fine. I was carrying a collecting net in my hands, and carefully freeing from the rock a gelatinous substance we had never seen before. The growths on these lava walls surprised us in every way. Obviously because of the special environment provided by the crater lake and the lava rock, a completely different symbiosis had developed here from that which was in the Sporades, along the Peloponnesus, or in Crete. I had even seen a species of fish that was new to us.

Startled, I jumped. A hand was put on my shoulder. It was Alfred. He had dived down to me, and was pointing at his film camera. Yes, of course, we had been planning to shoot the connecting scenes we lacked. Why was I breathing so fast?

These scenes had a history. After careful study of our scenario we had discovered that we still needed a number of important shots to fill in gaps. Above all, we needed pictures of my diving mishap near Elephteri. Heinz had taken some pictures of me being carried lifeless across the deck, but naturally we lacked what had taken place under water. And, after all, our film was supposed to depict the expedition truthfully in all its episodes. So we had decided to pose and shoot these scenes afterwards.

I did not feel quite easy in my mind about the matter. It was a bit unlikely that I should be writhing in my death throes on the ocean floor while Alfred took pictures from every angle. But, on the other hand, our film was supposed to be complete, and we could hardly be blamed for not filming the original of that particular scene.

While Alfred swam up to the surface I looked for a place that might do. These shots would have to match up with the scenes taken at the wreck. I tried to think whether my trunks, my cap, and the collecting net looked exactly as they did on that disastrous day. Everything was right. By a jutting part of the lava wall I stopped. This ramp looked exactly like the cliff at the entrance to the blossom gully below the wreck. I motioned to Alfred to hurry up. It was quite strange that I was breathing so fast. We must get this job finished.

Alfred dived and took up a position some thirty feet from me. As soon as he was ready I began to play my part. Just as I had done when the white spots appeared in my field of vision, I looked around uneasily. I picked a sponge and dropped it. Then I ducked a little, suddenly huddled, pushed off 'with my last ounce of strength'—and stiffened. Strange what happened to my body now. It revolved at an angle. It wasn't so easy being paralyzed and unconscious. I floated upwards with agonizing slowness.

To make sure, we repeated the scene three times. First the whole sequence, and then two series of close-ups. That was that. We nodded to each other, and swam back to the boat, Alfred leading, on the surface, and I following, fifteen feet down.

And then it happened.

So suddenly that I did not realize it myself, I lost consciousness. If I had lost my life on this occasion—and, as will be seen, it was a near thing—I would, as you might say, never have known it. An electric light switch seemed to have been turned off in me. There was a sudden end, without the slightest transition.

When I came to an hour had passed and I was lying on deck under a lot of blankets. This time, too, I owed my life to chance. For no particular reason Alfred had turned to look back at me as he was swimming, and to his horror had seen me blow out all my air and sink like a stone. Down into the utterly black, bottomless depths of the crater.

If he had turned two seconds later there would have been

no helping me. I would have fallen down and down, and Santorin would have been my last diving adventure. As it was, however, he raced after me and barely managed to catch me forty feet down and grab me by the air pouch from behind. As I had breathed out all my air, and had thus lost my buoyancy, it needed desperate exertion for him to pull me back to the surface. He appeared above water for only a moment, yelled piercingly, and sank away again. Luckily the boat was only twenty yards off; Joerg and Heinz dived right in and pulled us both out.

It was positively grotesque the way I kept shivering all over with cold in spite of the many blankets. Each limb did a dance of its own, quite beyond my power of control. I had suffered a so-called cold narcosis, such as has sometimes been observed in fliers who have had to ditch in the sea. If the body is chilled below 80 degrees you faint so quickly that you do not even notice it at all. As if a switch were snapped——

I had bitten the hard rubber mouthpiece clean through.

57

Heat . . .

The molecules, the smallest elements our world is made up of, tremble—that is what heat is. The more they tremble, the hotter it is; the colder it is, the less they tremble; if they stand perfectly still, absolute zero is reached. This is why there can be no cold deeper than 459 degrees below zero; the molecules cannot be any stiller than absolute stillness.

A lump of ice is warmed, its molecules tremble more and more, until finally they burst the bonds of solidity and the ice melts. It turns into water, and if we heat this further the trembling of the molecules grows so extreme that finally it bursts even the bonds of fluidity and the water evaporates. That is the secret of the three states of matter. Little trembling means solid; more trembling, liquid; still more trembling, gaseous. Under intense heat even hard iron melts; under still more intense heat it evaporates. With sufficient cold, air turns liquid; chilled still more, it freezes into crystals. Once upon a time all the matter of our earth was a fiery gas; one day all things on earth will be frozen, immobile.

When we heat a stove its molecules begin to tremble so violently that everything near also starts to tremble; the air, the walls, ourselves. That is why the room grows warm. Our spirits awaken, we grow active, and so it is with all other living beings. The higher (up to a certain point) the temperature rises, the faster the vital functions take place. For this reason the animals of the south reach sexual maturity earlier than their northern relatives. And since growth usually stops with sexual maturity the southern varieties, which thus have less time to grow, are, on the average, smaller. And since sexual maturity, reproduction, is in itself the functional fulfilment of a living being, the animals of the south do not live so long on the average as those in the north. This explains why very large sponges, stinging cnidaria and spiny echinodermata live in the polar seas and the icy depths of ocean. For this reason, too, human beings are usually larger in the north, whereas in the south the men are distinguished by their lively temperament and the women by their early bloom and withering.

The exceptions are the frogs, lizards, and snakes; in the south they grow to large sizes. But something else accounts for this. As they have no warmth of their own they stiffen in the cold, and thus have much less time in the north to search for food. These are forms born of starvation, nothing more.

Only the birds and mammals carry their own stoves with them. They preserve a constant body temperature, heating themselves by internal combustion. Naturally this requires fuel, that is to say, more food, and also more oxygen in order to burn this food in the tissues. So it is not surprising that the heat, which drives the blood stream, and thus transports food and oxygen throughout the body, is larger in the warm-blooded than in the cold-blooded animals. And for the same reason the warm-blooded animals of the north, which require the most heat, have exceptionally large hearts.

Very important is the mathematical law that says the volume of a body increases more rapidly than its surface area (the volume increases as the cube, the surface only as the square). Hence it follows that large animals have a comparatively small surface, and therefore lose less heat. This is the reason why the Arctic has developed such large warm-blooded animals as the polar bear, walrus, and whale. That is why small warm-blooded animals, because of their greater loss of heat, have a larger heart. And that, finally, is why the tropical creatures, to whom large surface and loss of heat do not matter, have long ears and tails.

One might suppose this also was the reason why the planktonic creatures that float in southern seas develop such long appendages. But plankton is not warm-blooded, so there must be another explanation. And indeed there is. The long appendages are necessary because the viscosity of water declines as its temperature rises. In order to float motionless even in tropic seas, then, these small organisms must increase their surface friction by enlarging their surfaces.

And if everything in nature thus seems to have some scientific reason, one more question: why are fish so especially resplendent in the tropics?

That, too, has its explanation. In the north the cold makes the struggle for existence extremely hard; hence only the most efficient—that is to say, the simplest—animal forms can survive. The tropics on the other hand, offer such a favourable environment that the most colourful and exotic creatures can survive there. These are, you might say, the 'de luxe models' of nature.

On the other hand, since such innumerable forms have developed in the tropics, they have been able to increase on only a very limited scale (which is why you will more easily

find ten different species in a coral reef than ten specimens of
the same species). In the north, on the contrary, where only a
few specimens have been able to hold their own, these have had
a chance to multiply all the more—hence the enormous
schools of herring, salmon and cod.

The molecules tremble—all this and much more is the result.
Our life moves within a small span. If the heat in our living
stove rises above 109 we die; if it falls below 80 we die likewise.
Less than 30 degrees embrace our feeling, loving, hoping, and
suffering—a very tiny difference in the trembling of the molecules!

58

In the evening the wind died down. The air grew so still that
we were able to eat by candlelight on the main deck. We stayed
up late, and our conversation revolved about the accident,
about death, chance, destiny, providence. As was bound to
happen, Xenophon now had to supply the last instalment of the
remarkable story of his life.

"So you came to Jerusalem?"

"Yes, I came to Jerusalem."

"Well, and then what?"

"I marched in through the Jaffa Gate, simply joined in
the main stream of people, and then got carried along through
the narrow lanes and bazaars."

"And?"

"Just think about my situation: I had no money, I was a
perfect stranger, I had no papers, and I had to go to the hospital
three days later with a severe case of jaundice. Out of the
thousand possibilities there were for living, eating, drinking,
and so on in the city, naturally I found out the best one—or,
rather, I didn't actually find it; it was a sort of ready-made
form that I slipped into, but in those days I wasn't advanced

enough to judge. I didn't need to act; things just happened to me.

"I'm standing in front of a sixty-foot garden wall in the middle of the old city when a kavass speaks to me—the kavasses always have handsome blue-embroidered clothes, and are important people. It was a hospice, conducted by an Austrian professor of geology; the staff were Catholic nuns from some Order or other. Well, ha, ha, this kavass fetched down the professor, and he talked to me and said, 'Yes, I've got a spot for you, just come along!' In the big garden behind there was a nice little gardener's house—I told you about that before— with a hen-house and a piggery and a lot of carpenter's tools, plus the lumber room of the whole hotel; anything that they didn't know what to do with got stuck in there. So there I lived. At supper the food was handed to me down in the bottom of the house through a peep-hole in the wall by an Arab girl with big black eyes the size of silver dollars, and in an echoing corridor stood a table for the staff, which was where I ate. And that was how it went on; I felt like a regular *Schnorrer*. Then three days later I went into the German Deaconess Hospital and lay there for thirty-six days. Once the head of the hotel came to visit me and said, 'Well, when you get out come back to me and you can rest for a couple of weeks.'

"And I actually did go back to him, and rested, and as luck would have it one day at one of the churches they couldn't find any altar boy for Mass. Now, you know I had to serve at Mass in the Vinzentinum every day, at six in the morning, so I knew the trade right well. I did it with dignity and care, didn't jump, didn't slouch, and made every genuflection just as it ought to be; I was assisting a suffragan bishop, and after the very first Mass people began saying, 'He does it better than the bishop.' And I helped him to take off his vestments in the sacristy—on the hill of Golgotha; any chaplain would have envied me—and he handed me ten piastres and asked politely if I would come back tomorrow.

"At the hotel they gave me a great reception, 'Why, we

thought you were Protestant because you never went to church!' And they became several degrees more polite. I remember I had a thin, white check coat and a nice long pair of trousers, and a pair of nice shoes, too. I slowly made my way in the altar-boy business. Everyone wants to say a Mass in Jerusalem, so there were a lot of priests and very few altar boys. In between I would clean cisterns, and so by early September I had accumulated quite a lot of money, really honestly earned money. But as a solution to the problem of how to get through the world without money, this wasn't it, because I knew perfectly well it was a purely local stroke of luck. And I'd probably have gone sooner if Nama hadn't bewitched me. She was a little Arab. I was nineteen at the time, you know. She must have put some kind of powder into my food: I fell simply madly in love with the girl. I watched how she used to go to the hen-house every day with the head sister, so I cut a hole in the netting and made a rope ladder that I could get up with. I always used to take a shower, naked, with a tin can, and I saw Nama watching me on the sly. That was how we came together; but let me tell you I was simply crazy. I tried various kinds of cure but nothing did any good. Then one day she got her long, black hair caught in the wire netting of one of the hen-houses, and like a flash I was up the rope ladder, through my secret passage, and had started to release her, and then it happened. I had barely touched her before we were both done for. Up above, meanwhile, the nun's white headdress kept moving to and fro: she didn't notice anything at all. This happened again fairly often.

"But one day I moved on, after all; I simply couldn't stand it. I was too well off. I meant to go from Jerusalem to Mersina, and from there straight across Asia Minor, through Anatolia and Georgia on foot, but a German I met kept me from leaving the ship at Mersina, and we both went on to Constantinople, where we tried to get a Russian visa. At first they were very friendly at the Consulate; we were both un-shaven, and we had practised *Heil, Moscow!* and scraps of

Russian. The secretary, a fat wench, takes us in to the head man, sits down on the desk with her back to the Consul, dips into his cigarettes, and collects four and a half pounds from each of us as advance against telegraph fees. They stalled us off for about two weeks, then told us the visas didn't cost anything, but we would have to make a contribution to the Red Cross. So then we decided to go home. At Sofia we separated. I took the road along the Danube, by ship as far as Mohacs, and because water travel got too tiresome I disembarked there and raced the last 150 miles to the Styrian frontier in a single week.

"I got back home in October; it was a very fine moment. It's evening, and I ring at the front door, and my mother opens it and says '*Mein Burscherl!*' Everything was just the same as it had always been. The same little living room, the same check tablecloth—only there was a considerable change in me, so that everything looked somehow different. But I left again pretty soon, and this time went direct to Greece. It was the summer of sixteen years ago, on June the twenty-first, that I first came to Zagora, on Mount Pelion, and by wandering in the neighbourhood I found out that you couldn't go any farther by land towards the north, towards the sea.

"I set straight out, and let me tell you that's a wonderful countryside. Leaping little brooks, rank meadows, beeches, oaks and plane trees, and nowhere a trace of human life. Only by one old, silvery-grey, bleached oak stood a tiny chapel, almost wider than it was high—it's a shame I wasn't able to show it to you; we could have reached it easily from Volos in two days. There was a tray with wax candles, wicks with cork floats, oil, and matches. I filled the eternal light, lit the floating wick, and sang, 'Hail, Mary, Star of the Sea!' Then I poured a little of the oil over some herbs I had gathered along the way; I ate of them reverently, and lay down at the feet of the Mother of God on the back of an icon I had laid down on the floor, and I decided she'd forgiven me. Then a couple of days later I turned up on the steep coast among the few fishermen who lived there, and I stayed with them and turned poacher. My boat, now, *Agios Nikolaios*, you should just have seen her! I held my course through every storm, and in the evening, when I would carry my fish across Pelion to Volos, I used to feel my heart swelling, because I knew I had really found what I was looking for."

59

THE boat moved off with gentle strokes of the oars, and we looked after it. In the bows crouched Joerg, stooping deep into the glass-bottomed box, peering downward. Aft, standing erect, was Xenophon, plying the oars in exact obedience to Joerg's left hand, with which he was setting the course. Between the two, neatly arrayed like cantaloupes in a basket, lay five bombs ready to throw, including the largest that had probably ever been made for poaching purposes.

Had we not got enough shark photographs even yet? No, we had nothing like enough. Above all, we lacked pictures showing man and shark together, to give some sense of scale. It was hard to get this kind of picture because it meant that one diver had to approach very close to the shark from just the right angle.

After five days' bad weather we had bright sunshine again at last. The Italian occupying squad at Santorin obligingly lent us a motor boat. Early in the morning we put out of the crater lake; a fisherman said he would show us some places where we could attract more than enough sharks. These good hunting grounds were supposed to be on the east coast of the island ring. And here we were at the first spot, and Joerg and Xenophon were exploring the terrain.

"*Maiatikos—Maiatikos——*" murmured the fisherman next to me. He was firmly convinced that here we must certainly meet 'May fish', big mackerel that came swarming along the coast just at this time of the year.

The boat was not fifty yards from the ship when Xenophon pointed aft with every sign of excitement, and we heard him talking to Joerg in a hoarse whisper. Joerg carefully lifted the glass-bottomed box into the boat, and now also looked aft. Then we saw him raising his hands and slowly clutching at the air as if he could barely contain his excitement. He went hastily to work at the bombs. And suddenly a big white package narrowly missed Xenophon's head and splashed into the water not ten feet beyond the boat.

The big bomb!

Although, as aforesaid, the boat was some fifty yards from us we ducked in spite of ourselves. That charge was big enough to sink a small submarine. The fisherman next to me rubbed his hands and giggled to himself. In the excitement Heinz opened his mouth and forgot to close it. Everyone waited, breathless. But for the moment nothing happened. Xenophon had moved the boat along with a cautious stroke of the oars, and then turned round, holding the basket with the cantaloupes above his head. Joerg stood frozen to stone, only his fingers clutching at the air again. Then at last came the explosion.

A dull, heavy blow made the ocean tremble, and rather slowly the water curved up, rose in a fat column, spread out like a gigantic blossom. But, impressive as this spectacle was, it was far outdone by what immediately followed in the boat. Scarcely had the rain of spray come down again before Joerg was hanging over the side again with the glass-bottomed box. And scarcely had he cast one glance downwards when he emitted an inhuman howl like a Sioux Indian who has caught and scalped his enemy and is brandishing the gory lock above his head. Xenophon, too, hastened to look through the glass-bottomed box, and diabolical laughter mingled with Joerg's yells. Quite beside themselves, the two danced about in the boat, which rocked alarmingly.

What had happened?

Our patience was to be sorely tried. No matter how loud we yelled to ask what was going on, the two dynamite fisher-

This shark was a born actor. Not a trace of stage fright

Suddenly I noticed that Xenophon was excitedly signalling us with the oar from above

A tuna was the cause of the excitement

It was to be killed with a bomb

men had completely forgotten our existence, and seemed, after the explosion, to have become deaf to all other sounds. They kept rowing round and round in circles, snatching the glass-bottomed box from each other, yelling and shaking themselves with delight.

Finally the boat came back.

"Indescribable!" yelled Joerg. "No, sir, you've never seen the like! You just won't believe it!"

"I've been a poacher for thirteen years but I've never seen anything like this!" yelled Xenophon. "This is a blast that has never been equalled except once to my knowledge, by the celebrated Garapagasos of Pyrgos, in February of ten years ago off Cape Kyme. Yes, sir, I always said Joerg was the boy!"

Little by little we, too, discovered what had happened. Xenophon had turned round while rowing, and had caught sight of a whole school of May fish following close upon the boat. The creatures were swimming near the surface, so that the water behind the boat gleamed like a silvery field. When Joerg tossed the big bomb and it started to sink, the fish swam inquisitively closer, and just at that moment it went off. All the fish were killed. Without a single exception they lay on the bottom among the seaweeds. Not one of them stirred. The whole bottom was literally covered with them.

"Xenophon estimates more than a thousand *oka*," said Joerg. "That's four thousand pounds of fish, you know."

"If only they don't come to life and swim off!" cried Heinz, who could hardly wait to see the fish himself.

"Ha, ha! They won't come to life; they'll never swim off!" said Xenophon. And once more he and Joerg rocked with laughter.

When we reached the spot we could understand their excitement. The spectacle of fifty or sixty fish, three or four feet long, lying on the bottom like sardines was really unique. But what was to be done with them? Not a single shark had appeared, so that in itself the blast had been perfectly futile.

o

Alfred went to the bottom in the diving gear, and tied the fish one after another by the tail to a long line. So they came up, one after another, and we stowed them in the boat, where they soon filled the whole deck. They weighed an average of twenty to forty-five pounds. I regarded them with sharply divided feelings. If our dynamiting had been hard to justify even so far, this last act was beyond all argument. I shuddered at the mere thought that any word of it might ever leak out. No, these fish must disappear at once. Possibly we could cut them in pieces and thus lure a few sharks after all by the scent of blood in the water.

But Xenophon would have none of this reasoning. We would salt the fish down, he said, and each of us would take a barrel or two home. The May fish, salted, was simply delicious, and we could live high for months. No, he would take care of everything; we need not worry at all; nobody would hear about it. If we brought fish home, it was really no wonder, considering our skill at underwater hunting, ha, ha! He asserted that the only problem was the salt; we needed at least 250 pounds, and we should have to get it from the Italians somehow, preferably for some scientific experiment, ha, ha, ha!

Against all these practical arguments I was powerless. So we hid our fish-laden ship in a little cove, bought the silence of the fishermen by three particularly plump specimens, invited the Italians for a run in the next couple of days—whereupon they gladly gave us the necessary 250 pounds of salt—and forthwith Xenophon went to work. With astonishing deftness he cut the fillets away from the bones, salted, rolled, and barrelled them, and kept laughing so merrily that he seemed like a new man.

"A thousand *oka* of fish—Psarathanas should have seen that!" he kept repeating.

"And all purely in the interests of science!" said Joerg, patting one of the full barrels.

60

My diving accident had happened on October the nineteenth, the great dynamiting took place three days later, and the subsequent week, from the twenty-third to the twenty-eighth, brought the high point of our expedition.

Not far from the spot where the May fish had flipped their last there was a place where enormous schools of small gopes kept filing past. Several poachers had already gathered there, and with them we dropped one bomb after another into the sea. The amazing thing was that the gopes came quite willingly to the slaughter. Scarcely had the thunder died away and the hecatombs sunk to the bottom or floated to the surface when new reinforcements would come pouring into the now vacant space. Probably they were attracted by the plankton, which were also killed.

We saw as many sharks as our hearts could desire. There were more and more from hour to hour. These sharks were obviously 'trained' not only to the sound but to the location of the blasts. In the course of our expedition we dropped bombs in regions not usually troubled with dynamite fishermen, and not once did we see any sharks. Here, on the other hand, and at the spots round Skiathos where poaching had been going on for twenty years, a sort of resident stock company of sharks and solitary tuna fish had grown up which would appear promptly at the table set for them at the sound of the gong. What these creatures did the rest of the day, and where they drifted about in the deep sea out yonder, heaven alone knew. Without an explosion we never saw a single one. But when a charge of dynamite went into the sea the first grey and blue shadows usually came whizzing up within ten seconds.

The most exciting moment for us was the one right after

the explosion, when we let ourselves slip down into the flickering fish soup. In their first rush the sharks would act fiercely. They came roaring up like a whirlwind—often straight at us. But they were interested not in people but in the savoury little gopes, and so they would always swerve, apparently surprised—as if you were eating peas and unexpectedly found a melon.

If ever our wildest plans were realized it was in those last days. The organization in the boat reached a pitch of perfection. Xenophon kept everything strictly in order, and managed the duels like the master of ceremonies in a quadrille. To his left lay the spare films in one water-proof pouch, to to the right the dynamite in another. Hanging overboard forward, one of us would peer down to the bottom, covered with countless dead fish. In the slanting light it would gleam below like a starry sky at night.

"Hold it, there are some more! Easy, easy, on the starboard bow, now!"

Cautiously two divers would push their finned legs over the gunwale. One to the right, the other to the left, so that the boat would not tip as they went over. They would have their breathing tubes in their mouths, the underwater cameras dangling on their chests. Then a blast would rumble against the boat, and before the rain of spray came down the two would be in the water, in the midst of the foam, heading downwards with hasty corkscrew turns.

For time was of the essence. The performance was short. Only in the first moment of excitement would the sharks rush pell-mell hither and thither, not caring whether you poked the camera right under their noses. Once they had calmed down it was considerably harder to come at them from a good angle. And since they ate rather from greed than from hunger they would soon scatter again.

The first ones came. One big, one little, one blue, one grey. The two divers communicated by frantic gestures. Each one would see on his own side a shark that seemed likely to him, and he would try to summon his companion over to his side. The visibility was twenty to twenty-five yards, though it was rather obscured by the dead fish, clustered here and there in thick, twitching clouds.

A tuna would shoot past. Quickly the camera would swing round, then a glance backward, and of course another shark was already arriving. No sign of the other diver. He would have swum after his shark, and be taking pictures somewhere else. The new shark would swim close above the bottom, picking up dead fish and shaking his head each time. Craning his neck sideways, the diver would strive to get the right focus on the brute. He would swim beside him with hasty fin strokes, rewind, and sight the camera again. Suddenly the buzz would sound a little higher. The film had run through; back to the surface.

Up there your partner would already be at the boat, furious because his camera was not running evenly. And, besides, some water had got in; not much, but enough. Xenophon had not screwed it up right. Hastily Xenophon would come rowing over and take both cameras to load new film. Almost no words would be exchanged. The two would wash out their masks, test their oxygen pressure gauges, and wait.

There, not fifty feet from the boat, a sharp dorsal fin appears above the waves—the dreaded 'black triangle'. And a little farther on, a dark point—the mouth of the shark, snapping at floating fish.

Already the two heads are under water. Yes, over yonder, rather hard to see, the ten-foot silhouette glides along just under the surface. Alfred, to whom one of the two heads belongs, surfaces again, followed by me, the owner of the other head. If only Xenophon would hurry a little! Wonder of wonders, the cameras are all ready. Hastily we fasten our neck straps and swim away from the boat. One diagonally to the left, the other to the right, to get the shark between us.

But while we are still pursuing this shark we see far below

us two others, grazing at leisure upon the fish meadow, and perhaps better suited to encirclement. A couple of quick gestures suffice to make the situation plain. We dive from opposite directions. In less than half a minute we are sixty-five feet down. We can scarcely feel the change in pressure; we have long since got used to that. Nor are we any longer conscious of manipulating the oxygen valve or focusing the camera; it is all automatic. Equally mechanical is swimming with the fins. If a shark passes above us we turn over on our backs and shoot from below; if a ray appears thirty feet below we plunge at him like hawks; when the film is gone we shoot upwards faster than the bubbles that move with us.

These two sharks were filmed, others were filmed, then we were back in the boat and Xenophon was helping us to undo our straps. With a few practised motions he changes the oxygen flasks and potassium cartridges for spares, and the other two boys put on the still wet gear and vanish in turn into the depths.

"You never swam up to that blue one right. By the way, did you see that fat one that came at you from behind?"

A brief shake of the head was the reply. In bathrobes, we crouched shivering in the boat. We would wait for an hour and recruit warmth, then the others would come up and we would go on. What might they be doing below? We gave it no thought. Were they in danger? We gave that no thought. It was magic, a mysterious fascination, to swim beside these creatures, so beautiful and supple that you could not help admiring them rather than be afraid of them.

The tuna fish, on the other hand, is clumsy in his impetuosity. He goes roaring along like a machine let loose, devours indiscriminately whatever comes within his sight, starts in alarm if you get too close to him, and then rushes blindly off.

The shark is the concentrated essence of felinity. His whole body is motion. His mighty tail fin barely sweeps the water, and he's gliding effortlessly along. For him there is no resistance. Eight or ten quick fin strokes, and he is flying through the sea at thirty-five, fifty, perhaps sixty miles an hour. And then a little turn and he swings aside. There's a fish before his maw: he surveys it with both eyes before he bites. Of course he does not turn over on his back, as people are always saying. There is something jolly in the way he snaps, in his pointed nose, in his supple motions. Something tremendously frolicsome—but the next moment he is lofty again, superior, almost arrogant. You approach him, and he never even notices. He swims quite casually on. What cares he for the vulgar herd? He is king of the sea, plays when he feels like it, takes what he wants, and swims on his way with no one knowing where it leads.

A big ray comes rocking and rolling along. He is as different from the shark as an elephant from a tiger. Assiduous but law-abiding, the elephant reaches for the lump of sugar with his trunk, and in the same naïve sort of way the giant ray stirs up the sand with his powerful pectoral wings in search of savoury little snails and shell-fish. At the same time his eyes have such a knowing look that he seems to be amused himself at the odd shape the Creator has embodied him in.

And how odd, after all, is what we are doing here!

We are swimming with fins alongside a giant ray, holding a box and pressing a button that makes a strip of film run behind a lens. The beams of light, reflected from the ray's body, flash through the lens and strike the film, leaving their traces there. The film goes into a bath, and the light traces turn into a picture of the ray. The whole thing is enlarged on paper and put in a newspaper, or the film is run before people who pay to see it. So the light traces bring in money. And with this money I pay for camera, ship, and expedition, and immediately we swim off somewhere else and the cycle begins anew.

But that is how life is. A constant cycle. You work in order to eat, and eat in order to work. And finally both are done with.

October 23. Early departure in order to meet the Italians

half-way and so prevent sight of the butchery on board. Unluckily the weather is not good, clouding over more and more. The water lies leaden grey and smooth; possibly rain is coming. While the others lie below decks singing I have to entertain the Italians. This time the fisherman guides us to another shark spot, where we anchor in dark water under a dark sky. Soon gopes appear. We drop bombs, and I see the first shark with the naked eye. Alfred and I are the first to dive, and we get into a terrific hurly-burly of sharks. At least five sharks round us, not in quite such a hurry as at Skiathos but swimming pleasantly and steadily. The water is very dark but we manage to get a splendid shark between us. Some of the sharks even swim straight at us. Wonderful! Sharks everywhere. They move about with their noses to the bottom, or snap up fish in motion. Among them, too, are small, fluttering rays. The Italians had hoped to go swimming and try the fins but they all stay out on account of the sharks. One shark goes swimming round Alfred right on the surface, and the men shout and wave their carbines. Very comical. We sink the fish heads, to serve as bait for tomorrow, then we have to quit because it grows very dark and starts to rain. We have shot a total of nine films. A wonderful take. On the way home it starts raining harder; the Italians shiver terribly, and we take them straight home to keep them away from the ship. Meanwhile Xenophon has finished his job. There are nine barrels in all; he plans to exchange one for tomato paste.

October 24. As the motor has to be overhauled first, we get a delayed start. The weather is overcast, with hope of sun, which, however, soon vanishes. The sea is calm, but then wind comes up. We go back to the same place; the bottom is already quite silver with dead fish. The first divers are Alfred and I again, but he is not quite ready when the bomb goes off. I immediately see three sharks, swimming in the snow flurry, one of them straight at my legs; I see a large shark swallowing a middle-sized May fish at one gulp. Then Alfred is there and the shark rhapsody begins again. Once a shark comes quite

Instantly we were in the water again, peering downward

The bite marks were like excisions made with a razor

Sailing into the crater lake of Santorin, one believes himself transported to the landscape of the Grand Canyon

Even under water the crater walls descend perpendicularly for about a thousand feet

I shuddered at the thought that something of this might become known. These fish had to disappear

close to Alfred from the front and I manage to photograph the scene. Heinz gives us a lot of trouble because he does not keep his distance properly. By four o'clock we are all exhausted. A total of thirteen descents, all the cartridges used up. We go home, hoping for better weather tomorrow.

October 25. Back to the same place, but a thick fog comes down and it is already raining when we arrive. Nevertheless we make a drop, but no sharks anywhere. Only Alfred goes into the water briefly to look for sponges, then we take off again. In the afternoon I successfully solder the film camera. Otherwise nothing.

October 26. Fine weather, but Xenophon believes there is a wind off-shore. Joerg has stomach-ache so we decide to stay there and pay a visit to the crater. Very pleasant. We take pictures in the fields of volcanic ash. In the afternoon Alfred and Xenophon go over to Thira to get tomato paste. Otherwise nothing in particular. Yesterday, incidentally, we had word that we are to be towed back. We hope it takes a while yet.

October 27. In the morning it is quite clear but when we reach the spot clouds are covering the sun again. Enough to drive you crazy. Finally we drop, though not at the appropriate moment, and there are numerous sharks round us, but just then a cloud comes. Finally the sun reappears and I am able to get some wonderful shots against the light. Two sharks circle round me close to the bottom, but Heinz stays cautiously above and somehow doesn't want to come down. I make frantic signs, but when he finally gets there of course the sharks have gone. Later Joerg approaches one shark fairly close with a spear. A great many dead fish. After lunch Joerg and I dive and get two fierce tuna fish between us that charge once at me and then once at Joerg and then again at me. We get a shark in our midst, and Heinz comes down at the same time with the harpoon. I swing the camera to and fro like mad. Wonderful lighting. A lucky thing the camera is working again.

October 28. Last day at Santorin. Cloudless sky. We are on the point of putting out when a boat arrives: we are to

P

report to the Italians; the coastguard ship is there to take us in tow. We go over disgustedly but contrive that we shall not be towed off until five o'clock. We go happily to our place; this time the water is quite calm and as smooth as a mirror. It is some while before we find gopes. At last, after we have observed a turtle above water, we see some and drop a bomb. Alfred and I dive, and immediately get two sharks between us. Incredible number of sharks round about; the bottom looks like a battlefield. We film and photograph to our hearts' content. Then Alfred points upwards; he has heard Joerg. The latter shows us a ray. Great excitement. We get him between us, wonderfully, burrowing like mad in the grass. Unfortunately we then scare him off into the depths. But Alfred's film was used up, anyway. We swim up and see sharks everywhere, some snapping for fish right beside the boat. The surface is so smooth that we no longer need the glass-bottomed box. Sharks everywhere. Then Joerg, with the harpoon, goes into the water with Alfred and I take the camera down, without any diving gear. I dive splendidly, no trouble at all, come down upon a shark and am filmed with him. Joerg, however, cannot get near any shark with the harpoon; perhaps they are afraid of the long rope. Once I see four sharks below me. Back to the surface; I'm shivering already. Shark fins are cutting the water everywhere now, some of them right by the boat. I film like a madman. Too bad we have no carbine! We try to bag a shark with dynamite but it doesn't bother them at all. If it doesn't land right on their heads they swim placidly on. Sharks below us all the time. Finally we drop a few more small charges and Alfred and I descend for the last time. It is the maddest shark race we have ever seen. We count seventeen sharks in our field of vision at one time. Four sharks together swim between us, a regular shark rush; no matter where we look there are sharks. Alfred and I are working together splendidly, and we get the creatures between us without difficulty. I try to catch one particularly fat shark by the tail and almost succeed. Finally there are fewer, that is, there are only three or four around, and our films are used up. Exactly at five o'clock we get home, and so does the ship. Heinz, who had stayed on board, has traded for wine instead of tomato paste. Fifty gallons. Bon voyage!

61

LIKE a golden double sail Santorin rose behind us above the evening sea. As we were in tow to another ship, the *Sultana* glided soundlessly, and faster than ever before, through the waves. We were all on the afterdeck; Dr. Beckh was discussing the evening's menu with Papa Jorgi, Joerg and Alfred were playing cards, Xenophon was looking over Joerg's shoulder and Heinz over Alfred's.

And so our expedition was at an end. In Milos we would have one day, and then back to the Piraeus. Then there would be nothing more for us to do but pack our numerous boxes and liquidate the vessel.

"No, it isn't that easy!" cried Alfred. "That was my king. No cheating, now!"

"The king is mine," Joerg replied. "You should stack your tricks more carefully."

"Go on, Joerg! I saw you slipping it away myself!" Heinz butts in.

"Shut up!"

"Joerg, hand over that king. You can't get away with it."

"Whose was the king?" Joerg turns to Xenophon.

"The king was Joerg's," declares Xenophon categorically.

No, our expedition had brought no end. On the contrary, the whole of it had been only a beginning, a prelude. Our dynamiting, true enough, had been highly deplorable but at least it had brought us interesting observations and photographs, and so far as the diving method we had developed was concerned, it offered significant new opportunities to science.

To extend it further would be our next job. First of all we must develop a waterproof rubber suit by way of protection against cold, such that wool could be worn under it, and so close-fitting that it would neither hamper swimming nor form painful wrinkles under high pressure. If we succeeded we would be able in future to work even in winter and in the colder regions of the sea. And if we further succeeded in closing the suit over our heads and heating it electrically we should be able to swim in the Arctic oceans.

Then, in order to reach greater depths, we would have to give up breathing pure oxygen. To counteract its poisons at high pressures we should need to dilute it with some neutral gas. Hydrogen was suitable but problematical, because when mixed with oxygen it creates an explosive gas. Successful experiments had already been made in America with helium, so helium it should be. The only difficulty was in designing automatic valves that would vary the proportion of oxygen and helium according to the depth. If this was accomplished there was theoretically no reason why we could not, with our small gear, reach depths down to 325 feet by free swimming. Here the waterproof suit would still be essential, though, because at great depths the water even in the warmest seas is extremely cold.

Obviously in future we would need better weapons, easily portable underwater spotlights for colour shots, and a small head lamp, so that we could hunt and observe even at night. In regard to electrical fishing, we should have to study the possibility of doing it in the sea through the design of suitable directional short-wave transmitters. And the same for ultra-high-frequency gear.

A special problem was the library. Previous research expeditions had always decided that it is impracticable to carry aboard ship the entire special literature needed for identifying the catch. Most of the publications are too rare and too expensive. The best anyone had been able to do, therefore, was to collect and preserve during the expeditions, and to work on the material at home. This, however, had the disadvantage that the most interesting questions usually do not arise until the results are being studied, and it is generally a long time before another expedition goes back to the same area. It would surely be far better to do your studying on the spot. I calculated that with ten assistants one could microfilm the entire literature of oceanic biology in less than three months, and then the films could be arranged on reels according to the various subjects. Only a copy of this film library would be taken on board; the negative would remain at home in safety. Reading and reference would take place at special stands, where the reel would be mounted and the desired page would be projected from below on to a ground-glass screen. The leaves would be turned by pressing a button, and through proper copying one could have the type white on black, which would be easier on the eyes. Such a library could be stowed in a fairly small space aboard ship, and the costs could be recovered by selling copies to other small institutions that could not afford a complete library.

There were possibilities, too, for observation and photography in the deep sea. William Beebe's bathysphere and the underwater balloon planned by Picard were tools extremely expensive to use, but was it absolutely necessary to descend to those dark regions in person? Might not one accomplish the same thing as well, if not better, by lowering a television camera into the depths? Modern television gear could be housed in a ball less than two and a half feet in internal diameter, and—since the surface and hence surface pressure increases as the square of the diameter—so small a sphere could much more easily be made to resist pressures at depths below thirty thousand feet. Remote-controlled still and film cameras, high-powered floodlights, and the television gear could be housed in five or six such spheres, and these could be deployed in a quarter-circle round some sort of bait, and coupled with a remote-controlled electric trap in such a way that the creatures thus attracted could not only be observed, filmed, and photographed from above but could also be bagged. Since a system of this kind would not be so heavy by far as Beebe's bathysphere it would not need nearly such heavy cables, and thus its weight would also be reduced. The entire arrangement could be let down from a vessel of moderate size, and any rocking of the ship could be compensated for by an arrangement of buoys that would deflect the cable as necessary. Sitting before the television screen in a darkened room, we could penetrate the deep sea at our ease, and the spheres would also be very suitable for seeking out sunken ships as well as for observation in shallow water, say to study the nocturnal life of a coral reef.

The oceans lie infinitely far-flung and infinitely mysterious: their exploitation is perhaps the greatest economic undertaking that still awaits execution. The continents on which we so proudly promenade constitute altogether scarcely a third of the earth's surface, and even of this scant third only part can be cultivated, for it includes vast deserts, steppes, mountain ranges, jungles, swamps, and the polar ice. Perhaps clearing, irrigation, and scientific manipulation of climate will make some further areas useful; but nothing can be done about the fact that land is fertile only at one level—that you cannot pasture cattle fifty feet above a wheat field and plant potatoes fifty feet below.

Quite otherwise the sea. Not only do the oceans cover almost seventy per cent of our earth's surface; they average some thirteen thousand feet deep and almost all of this vast space is full of living beings now beyond our reach. Consider for a moment: a ploughed field thirteen thousand feet deep where food can grow, over an area twice as big as all the lands together!

More than that. The creatures of the sea are considerably more prolific than those that feed us on land. A cow can give birth to only a limited number of calves; if you slaughter too many the herd is bound to die out. One pair of fish, on the other hand, produces tens of thousands, nay millions, of fertile eggs;

of the young that hatch, however, only an average of two reach maturity. Why is this? A perfectly simple, logical conclusion: because if two parents were to produce an average of more than two adult descendants there would bound to be more and more fish with each generation, so that the sea would long since have overflowed with fish. Every oceanic area—like every region on land—can support only a limited number of organisms; the surplus is bound to perish and serve the others as food. Out of tens of thousands and millions, then, never more than two survivors! Hence we see that we may catch far more fish than we can slaughter calves without running any risk of exterminating the finny herds.

A difficult situation is that of the whale which, being a mammal, bears only a small number of living young. But why do we hunt the whale? Its fat, the main thing that interests us, is by no means its personal product; on the contrary, it merely stores up in its *embonpoint* the fat of tiny plankton creatures, primarily winged snails, which it filters out of the sea water with its gigantic maw. And even these do not themselves create the fat, but devour it with tiny crabs, and these again with tiny algae, which produce it in their microscopic bodies as a reservoir of power and in order to float better. Instead, then, of catching the whale, that storehouse of fat, we might equally well lay the real fat producers under contribution. Many things have already been accomplished that seemed impossible to previous generations. Is it not conceivable that some day oceans will be cultivated like fields? That even in the sea we may sow, manure, and harvest?

When we consider what modern chemists and nutrition specialists are producing out of the refuse it seems likely that they might also succeed in treating the produce of the sea, highly nutritious in any case, to create palatable and long-lasting foodstuffs. Surely the sustenance of an ever increasing humanity could be assured out of the oceans—though not with present-day methods of fishing. Strange though it be, in regard to the sea man is still a nomad. He roams its surface and lowers nets and lines into the deep where there happen to be abundant fish, but as yet there is not the slightest thought of any profitable exploitation or cultivation of oceanic resources. Nets, hooks, harpoons, and seines have indeed been highly perfected, but with such methods we are still practically in prehistoric times, and this in an age when science is already actively influencing the whirl of the electron and the breeding of the weather. Whether the atomic forces whose utilization is being carried forward today at such huge expense will really be useful to mankind still remains highly questionable. But that the opening up of the oceans and its riches can only be a blessing in the struggle against hunger and war is surely beyond all doubt.

Endlessly broad and mysterious lays the ocean—what an enormous field of endeavour! Only a properly equipped vessel is needed for us to begin: off to the Red Sea, the Indian Ocean, the coral islands of the South Seas, and the Great Barrier Reef of Australia; off to the icy coasts of Patagonia and the Antarctic, to Galápagos, to the Philippine Trench, to the coasts of Greenland——

"When you lose you have to pay up; that's all there is to it," I heard Joerg telling Alfred.

Fiery red like a golden double sail, Santorin stood far behind us above the evening sea.

62

THE two elements of beauty—force and harmony—are the deepest identifiable roots of creation in general. Everything can be traced to force and harmony; all matter, everything we see and feel about us, is, as modern physics recognizes, nothing more than force in the guise of various harmonies. Force becomes matter, waves become atoms—this is hard for the mind to grasp, but once we have grasped it it fills us with joy.

The greatly feared "black triangle" and, in front of it, the pointed snout of the shark, snapping at fish

Scarcely has the hecatomb of dead gopes sunk down, when new ones come streaming in

It takes a lot of patience to get man and shark into the same picture

I tried to seize the tail of a particularly big one. Then there were only three or four sharks left in the vicinity, and our films were used up as well

In search of God? Very well: the ultimate, most enigmatic, most divine thing in the world, force and harmony, is in us, above us; all of us and everything that moves us are manifestations of this ultimate, this divine enigma.

When living beings first emerged they soon divided into two sexes. This is something absolutely necessary, even for those tiny forms that multiply, like a drop of water, by simple partition. For every being has its own special harmony, its special identity of shape and behaviour determined by the heredity factors—tiny chemical particles at whose command the individual grows according to the nature of its species. They are the musical score by which force, the ultimate motive power, conducts the living symphony of creation. This score must never be lost, and since that could not be indefinitely avoided after constant divisions, from time to time two individuals of the species must fuse into one, so that what the one has lost the other may replace.

And lo! When nature reached its highest development in a man the two underlying features of creation were apportioned to the two sexes. The feminine became the symbol of harmony, the masculine the symbol of force, and when love urges the two to unite it symbolizes the fusion of the two inscrutable, divine elements.

And the meaning of existence? If finite man can ask any such infinite question, is not that meaning simply in the search for harmony within and without?

63

THE world spins like a top, and like tops we spin also. One moment it is black, the next white, one moment the world is beautiful, then ugly, one moment we think we know why we are alive, the next we have our doubts. We crouch like mice, one here, one there, looking for warmth, safety, and bacon, and the world turns and turns, and since we have our ticket for the performance we watch it and participate as best we can.

Faster than we had imagined, we were back at the South Station in Vienna, shaking hands for the last time and scattering before the harsh winds of war. In the spring I had one more chance to get back to the sea for a few months, this time near Naples. I arrived there with part of the Greek collections, which I had brought for comparison. I was the last and only guest at the famous Zoological Station, so that the whole institution, with all its equipment and its marvellous library, was at my disposal. Outside the window, blossoming trees, beyond those the ocean, in the distance Vesuvius and Capri—but the daily noon bombing raid ensured that even here the war should not be forgotten.

As soon as the sea warmed up and the Italian authorities gave me a diving permit, I moved over to Capri and set up my headquarters at the Blue Grotto. What a joy to find my favourite orchids down below there, and exactly in the part of the cave where my theories, developed meanwhile, told me they should have been! Decked out like a Christmas tree with tweezers, scalpels, a collecting case, a magnifying glass, and a school slate and chalk, I worked down in the blue twilight amid a magnificence that almost put the Greek caves to shame. No student working at the Zoological Station should fail to have a look at the underwater part of this marvellous grotto.

Once, when high seas rendered the normal entrance impassable, I had myself put down outside and swam through the second, submarine, entrance, which produces the celebrated colour effect. Far to the rear of the tremendous underwater chamber I came on an alcove so colourfully adorned that I involuntarily gave a cry of surprise. The breathing tube came within an ace of dropping from my mouth. Only afterwards did I realize what this would have meant. My breathing pouch would instantly have filled with water, and as I was almost sixty-five feet down and far to the rear, with my increased weight I could scarcely have regained daylight.

*   *   *   *   *   *

A strange fate was in store for my Greek collections. As I have said, I had brought them to Naples in numerous boxes, and several more new boxes had arrived at Capri. Finally, with the war front coming dangerously near, I had to make up my mind to leave. As there had been a heavy raid during the night it was only with difficulty that I got a truck to take the boxes, twelve in all, to the station. There they were stowed in an express car, and the train was to leave in two hours.

Howling sirens—air-raid warning!

Everyone poured into the tunnel. When the bombing slackened off after an hour or so I could stand it no longer; I rushed up, straight through the railway yards, where brisk fires were blazing everywhere. When I finally got to where I could see my train I saw it was ablaze. It and the train next to it.

I raced through this flaming lane and saw, to my relief, that my car was the only one not yet burning. The locomotive in front was on fire, and to the rear all the cars were ablaze, but the first flames were just hesitantly licking at mine. This did little good, however, because the car was locked and I had no key to open it.

This left me about fifteen minutes. If by then I succeeded in finding a key I could save the boxes. If not, my whole work would be in vain, and irreplaceable parts of the collection would be lost, to say nothing of what it might mean to my doctorate thesis.

I ran hither and thither, but in the whole railway yard there seemed to be no one who had a key. Finally I encountered a man who had an axe; he came with me and with this axe I managed to penetrate the vestibule and the grating of the car, which was now blazing. The door could not be opened from inside but I was able to knock out the gratings over the window. Through these I shoved out one box after another, and the helpful Italian received them outside.

Suddenly the man began waving his arms like a lunatic. I could not see what he wanted; he was trying by every means to urge me to get out of the car. I thought he had been frightened by the oxygen flasks in the second goods truck, which were exploding one after another, and I tried to explain to him there there was no danger because these flasks are of a metal that doesn't splinter. But by then he had gone, casting one last look back at me as though I were a soul on its way to purgatory.

Now I had to drop the remaining boxes out of the window —but broken collections would be better than burnt ones. The last three I simply could not manage. I succeeded in raising them only as high as my stomach, then fell over backwards with the box on top of me. So I gave up and jumped outside with a sigh of relief.

Then I saw why the Italian had executed his wild dance. On the other neighbouring track, hidden by our train, stood a petrol train, and here, too, the fire was at work. Indeed, the whole raid, as I later learned, had been aimed precisely at this petrol shipment. So it had all been for nothing, after all, for when the explosion came the boxes would be destroyed. And alone I could not possibly haul them out of danger.

Once more I raced about the railway yard, but not a soul was ready to help. Everyone was talking about the imminent explosion. A fire brigade that had been summoned presented a tragi-comic spectacle. Eight men were standing round one hose, each one yelling at the other seven that they were all cowards, and at the same time all eight kept moving—to the rear.

Suddenly, as if he had sprung up out of the earth, a Neapolitan lad stood beside me. He was perhaps fourteen years old, completely ragged and dirty, barefoot. In great excitement he positively fell upon my neck, crying "*Kamerat! Kamerat!*" This boy was willing to help.

Barefoot he ran across the thousand bits of broken glass that covered the ground between the two burning trains. As he was not strong, and I was completely exhausted, we could carry the boxes only fifty or sixty feet at a time. Then we had to put them down and recover our breath. It was agonizingly slow work. With the last boxes, however, three more boys of the same age, whose chieftain he obviously was, helped us. And so everything was brought to safety.

The explosion, devastating everything around, took place exactly eight minutes later.

My taking of a degree at the Friedrich Wilhelm University in Berlin occurred in the following fashion:

I was supposed to go to the Dean's office in the morning to receive the grade on my thesis and my diploma, but when I came out of the Metropolitan Rapid Transit and walked along Unter den Linden to the university I discovered that the university no longer existed. It had been completely bombed out. Only smoking walls remained.

As I approached I saw a man painfully lugging a heavy box on his back. I lent him a hand, and when we put down the box at its destination I recognized the man as Professor Bieberbach—His Respectability the Dean.

Without a word we lugged a few more salvaged pieces of furniture into a shed, where they would be sheltered from the steadily streaming rain. Then Professor Bieberbach halted suddenly.

"I suppose you're worried about your thesis?" he asked. "Well, let me reassure you; it was saved, and we can have a try at getting it."

Handing me a shovel, he went across the former lawn of the back courtyard, now sprinkled with fragments. If my thesis still existed, I owed it to a female assistant, whose presence of mind had saved the Dean's office safe. It was so heavy that it took eight men to move it, and when the university was on fire, and the auxiliary air-raid crews came and asked what was in this monster, she promptly declared it contained one hundred thousand marks in bank notes.

"If she'd said it was only doctors' dissertations," Professor Bieberbach went on, "the men would probably have said,

'All right, let 'em write 'em over again!' But as it was, they actually lugged the huge thing to the window and threw it out—there it is."

The safe, falling from the third-floor window, had dug into the soft lawn like a bomb. In the rain His Respectability the Dean and I started shovelling until the door of the safe was free. Then he took the keys from his pocket and the door opened at once.

The contents were undamaged. On top was my thesis.

"Your study of the Reteporidae was graded *summa cum laude,* a mark this university has not given to any zoologist for eight years. Congratulations, Herr Doktor!"

Dismal and sooty, the empty walls of the university reached towards the sky.

Recently I paid a visit to Xenophon, who is now a charcoal burner in the Styrian mountains. He had carefully described the way, and said I could not miss it. I was to go from the station to the pasture farm, then up the ditch for about an hour, till I came to a big woodpile, and from there to the left across the brook and up the gravel slope through the woods.

I had just reached the woodpile and crossed the brook when, from far above, I heard trampling and horrible singing. High up on the slope appeared a sledge, heavily laden with charcoal bags—Xenophon was between the curved runners in front—charging downwards at a terrifying pace.

When Xenophon caught sight of me he rushed over joyfully. He had not changed a bit. But the knotty oak had grown a little knottier. Carefully he piled the charcoal bags in neat rows one on top of another—I could not help being reminded of the little basket with the bombs—and then, dragging the sledge behind us, we walked into the woods.

There was much to tell. Joerg was in Vienna, Alfred in Hamburg, of Heinz I knew only that he had married, and I had heard nothing more at all of Dr. Beckh. And our ship, the *Universitas?* Well, unfortunately she was gone. And the equipment? Yes, unfortunately that was almost all gone, too.

"You knew the *Universitas* was used as a munitions transport afterwards and blew up, didn't you?"

Yes, that I knew.

"See that tin can over there?" We were standing by a stout tree below which a tin vessel stood like a small monument on a pedestal. "I made my start here two years ago with that; it was all I had. I used to heat up my food in it, and I slept under that tree. At first the peasants laughed at me and at my charcoal burning, but I've really settled in quite nicely in these two years. First I built that little hut"—a sloping board roof rose above a pit in the ground some distance away— "and then, last autumn, the big one that you're about to see, a regular palace. And I've got my own man working for me regularly, and if you stay with us today—you know perfectly well I shan't let you go—we'll give you a piece of meat roasted on the spit that will just melt in your mouth!"

We went into the clearing where the big kiln stood— smoking—and beyond it Xenophon's new hut. We circled several times round it duly to admire everything. It was indeed a little luxury villa he had built, though it was perhaps a bit odd that there were no windows.

"Oh, well, windows," said Xenophon disdainfully. "Either you're outside, and then you're out, or you're inside, and then you're in!

"Though I must say," he remarked later, as we were sitting in the hut and he was making coffee in a gigantic pot on a little stove, "now that everything's beginning to settle down again I often have an itch to chuck it all and start something new. How about it, old boy? When do we sail?"

And in the evening, before he put out the candle, he turned to me once more. "Remember the fifteenth of June? I was right after all."

"Why, when was that?"

"You know, that evening in Planit, when I told you that true insight is deadly. And you simply split your sides laughing!"

"Yes, and——?"

"Well, look at the world and this wonderful science of yours and where it's leading to! We get a newspaper up here only now and then, but I can tell you it's plenty for me. No, old boy, I'm right: true insight is deadly. Once you catch on to the last dodge there'll come a big bang, and that'll be it!"

The candle flickered and went out.

THE END

Dr. Hans Hass on the crater lake of Santorin.